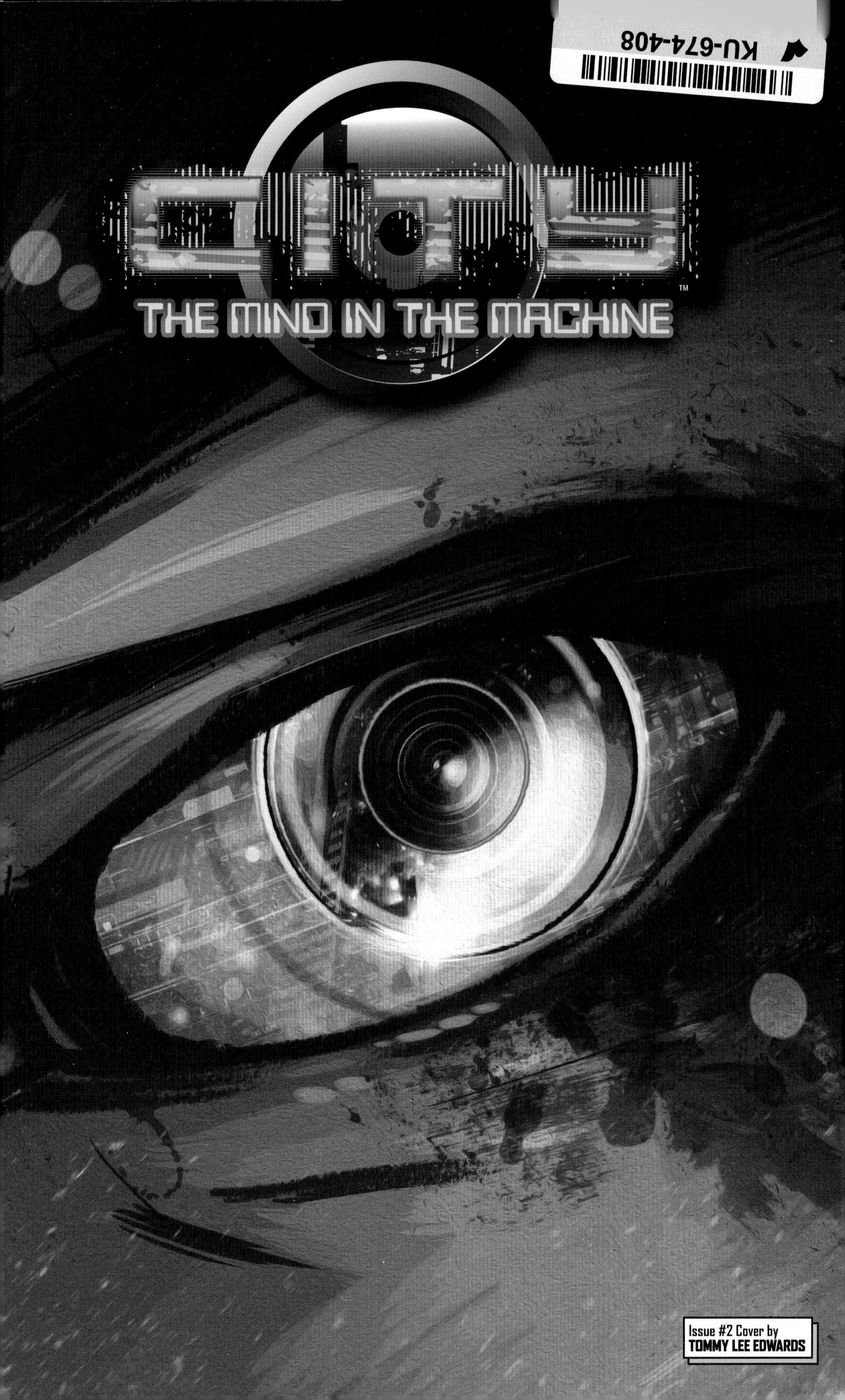
CITY™
THE MIND IN THE MACHINE
Issue #2 Cover by
TOMMY LEE EDWARDS

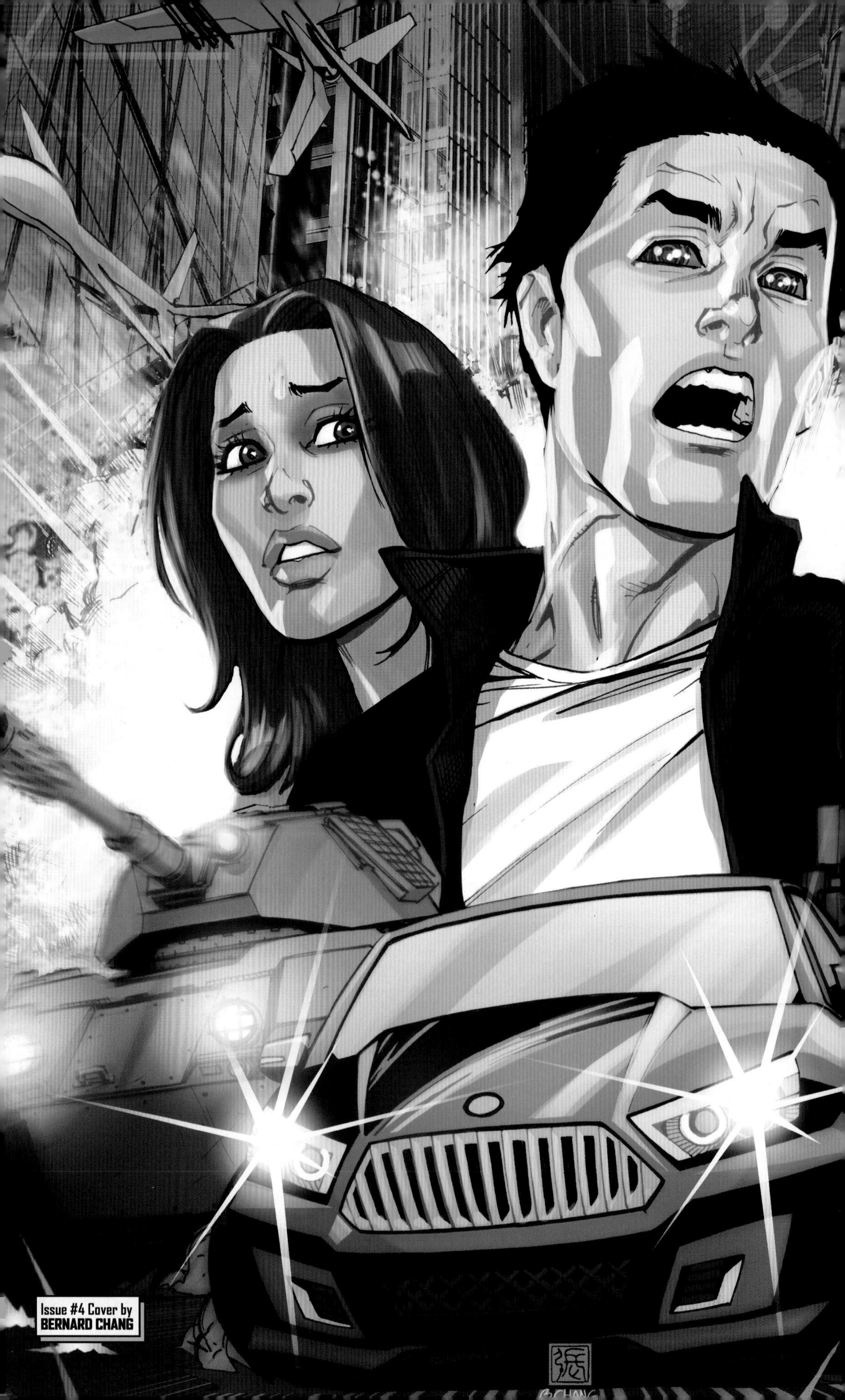

Issue #4 Cover by
BERNARD CHANG

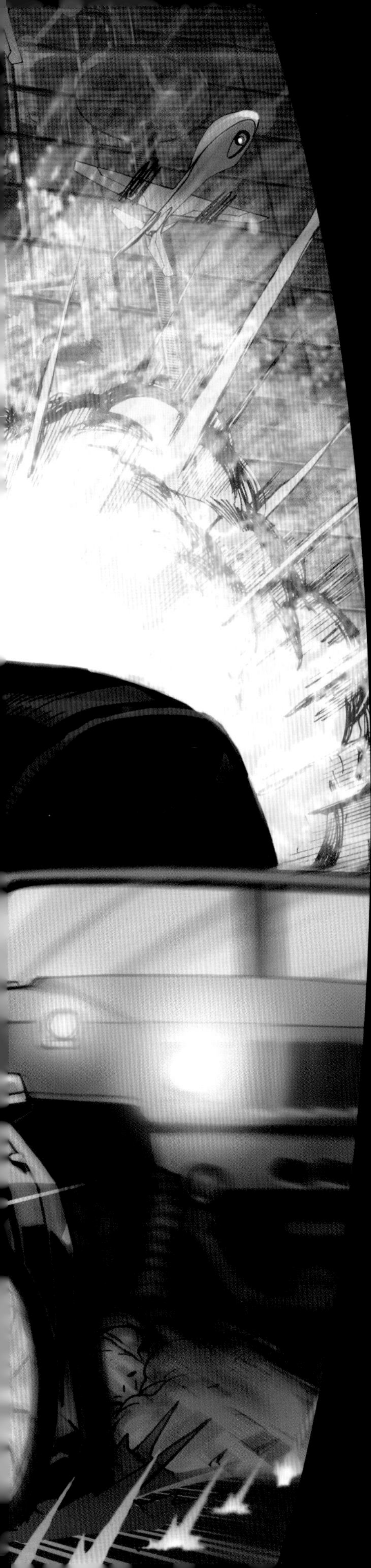

Written by
ERIC GARCIA

Pencils and Inks
JAVIER FERNANDEZ, DREW MOSS, and MICHAEL MONTENAT

Colorists
MARK ENGLERT and DOUGLAS A. SIROIS

Letters
TROY PETERI

Story Editor
RENAE GEERLINGS

IDW Publishing Edits
SARAH GAYDOS

Design
STEVE BLACKWELL

Trade Cover Art by
BERNARD CHANG

DARBY POP™
PUBLISHING

President
JEFF KLINE

Editor In Chief
DAVID WOHL

Managing Editor
RENAE GEERLINGS

VP of Business Development
MARK WHEELER

Marketing Director
JOSHUA COZINE

Legal Counsel
TOM COLLIER

Comptroller
LOIS M. BOTCHETT

Marketing Associate
KRISTINE CHESTER

LOVE US? HATE US?

Send an email to FANMAIL@DARBYPOP.COM to let us know what you think!

Become our fan on Facebook **facebook.com/idwpublishing**
Follow us on Twitter **@idwpublishing**
Check us out on YouTube **youtube.com/idwpublishing**
www.IDWPUBLISHING.com

ISBN: 978-1-63140-042-1
17 16 15 14 1 2 3 4

IDW®

IDW founded by Ted Adams, Alex Garner, Kris Oprisko, and Robbie Robbins

Ted Adams, CEO & Publisher • Greg Goldstein, President & COO
Robbie Robbins, EVP/Sr. Graphic Artist • Chris Ryall, Chief Creative Officer/Editor-in-Chief
Matthew Ruzicka, CPA, Chief Financial Officer • Alan Payne, VP of Sales
Dirk Wood, VP of Marketing • Lorelei Bunjes, VP of Digital Services

Originally published as CITY: THE MIND IN THE MACHINE issues #1–4.

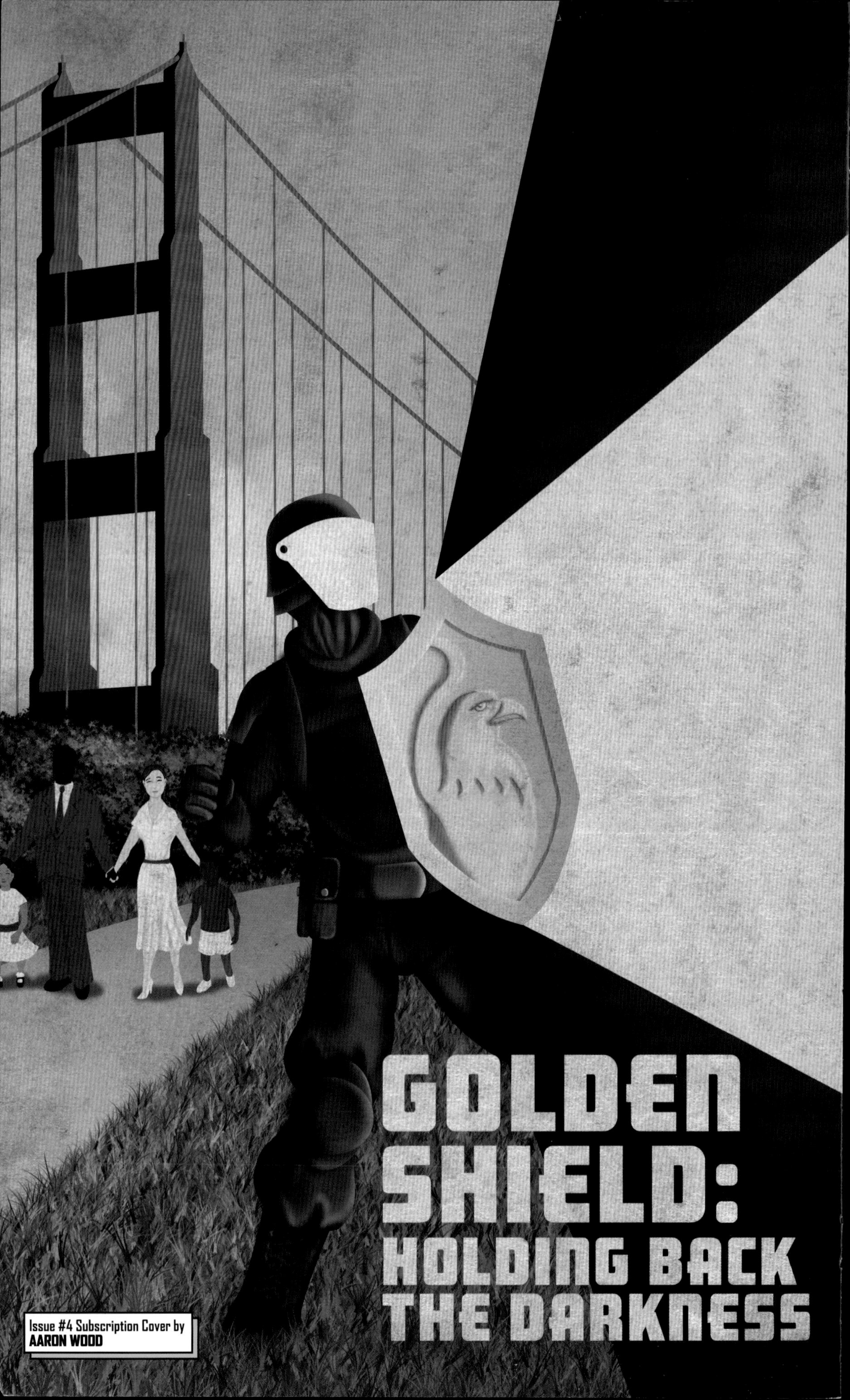
GOLDEN
SHIELD:
HOLDING BACK
THE DARKNESS
Issue #4 Subscription Cover by
AARON WOOD

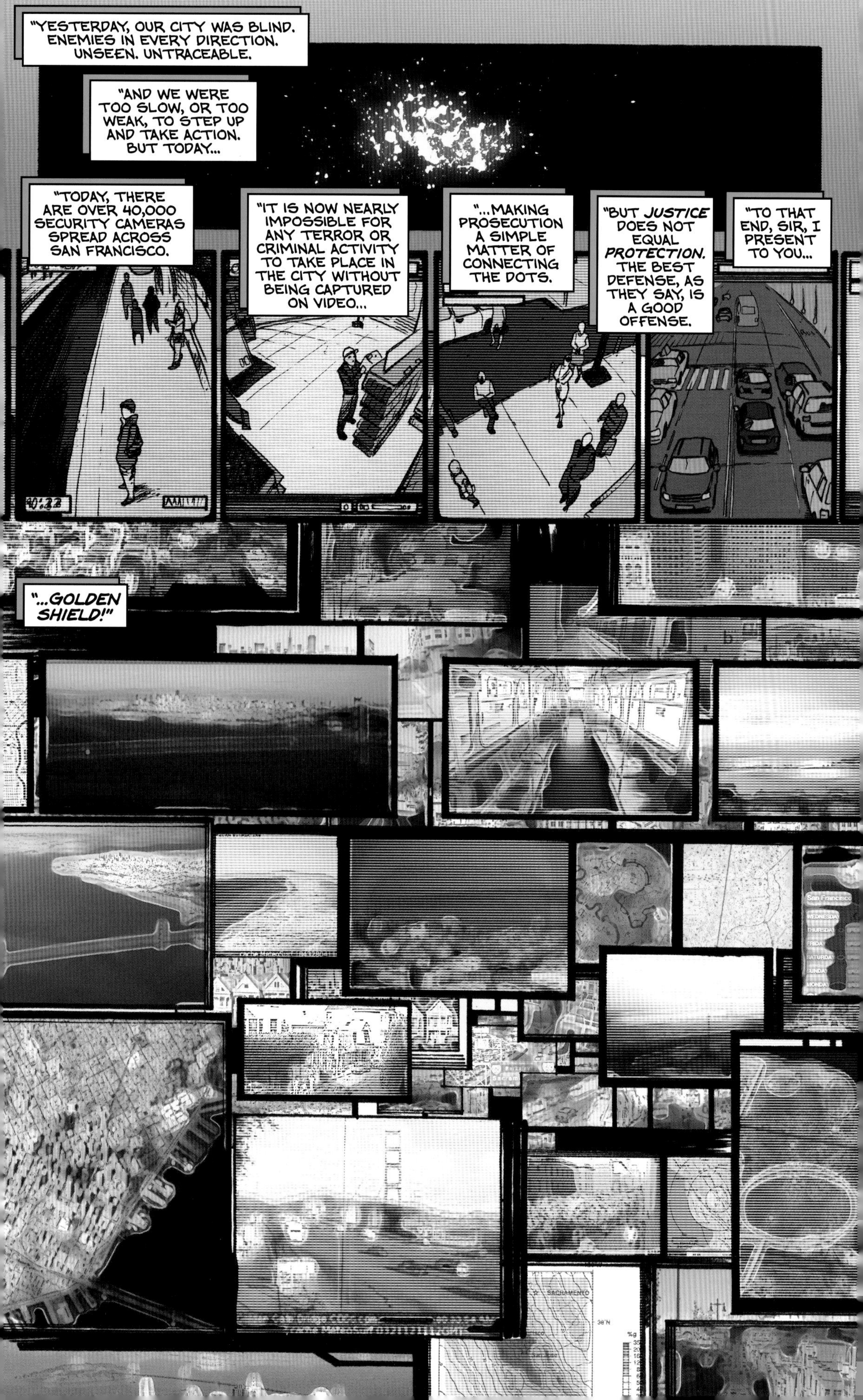
"YESTERDAY, OUR CITY WAS BLIND. ENEMIES IN EVERY DIRECTION. UNSEEN. UNTRACEABLE.
"AND WE WERE TOO SLOW, OR TOO WEAK, TO STEP UP AND TAKE ACTION. BUT TODAY...
"TODAY, THERE ARE OVER 40,000 SECURITY CAMERAS SPREAD ACROSS SAN FRANCISCO.
"IT IS NOW NEARLY IMPOSSIBLE FOR ANY TERROR OR CRIMINAL ACTIVITY TO TAKE PLACE IN THE CITY WITHOUT BEING CAPTURED ON VIDEO...
"...MAKING PROSECUTION A SIMPLE MATTER OF CONNECTING THE DOTS.
"BUT *JUSTICE* DOES NOT EQUAL *PROTECTION*. THE BEST DEFENSE, AS THEY SAY, IS A GOOD OFFENSE.
"TO THAT END, SIR, I PRESENT TO YOU...
"...GOLDEN SHIELD!"

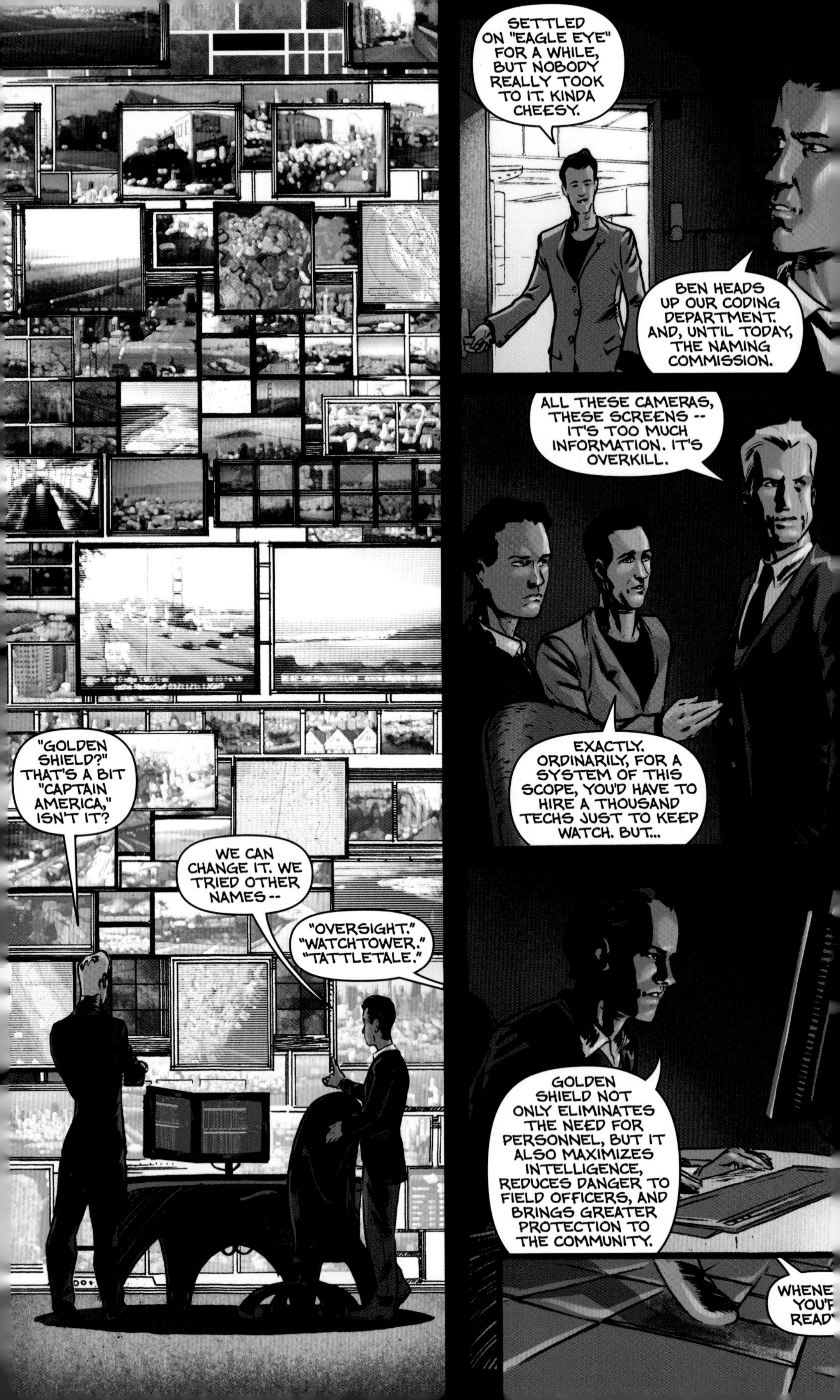
"GOLDEN SHIELD?" THAT'S A BIT "CAPTAIN AMERICA," ISN'T IT?
WE CAN CHANGE IT. WE TRIED OTHER NAMES --
"OVERSIGHT." "WATCHTOWER." "TATTLETALE."
SETTLED ON "EAGLE EYE" FOR A WHILE, BUT NOBODY REALLY TOOK TO IT. KINDA CHEESY.
BEN HEADS UP OUR CODING DEPARTMENT. AND, UNTIL TODAY, THE NAMING COMMISSION.
ALL THESE CAMERAS, THESE SCREENS -- IT'S TOO MUCH INFORMATION. IT'S OVERKILL.
EXACTLY. ORDINARILY, FOR A SYSTEM OF THIS SCOPE, YOU'D HAVE TO HIRE A THOUSAND TECHS JUST TO KEEP WATCH. BUT...
GOLDEN SHIELD NOT ONLY ELIMINATES THE NEED FOR PERSONNEL, BUT IT ALSO MAXIMIZES INTELLIGENCE, REDUCES DANGER TO FIELD OFFICERS, AND BRINGS GREATER PROTECTION TO THE COMMUNITY.

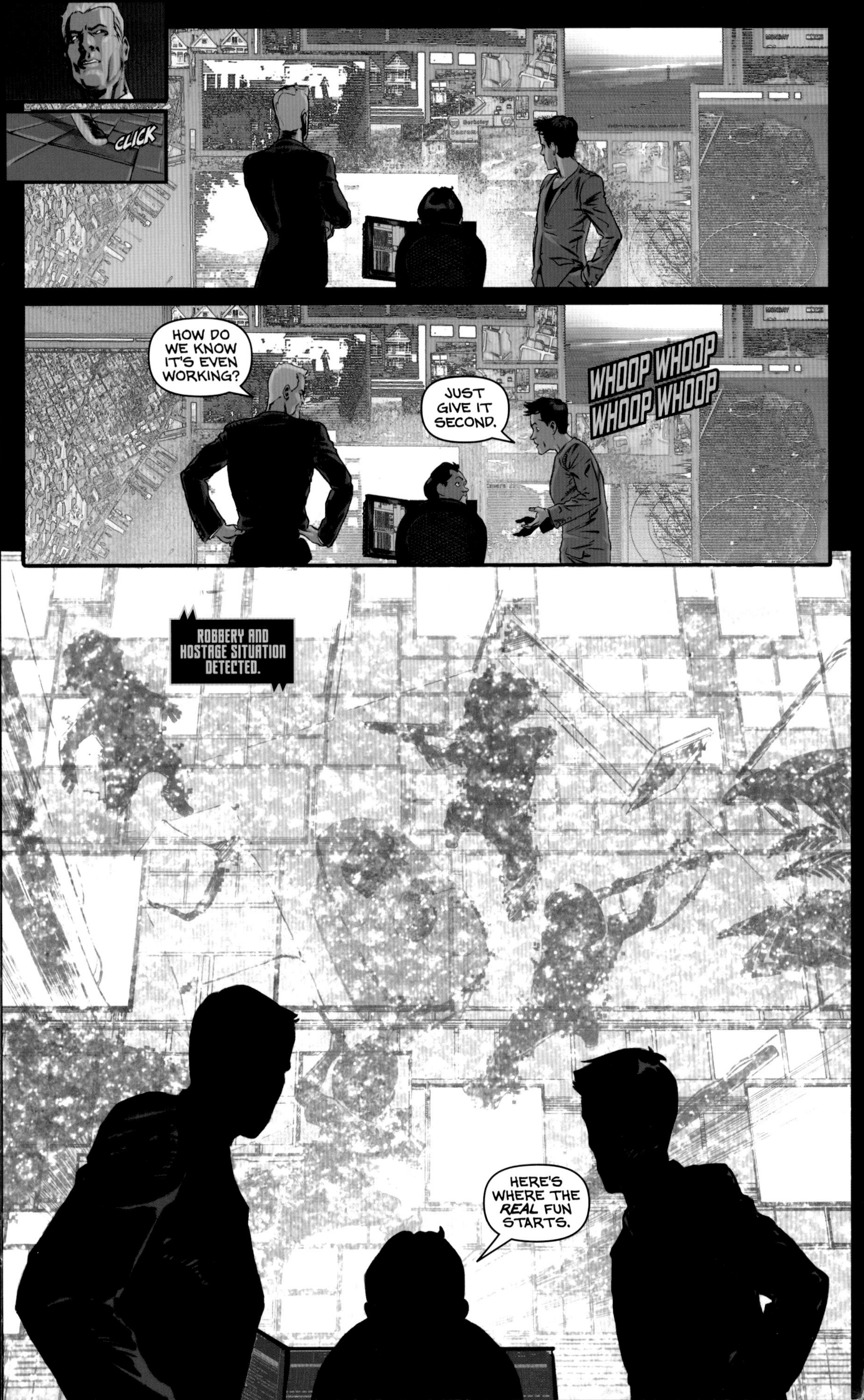
CLICK
HOW DO WE KNOW IT'S EVEN WORKING?
JUST GIVE IT SECOND.
WHOOP WHOOP WHOOP WHOOP
ROBBERY AND HOSTAGE SITUATION DETECTED.
HERE'S WHERE THE *REAL* FUN STARTS.

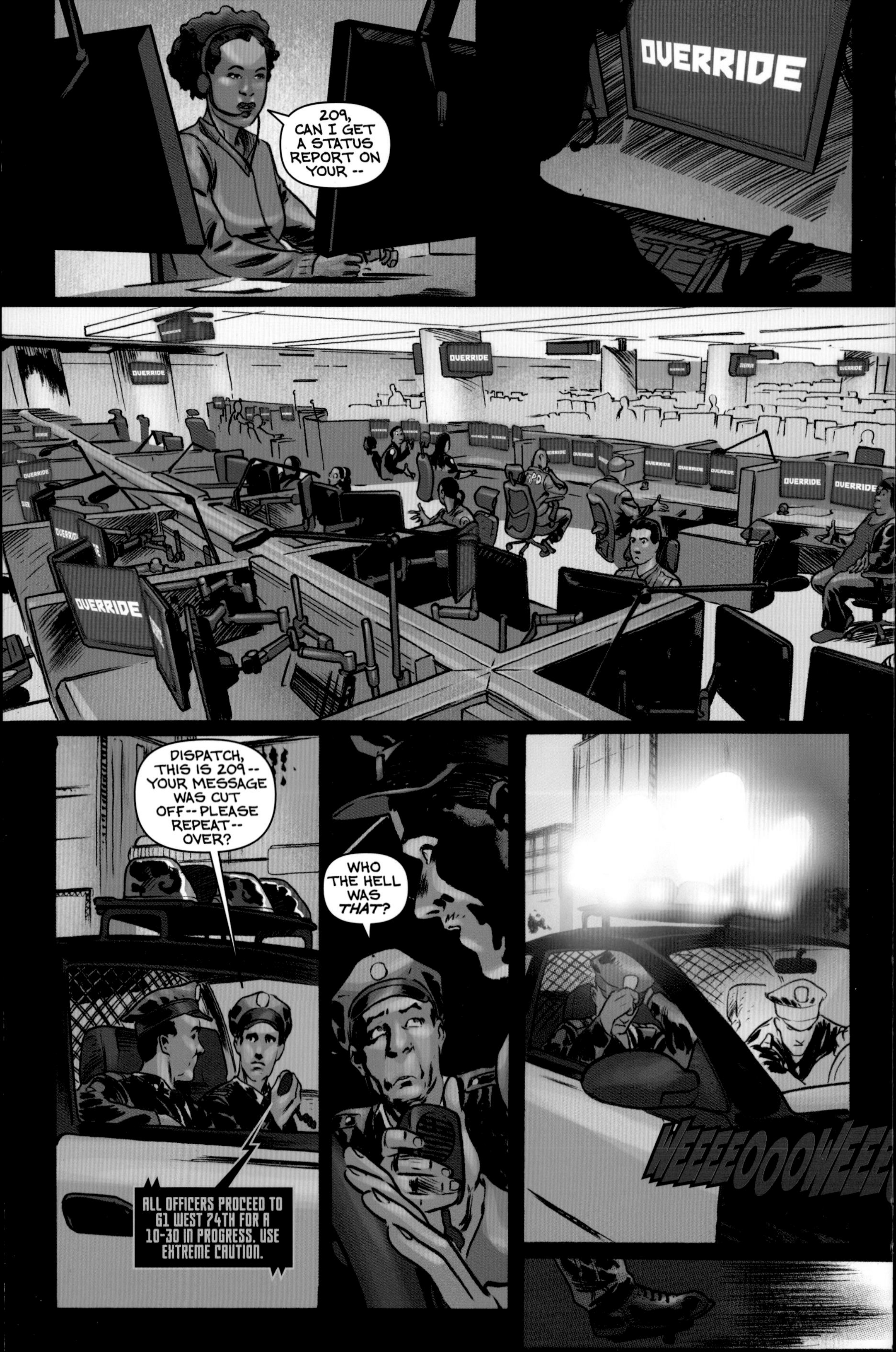
209, CAN I GET A STATUS REPORT ON YOUR --
OVERRIDE
OVERRIDE
DISPATCH, THIS IS 209 -- YOUR MESSAGE WAS CUT OFF -- PLEASE REPEAT -- OVER?
ALL OFFICERS PROCEED TO 61 WEST 74TH FOR A 10-30 IN PROGRESS. USE EXTREME CAUTION.
WHO THE HELL WAS THAT?
WEEEOOOWEEE

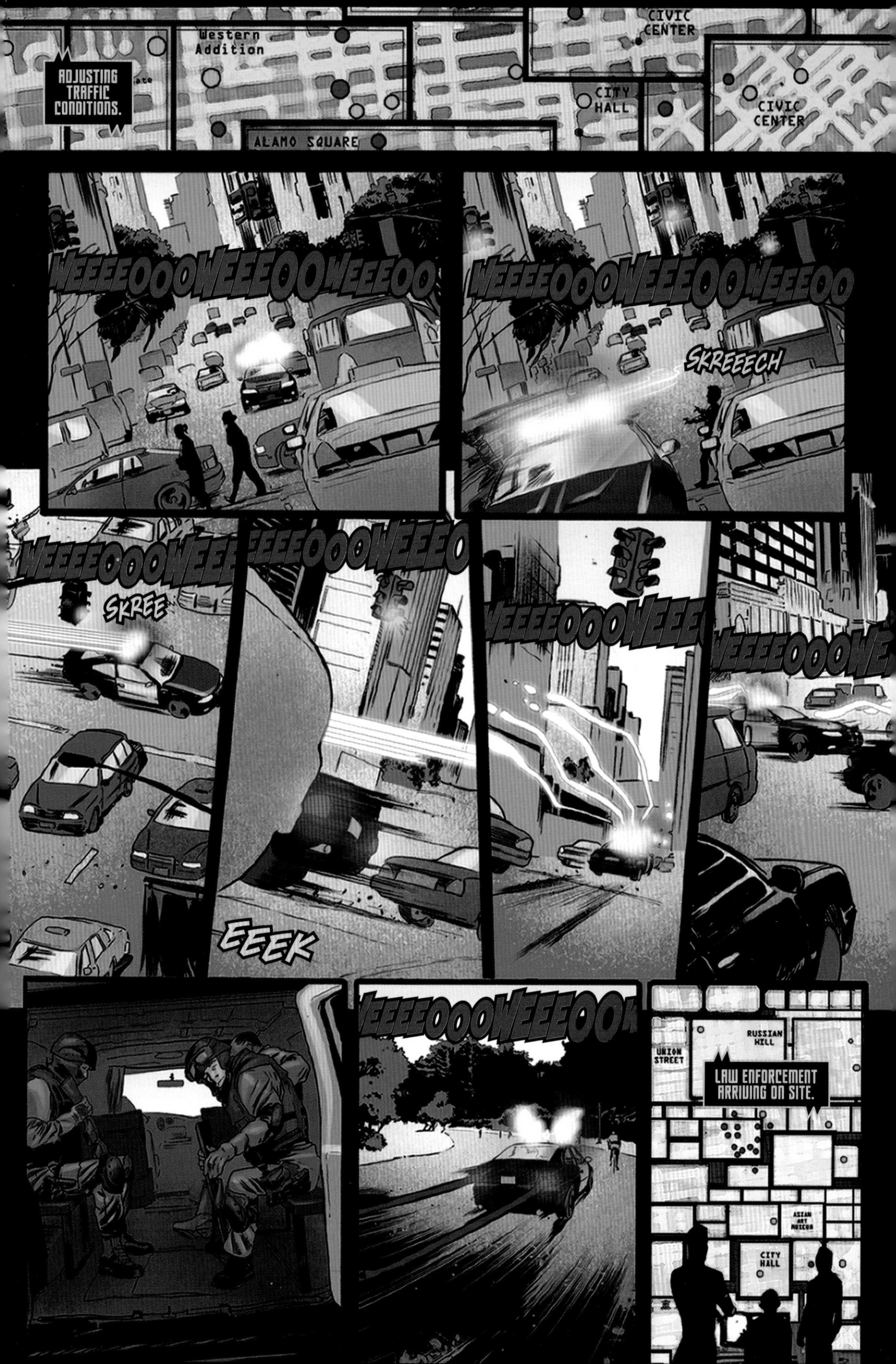

ADJUSTING TRAFFIC CONDITIONS.
Western Addition
CIVIC CENTER
CITY HALL
CIVIC CENTER
ALAMO SQUARE
WEEEEOOOWEEEOOWEEEOO
WEEEEOOOWEEEOOWEEEOO
SKREEECH
SKREE
EEEK
LAW ENFORCEMENT ARRIVING ON SITE.
RUSSIAN HILL
UNION STREET
ASIAN ART MUSEUM
CITY HALL

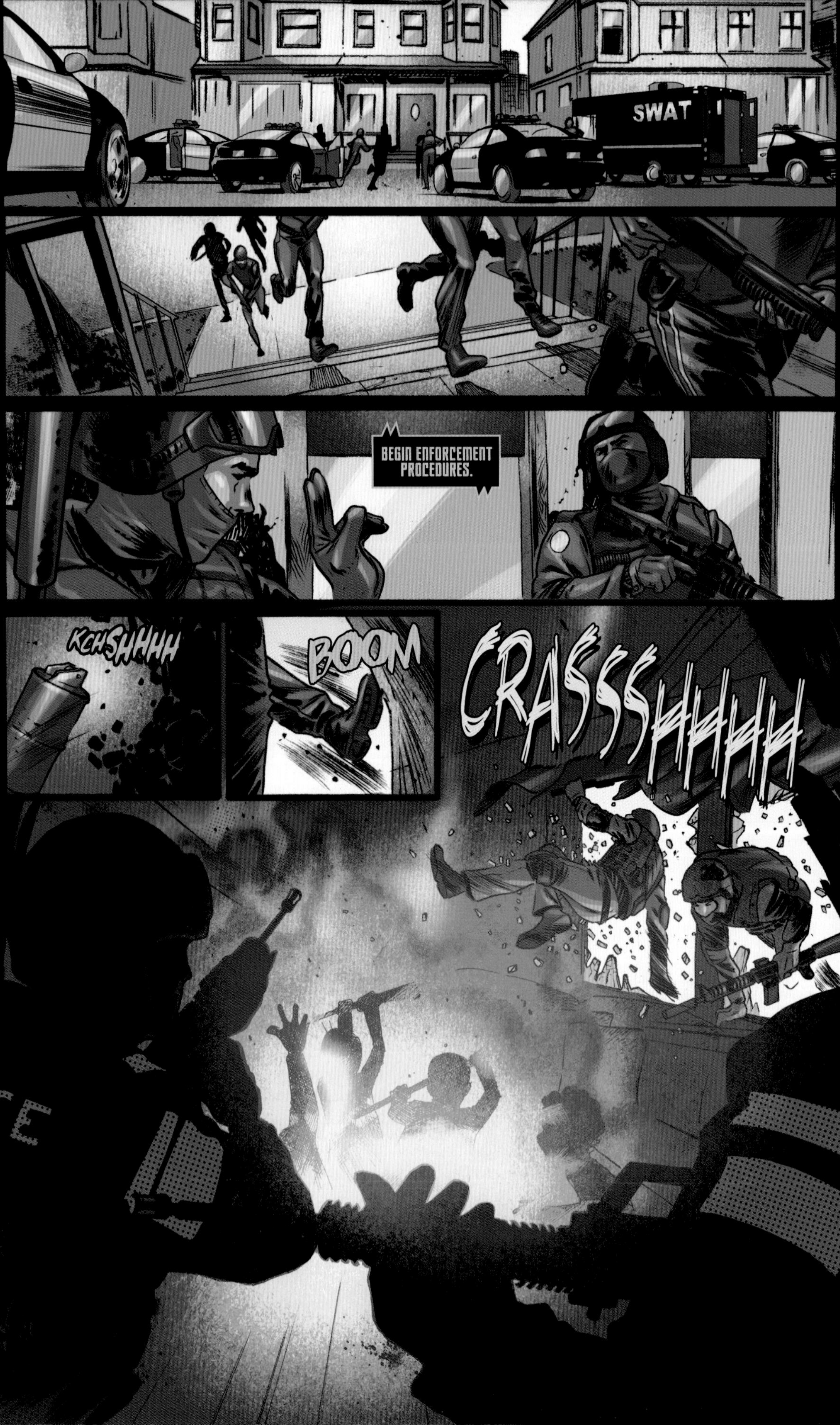
SWAT
BEGIN ENFORCEMENT PROCEDURES.
KCHSHHHH
BOOM
CRASSSHHHH

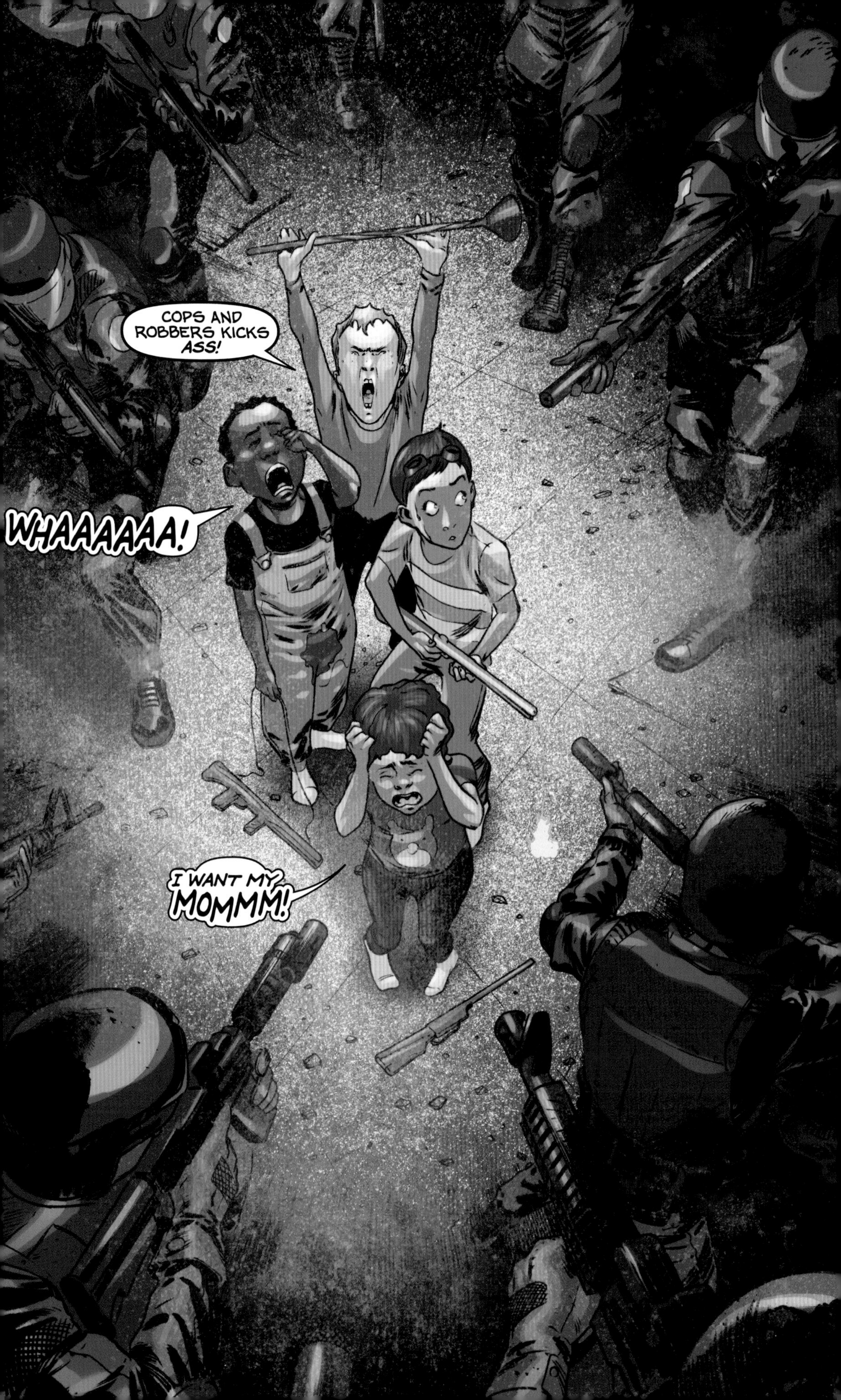
COPS AND ROBBERS KICKS ASS!
WHAAAAAA!
I WANT MY MOMMM!

IF YOU'LL JUST GIVE IT ONE MORE TEST--

HOMELAND'S UNDER ENOUGH SCRUTINY. I CAN'T BUY A PROGRAM THAT'S GONNA BRING LAWSUITS RAINING DOWN ON US.

I CAN FIX IT. GIVE ME A MONTH.

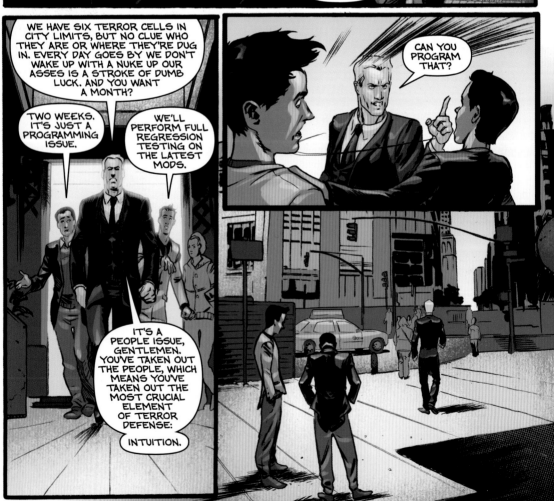

WE HAVE SIX TERROR CELLS IN CITY LIMITS, BUT NO CLUE WHO THEY ARE OR WHERE THEY'RE DUG IN. EVERY DAY GOES BY WE DON'T WAKE UP WITH A NUKE UP OUR ASSES IS A STROKE OF DUMB LUCK. AND YOU WANT A MONTH?

CAN YOU PROGRAM THAT?

TWO WEEKS. IT'S JUST A PROGRAMMING ISSUE.

WE'LL PERFORM FULL REGRESSION TESTING ON THE LATEST MODS.

IT'S A PEOPLE ISSUE, GENTLEMEN. YOU'VE TAKEN OUT THE PEOPLE, WHICH MEANS YOU'VE TAKEN OUT THE MOST CRUCIAL ELEMENT OF TERROR DEFENSE:

INTUITION.

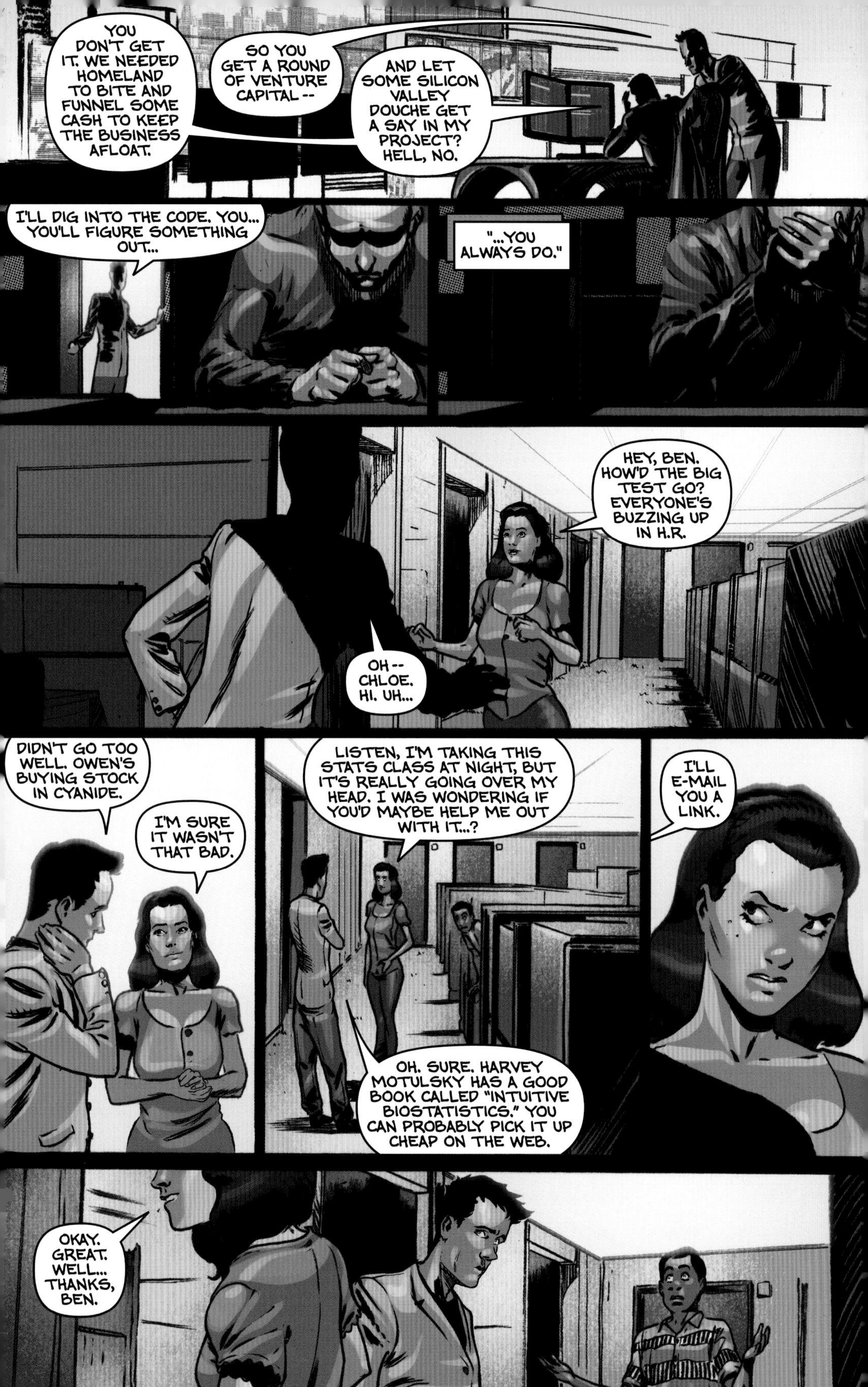
YOU DON'T GET IT. WE NEEDED HOMELAND TO BITE AND FUNNEL SOME CASH TO KEEP THE BUSINESS AFLOAT.
SO YOU GET A ROUND OF VENTURE CAPITAL --
AND LET SOME SILICON VALLEY DOUCHE GET A SAY IN MY PROJECT? HELL, NO.
I'LL DIG INTO THE CODE. YOU... YOU'LL FIGURE SOMETHING OUT...
"...YOU ALWAYS DO."
HEY, BEN. HOW'D THE BIG TEST GO? EVERYONE'S BUZZING UP IN H.R.
OH -- CHLOE. HI. UH...
DIDN'T GO TOO WELL. OWEN'S BUYING STOCK IN CYANIDE.
I'M SURE IT WASN'T THAT BAD.
LISTEN, I'M TAKING THIS STATS CLASS AT NIGHT, BUT IT'S REALLY GOING OVER MY HEAD. I WAS WONDERING IF YOU'D MAYBE HELP ME OUT WITH IT...?
OH. SURE. HARVEY MOTULSKY HAS A GOOD BOOK CALLED "INTUITIVE BIOSTATISTICS." YOU CAN PROBABLY PICK IT UP CHEAP ON THE WEB.
I'LL E-MAIL YOU A LINK.
OKAY. GREAT. WELL... THANKS, BEN.

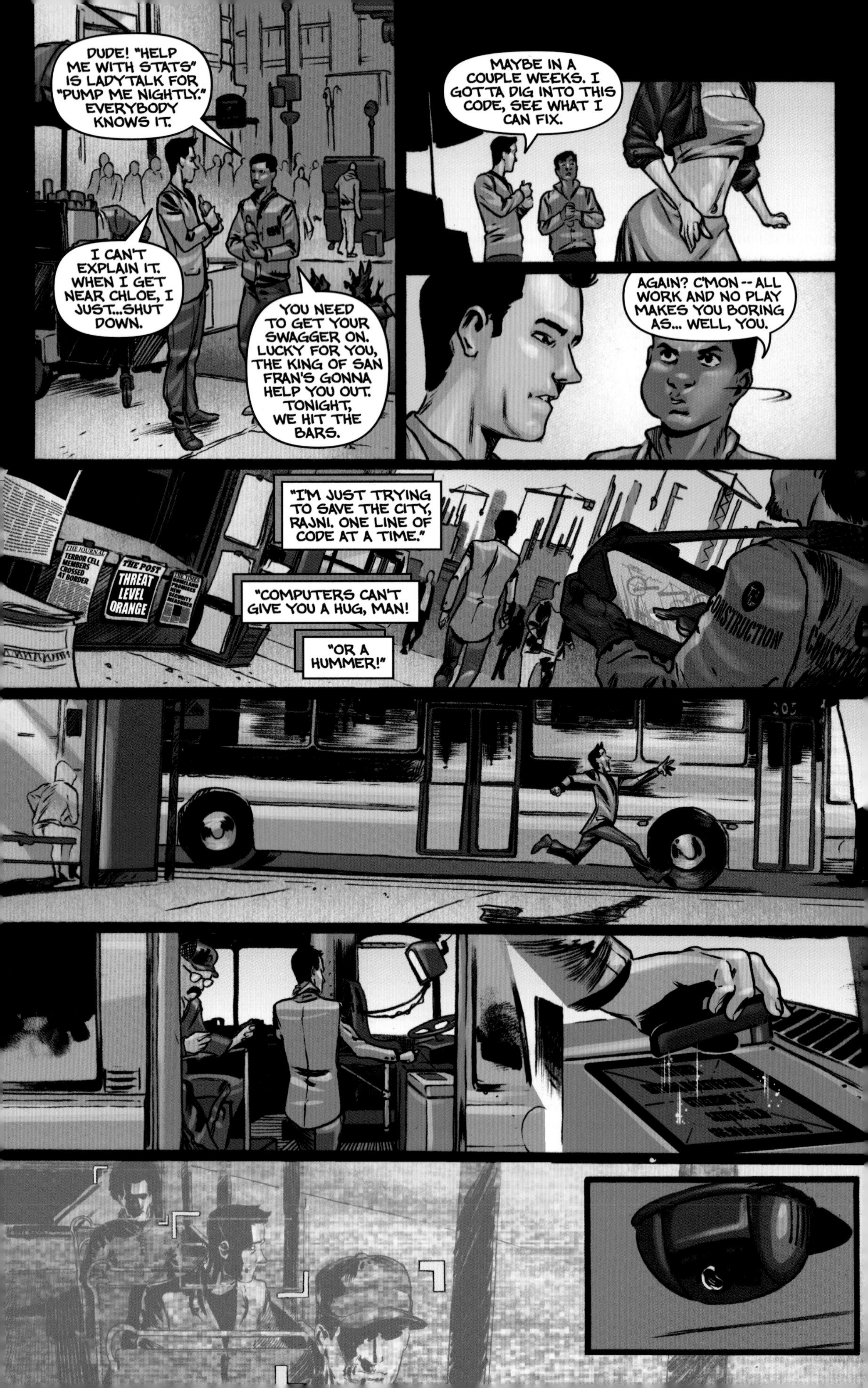
DUDE! "HELP ME WITH STATS" IS LADYTALK FOR "PUMP ME NIGHTLY." EVERYBODY KNOWS IT.
I CAN'T EXPLAIN IT. WHEN I GET NEAR CHLOE, I JUST...SHUT DOWN.
YOU NEED TO GET YOUR SWAGGER ON. LUCKY FOR YOU, THE KING OF SAN FRAN'S GONNA HELP YOU OUT. TONIGHT, WE HIT THE BARS.
MAYBE IN A COUPLE WEEKS. I GOTTA DIG INTO THIS CODE, SEE WHAT I CAN FIX.
AGAIN? C'MON -- ALL WORK AND NO PLAY MAKES YOU BORING AS... WELL, YOU.
THE JOURNAL
TERROR CELL MEMBERS CROSSED AT BORDER
THE POST
THREAT LEVEL ORANGE
THE TIMES
"I'M JUST TRYING TO SAVE THE CITY, RAJNI. ONE LINE OF CODE AT A TIME."
"COMPUTERS CAN'T GIVE YOU A HUG, MAN!
"OR A HUMMER!"
CONSTRUCTION
CONSTRUCTION

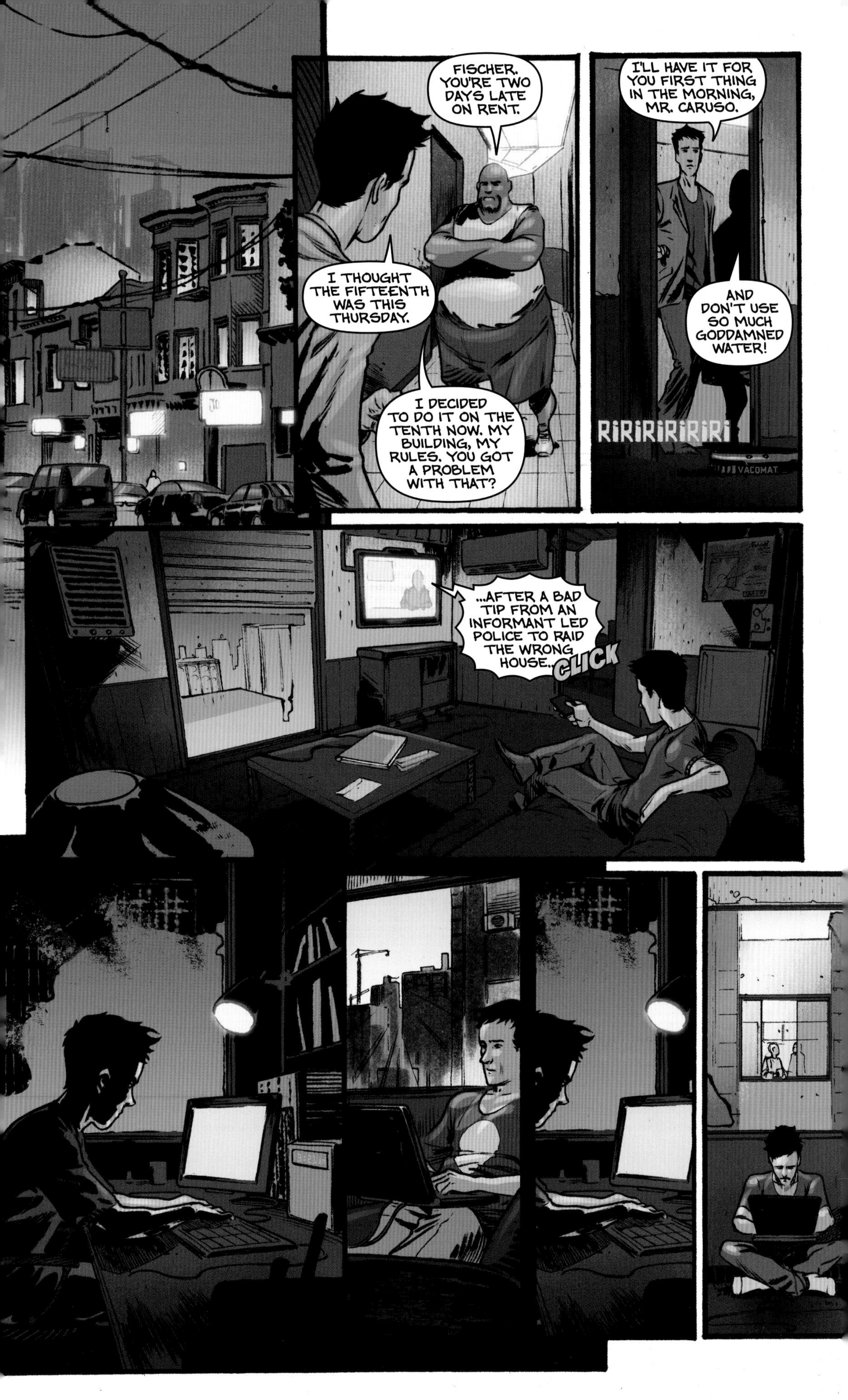
FISCHER. YOU'RE TWO DAYS LATE ON RENT.
I THOUGHT THE FIFTEENTH WAS THIS THURSDAY.
I DECIDED TO DO IT ON THE TENTH NOW. MY BUILDING, MY RULES. YOU GOT A PROBLEM WITH THAT?
I'LL HAVE IT FOR YOU FIRST THING IN THE MORNING, MR. CARUSO.
AND DON'T USE SO MUCH GODDAMNED WATER!
RiRiRiRiRiRi
VACOMAT
...AFTER A BAD TIP FROM AN INFORMANT LED POLICE TO RAID THE WRONG HOUSE...
CLICK

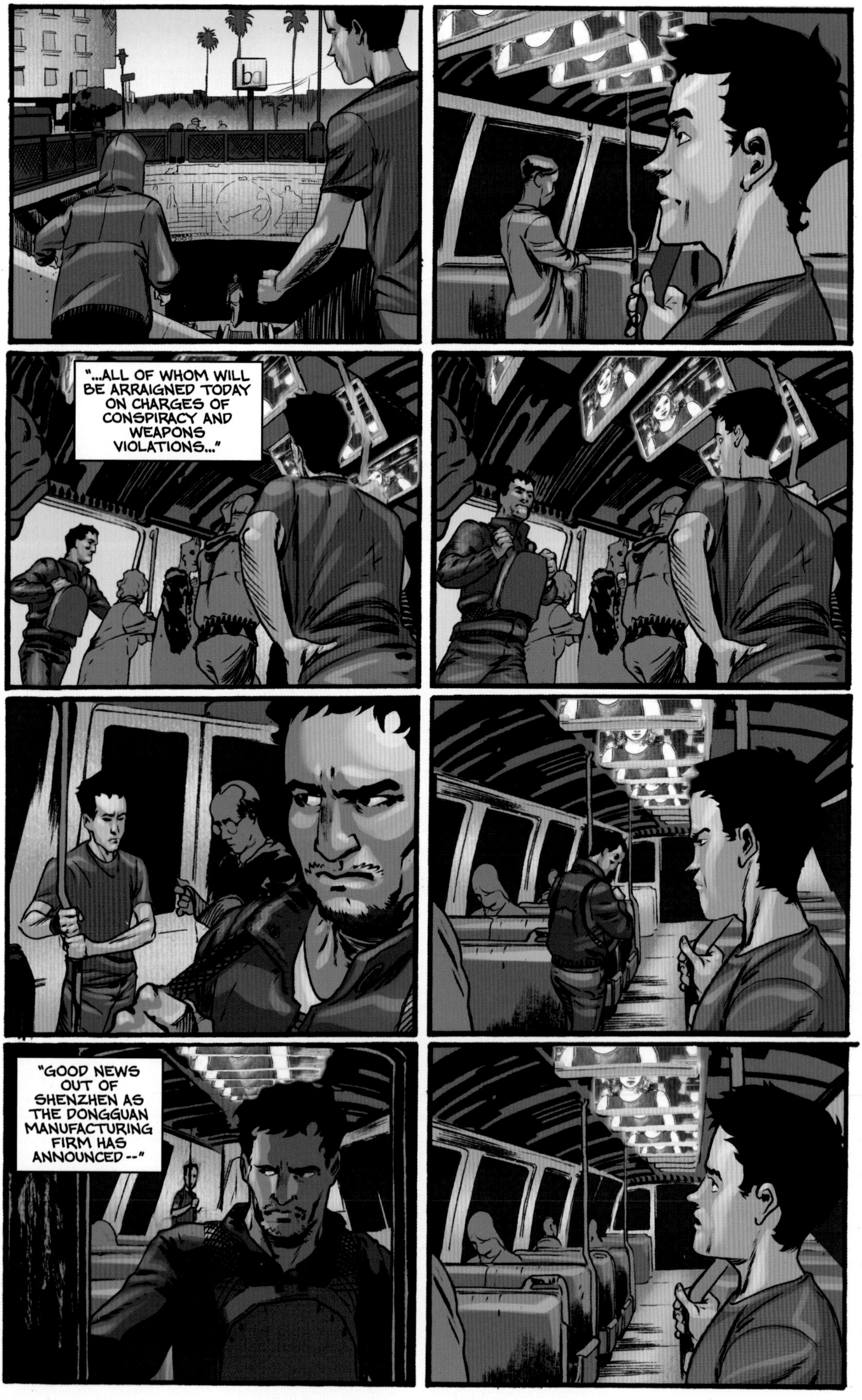
"...ALL OF WHOM WILL BE ARRAIGNED TODAY ON CHARGES OF CONSPIRACY AND WEAPONS VIOLATIONS..."
"GOOD NEWS OUT OF SHENZHEN AS THE DONGGUAN MANUFACTURING FIRM HAS ANNOUNCED --"

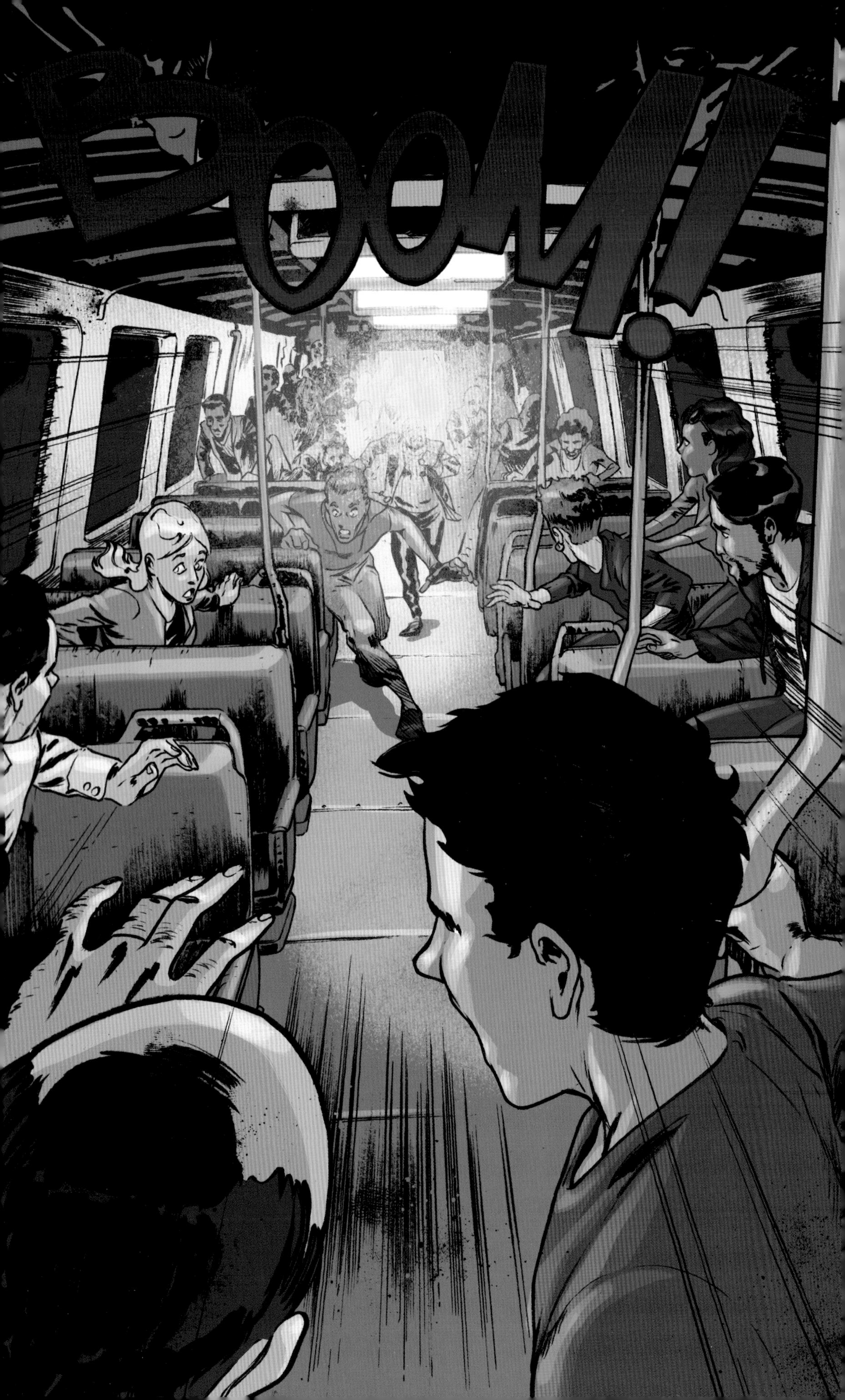
BOOM!

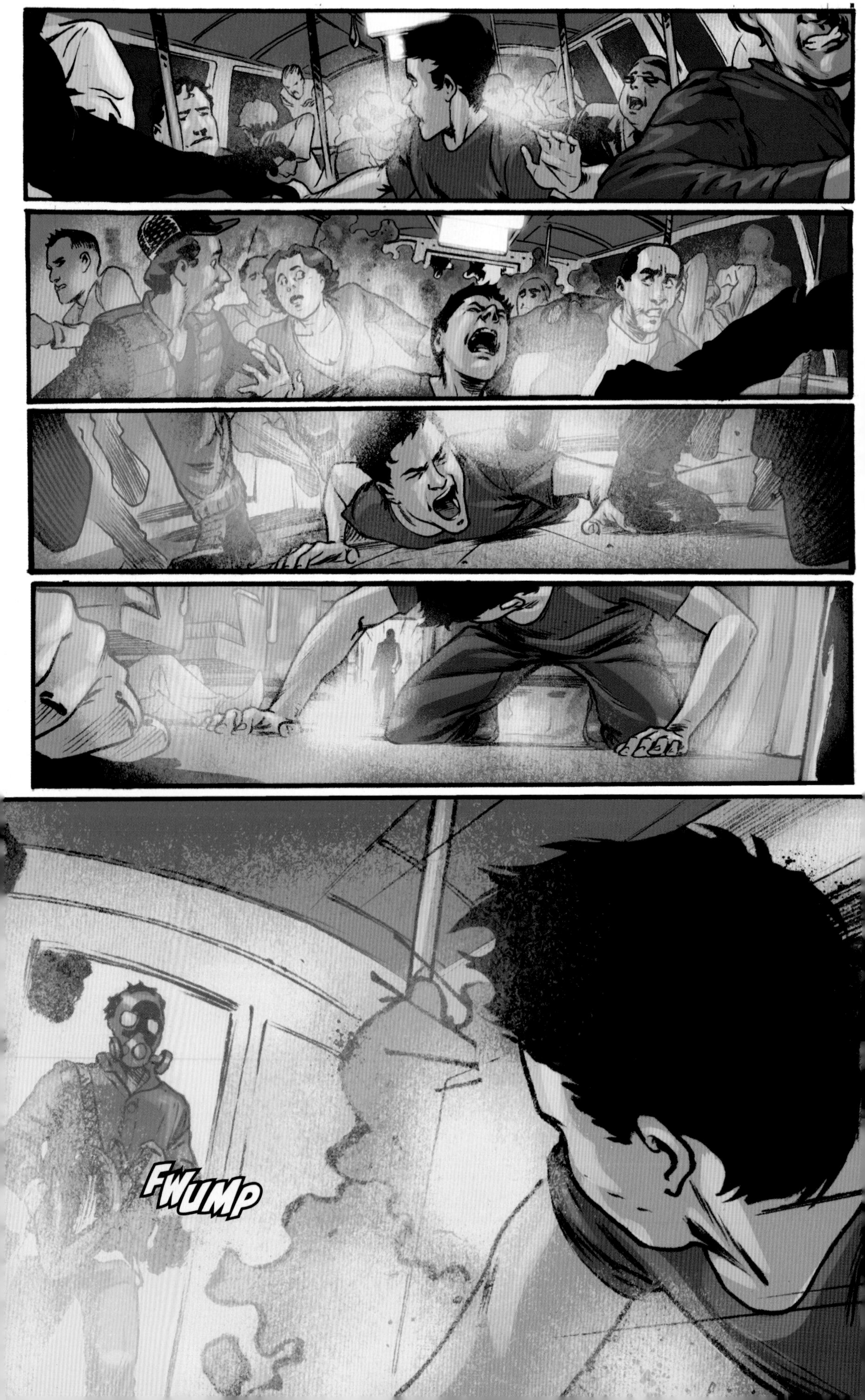
FWUMP

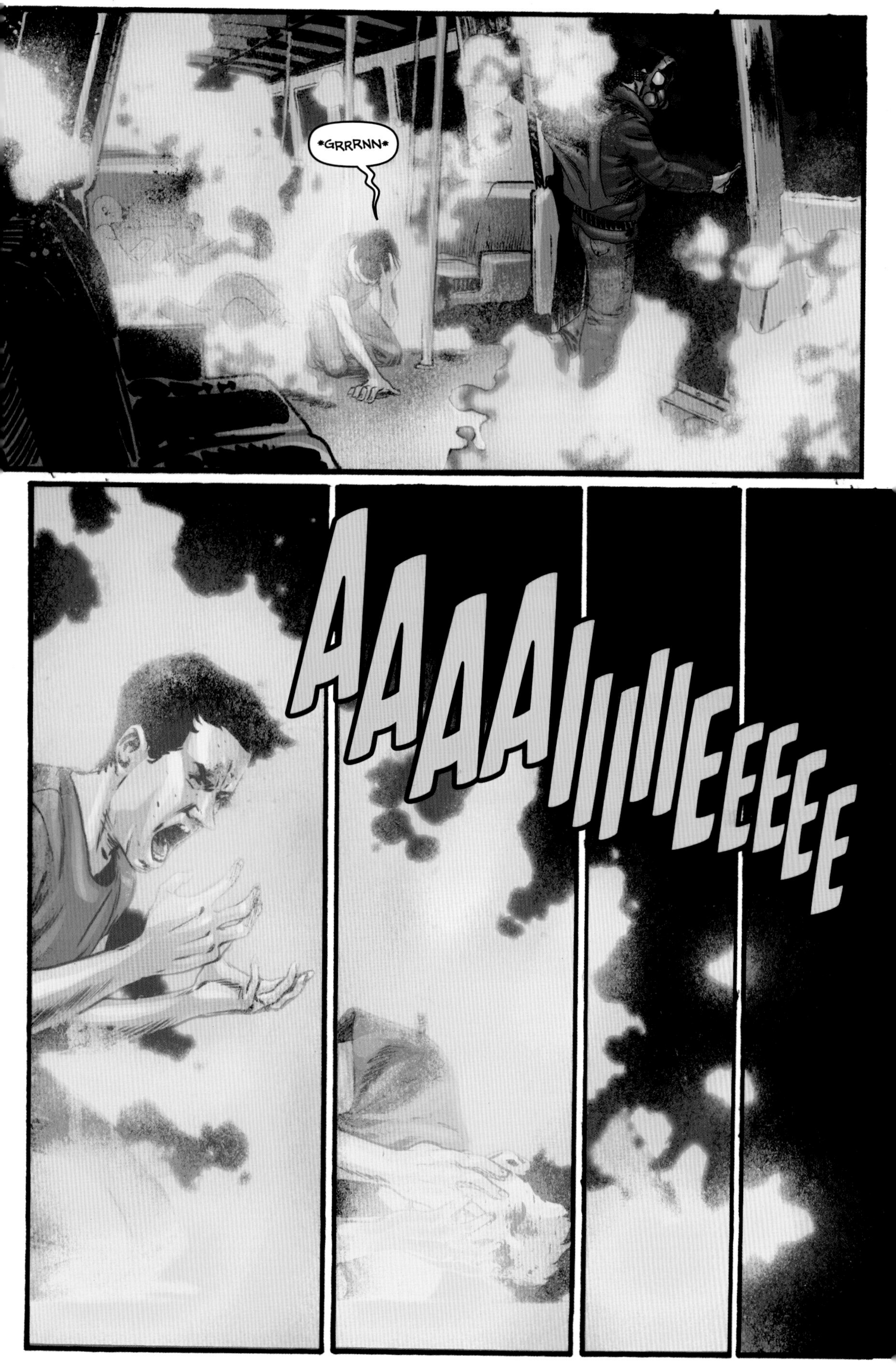
GRRRNN
AAAAIIIIIEEEEEE

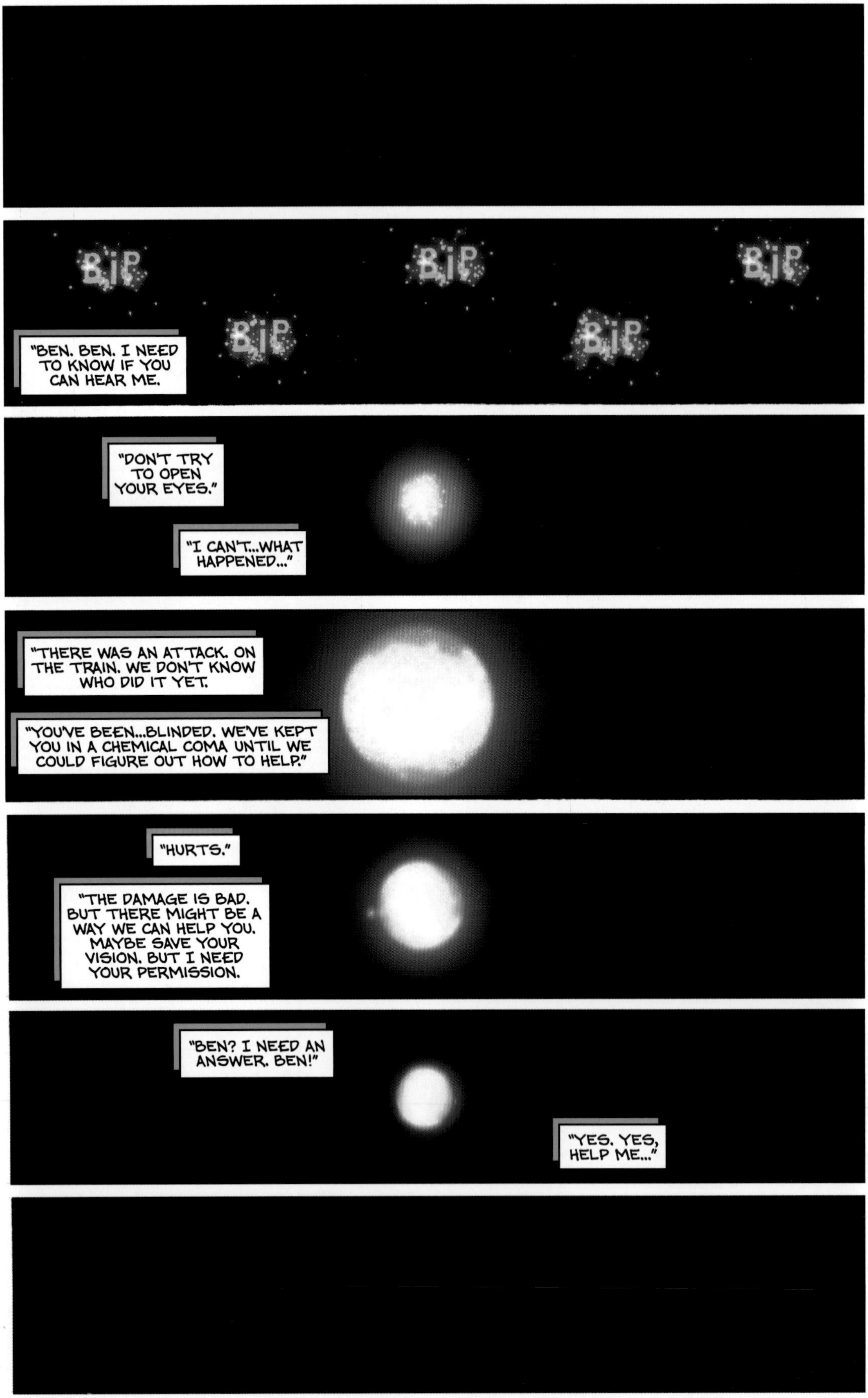
BIP
BIP
BIP
BIP
BIP
"BEN. BEN. I NEED TO KNOW IF YOU CAN HEAR ME.
"DON'T TRY TO OPEN YOUR EYES."
"I CAN'T...WHAT HAPPENED..."
"THERE WAS AN ATTACK. ON THE TRAIN. WE DON'T KNOW WHO DID IT YET.
"YOU'VE BEEN...BLINDED. WE'VE KEPT YOU IN A CHEMICAL COMA UNTIL WE COULD FIGURE OUT HOW TO HELP."
"HURTS."
"THE DAMAGE IS BAD. BUT THERE MIGHT BE A WAY WE CAN HELP YOU. MAYBE SAVE YOUR VISION. BUT I NEED YOUR PERMISSION.
"BEN? I NEED AN ANSWER. BEN!"
"YES. YES, HELP ME..."

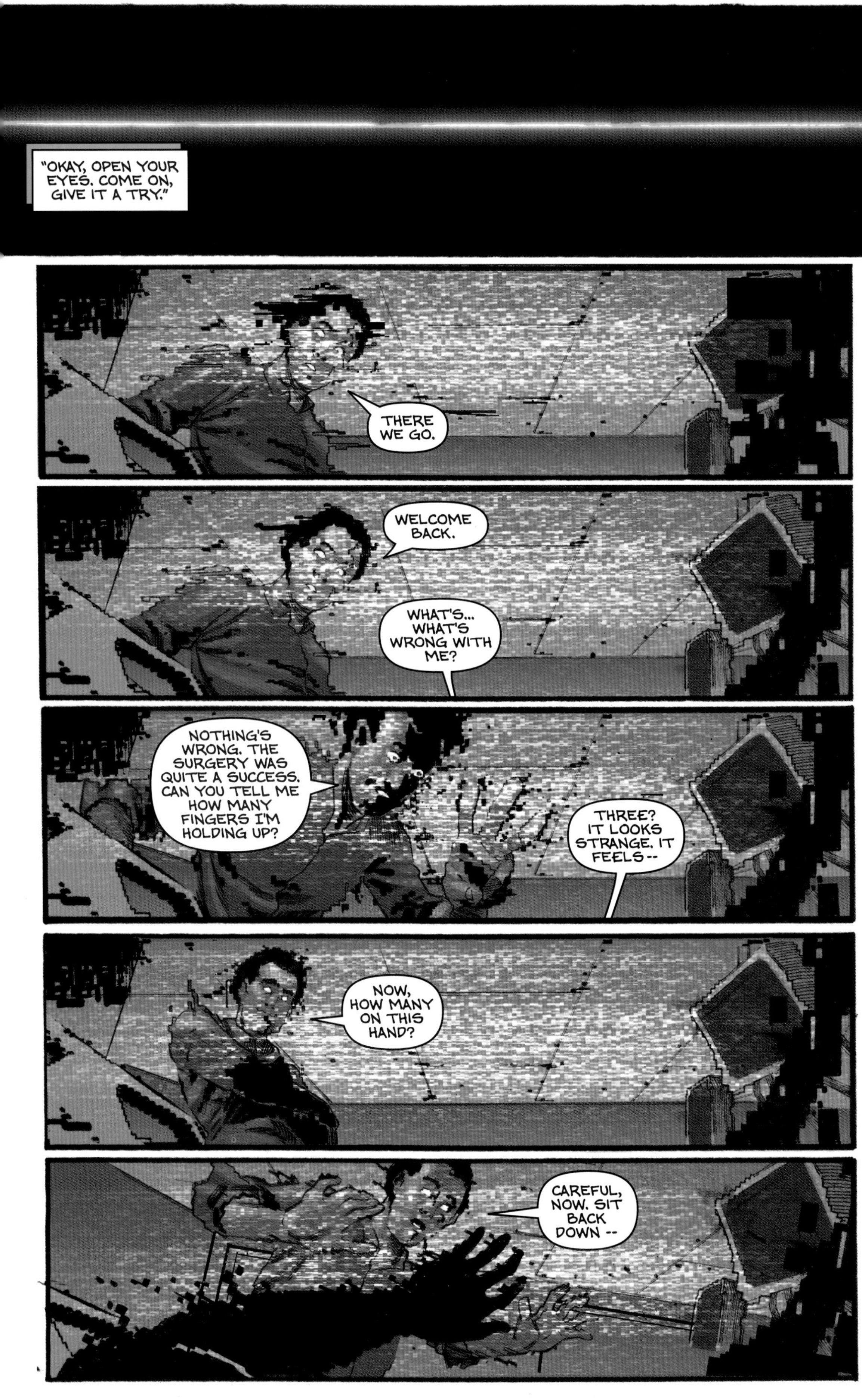
"OKAY, OPEN YOUR EYES. COME ON, GIVE IT A TRY."
THERE WE GO.
WELCOME BACK.
WHAT'S... WHAT'S WRONG WITH ME?
NOTHING'S WRONG. THE SURGERY WAS QUITE A SUCCESS. CAN YOU TELL ME HOW MANY FINGERS I'M HOLDING UP?
THREE? IT LOOKS STRANGE. IT FEELS --
NOW, HOW MANY ON THIS HAND?
CAREFUL, NOW. SIT BACK DOWN --

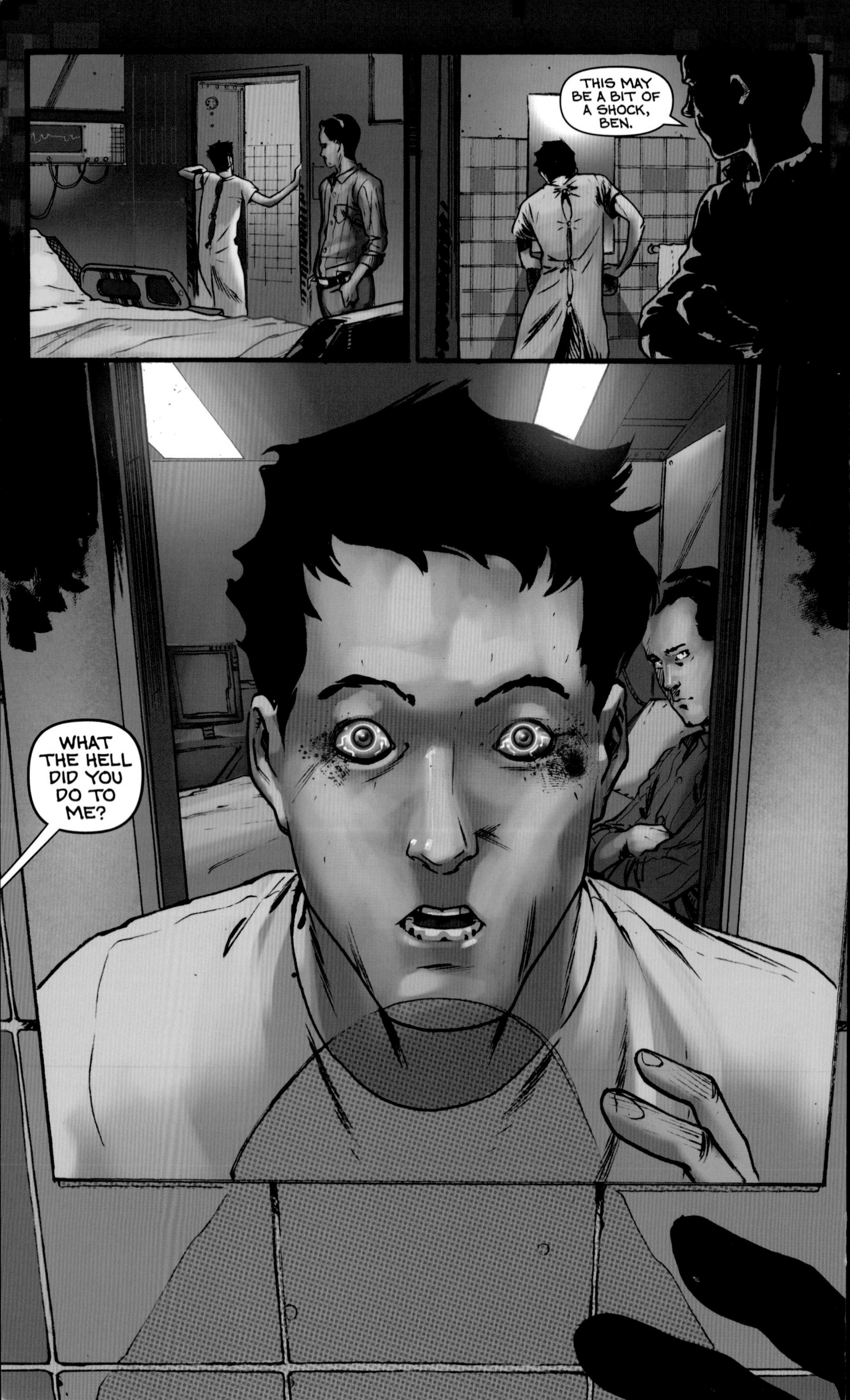
THIS MAY BE A BIT OF A SHOCK, BEN.
WHAT THE HELL DID YOU DO TO ME?

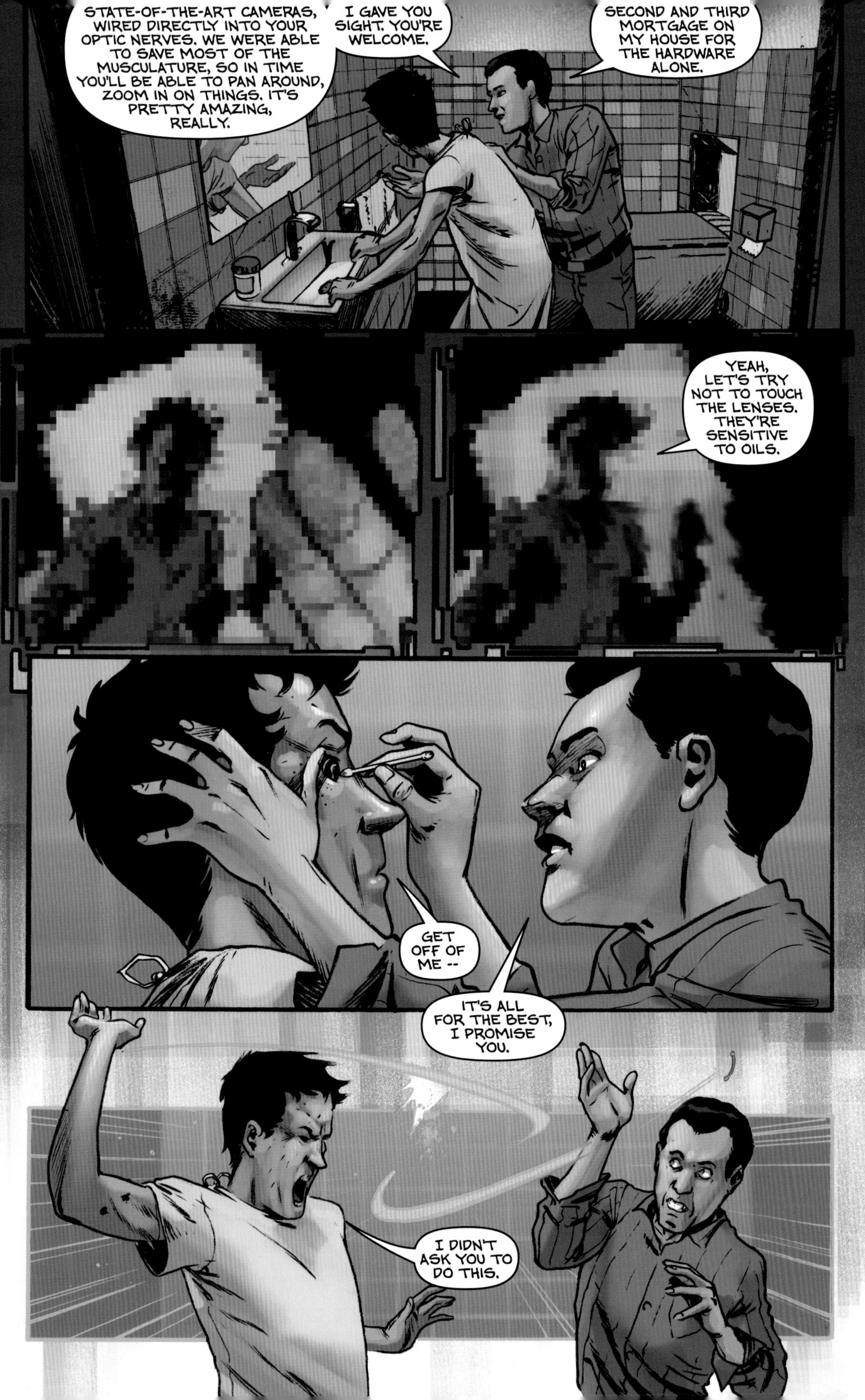
STATE-OF-THE-ART CAMERAS, WIRED DIRECTLY INTO YOUR OPTIC NERVES. WE WERE ABLE TO SAVE MOST OF THE MUSCULATURE, SO IN TIME YOU'LL BE ABLE TO PAN AROUND, ZOOM IN ON THINGS. IT'S PRETTY AMAZING, REALLY.
I GAVE YOU SIGHT. YOU'RE WELCOME.
SECOND AND THIRD MORTGAGE ON MY HOUSE FOR THE HARDWARE ALONE.
YEAH, LET'S TRY NOT TO TOUCH THE LENSES. THEY'RE SENSITIVE TO OILS.
GET OFF OF ME --
IT'S ALL FOR THE BEST, I PROMISE YOU.
I DIDN'T ASK YOU TO DO THIS.

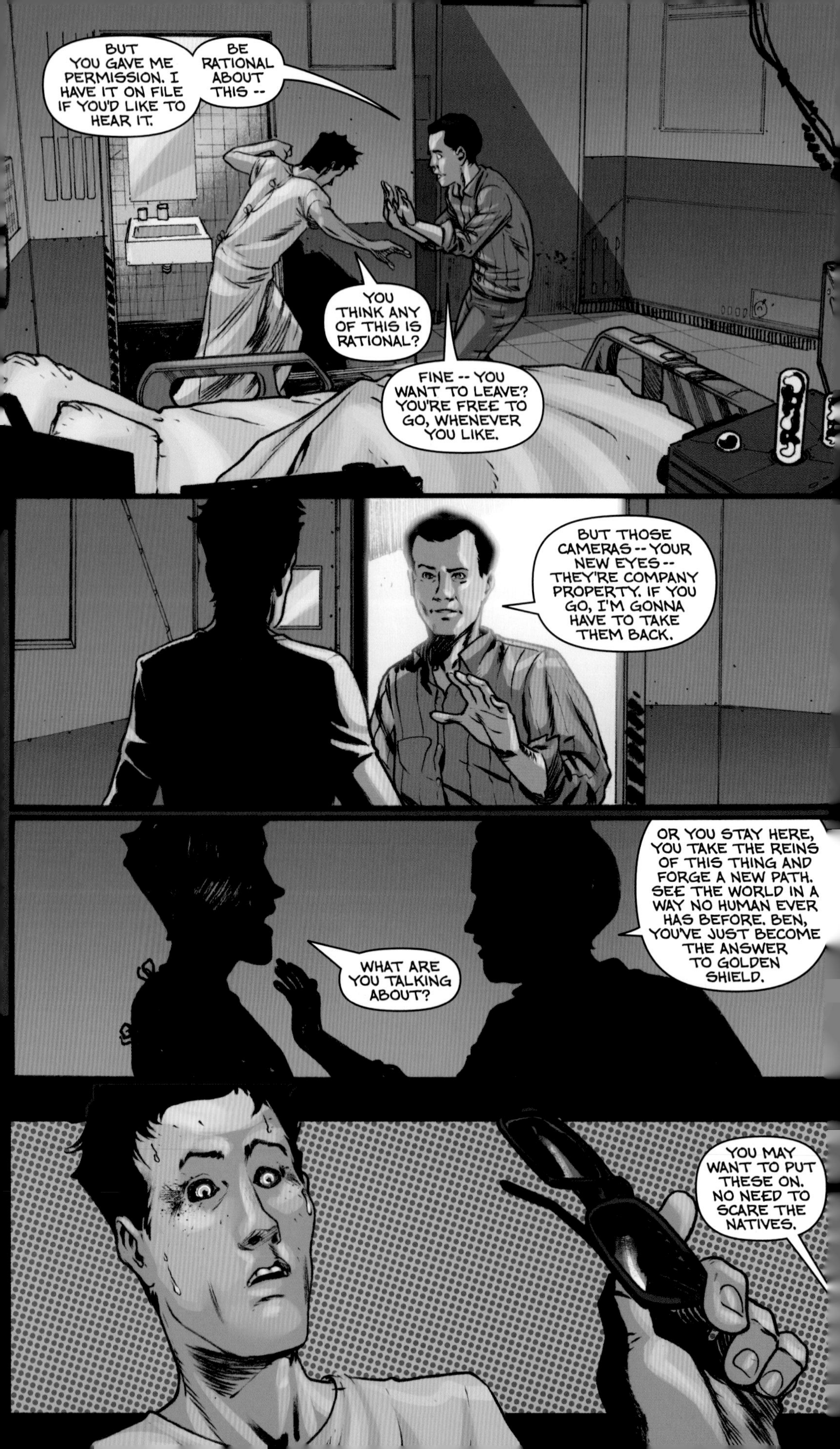
BUT YOU GAVE ME PERMISSION. I HAVE IT ON FILE IF YOU'D LIKE TO HEAR IT.
BE RATIONAL ABOUT THIS --
YOU THINK ANY OF THIS IS RATIONAL?
FINE -- YOU WANT TO LEAVE? YOU'RE FREE TO GO, WHENEVER YOU LIKE.
BUT THOSE CAMERAS -- YOUR NEW EYES -- THEY'RE COMPANY PROPERTY. IF YOU GO, I'M GONNA HAVE TO TAKE THEM BACK.
OR YOU STAY HERE, YOU TAKE THE REINS OF THIS THING AND FORGE A NEW PATH. SEE THE WORLD IN A WAY NO HUMAN EVER HAS BEFORE. BEN, YOU'VE JUST BECOME THE ANSWER TO GOLDEN SHIELD.
WHAT ARE YOU TALKING ABOUT?
YOU MAY WANT TO PUT THESE ON. NO NEED TO SCARE THE NATIVES.

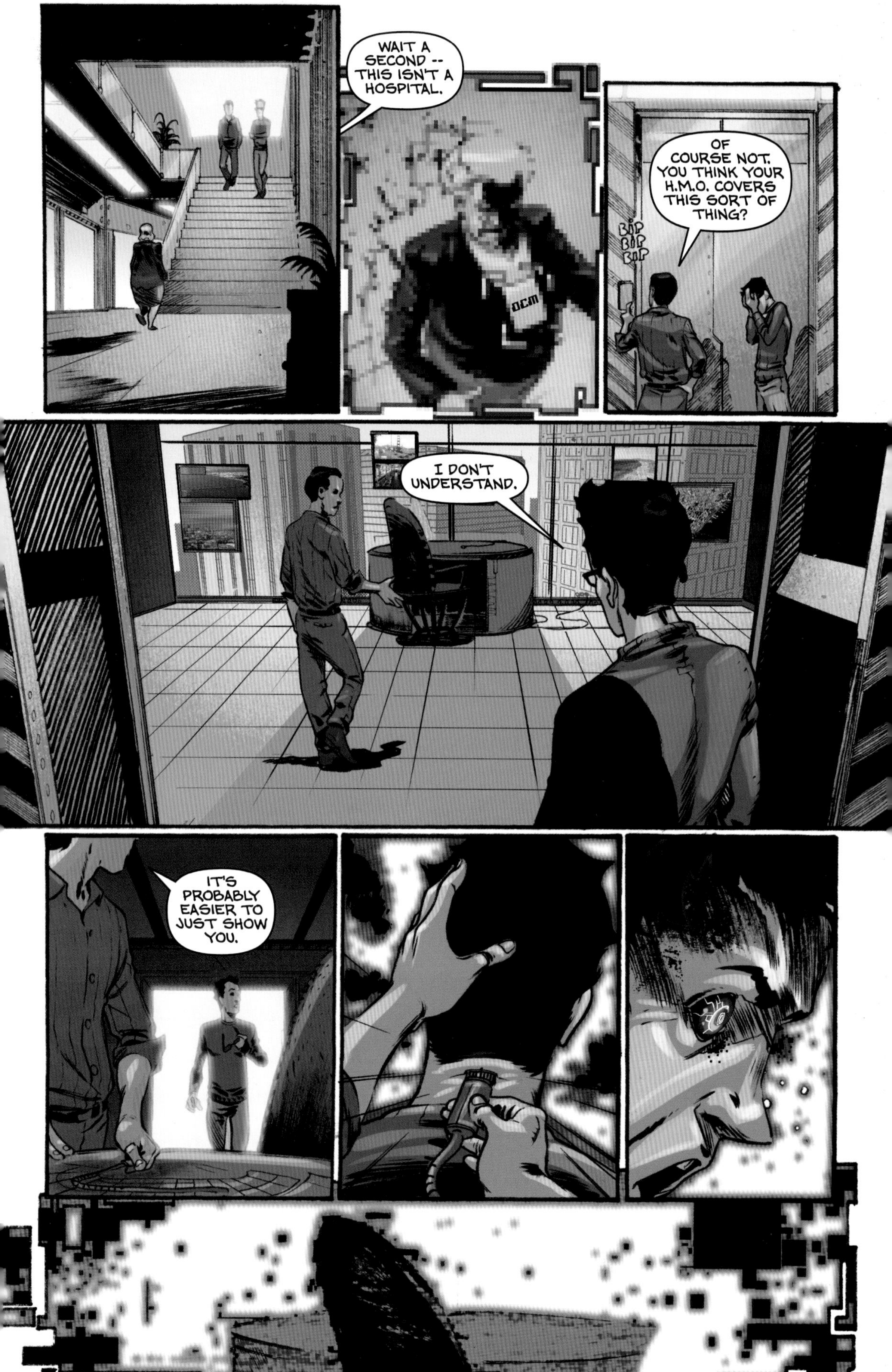
WAIT A SECOND -- THIS ISN'T A HOSPITAL.
OCM
BIP BIP BIP
OF COURSE NOT. YOU THINK YOUR H.M.O. COVERS THIS SORT OF THING?
I DON'T UNDERSTAND.
IT'S PROBABLY EASIER TO JUST SHOW YOU.

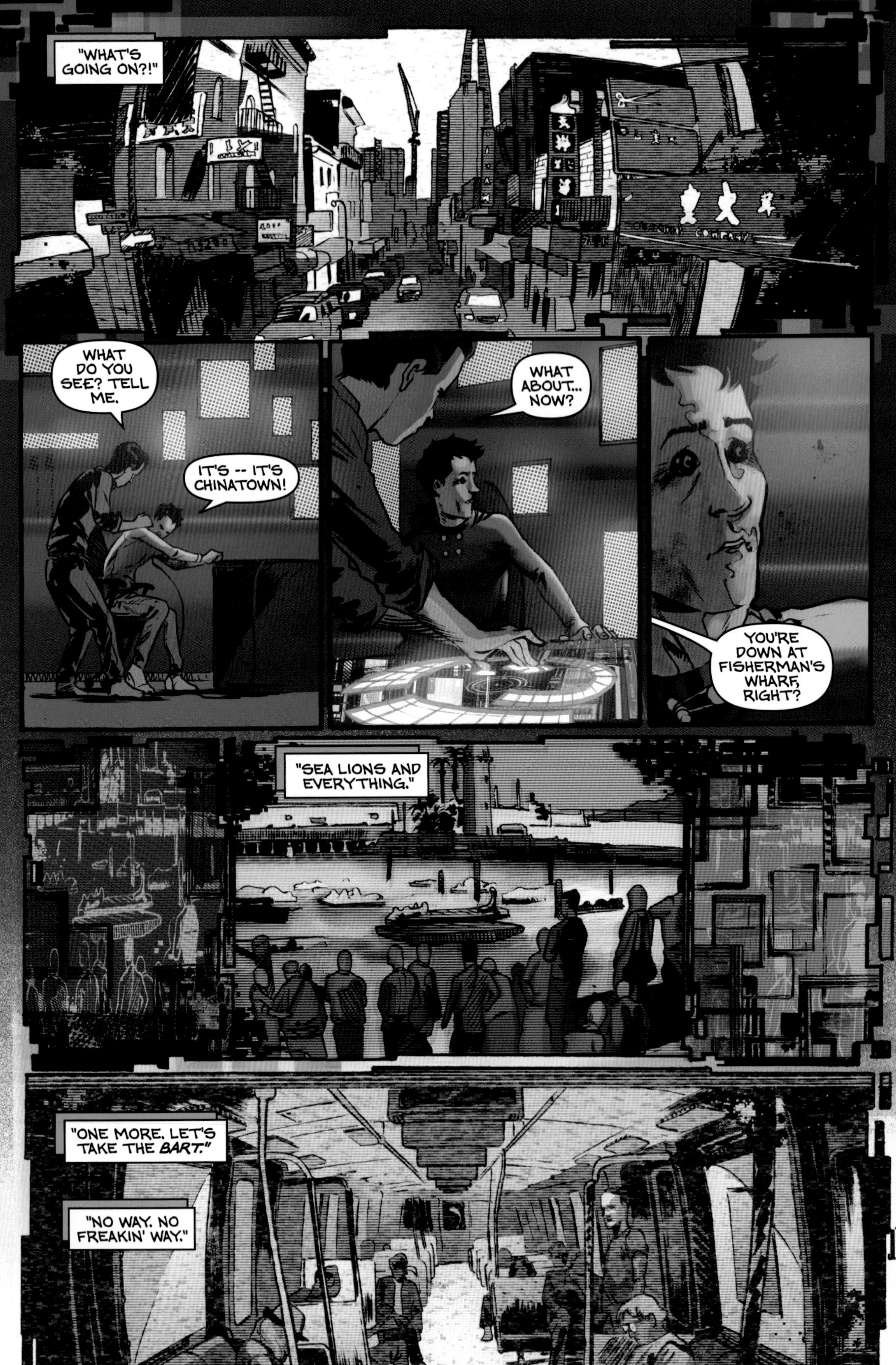
"WHAT'S GOING ON?!"
WHAT DO YOU SEE? TELL ME.
IT'S -- IT'S CHINATOWN!
WHAT ABOUT... NOW?
YOU'RE DOWN AT FISHERMAN'S WHARF, RIGHT?
"SEA LIONS AND EVERYTHING."
"ONE MORE. LET'S TAKE THE *BART.*"
"NO WAY. NO FREAKIN' WAY."

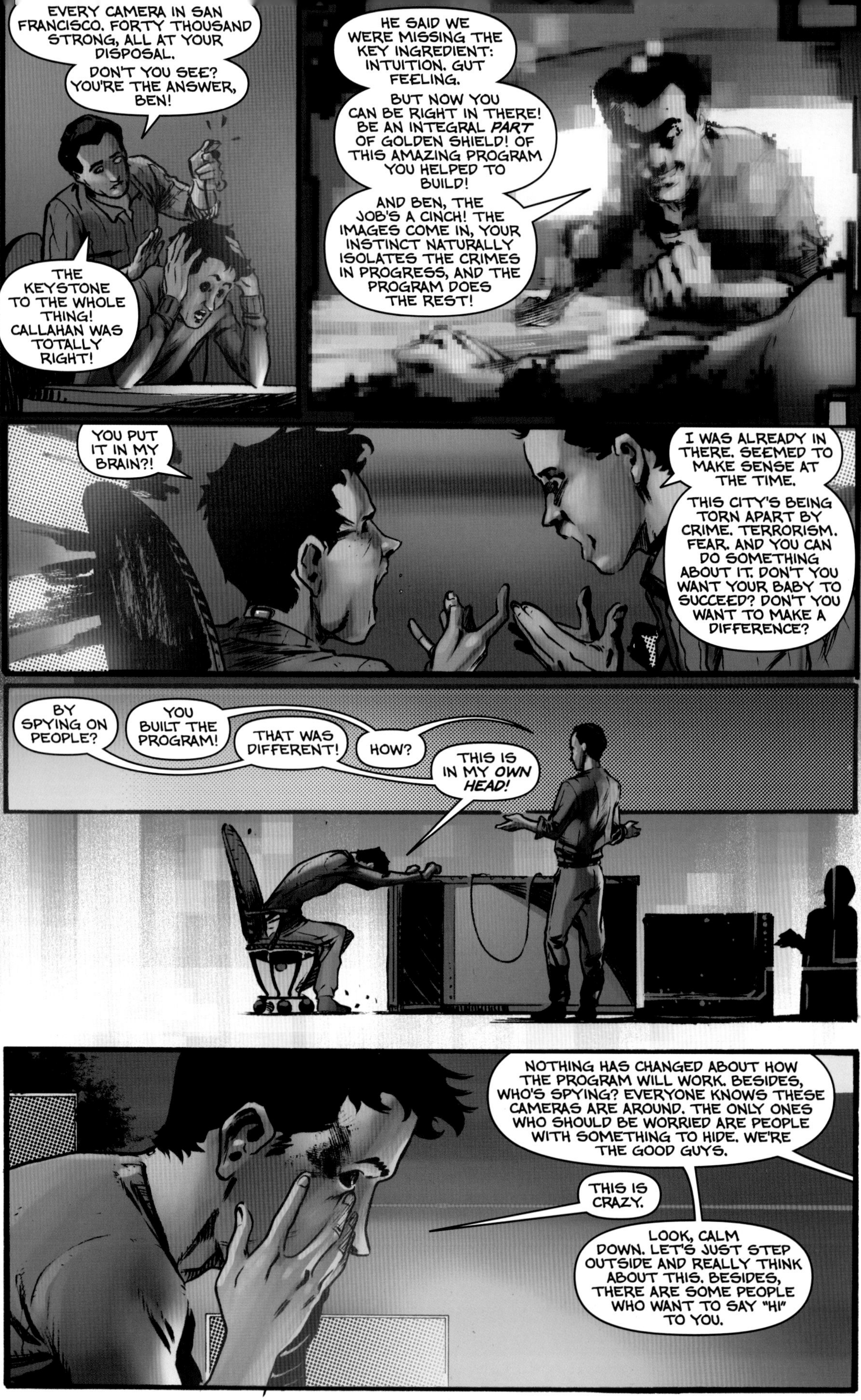
EVERY CAMERA IN SAN FRANCISCO. FORTY THOUSAND STRONG, ALL AT YOUR DISPOSAL.
DON'T YOU SEE? YOU'RE THE ANSWER, BEN!
THE KEYSTONE TO THE WHOLE THING! CALLAHAN WAS TOTALLY RIGHT!
HE SAID WE WERE MISSING THE KEY INGREDIENT: INTUITION. GUT FEELING.
BUT NOW YOU CAN BE RIGHT IN THERE! BE AN INTEGRAL *PART* OF GOLDEN SHIELD! OF THIS AMAZING PROGRAM YOU HELPED TO BUILD!
AND BEN, THE JOB'S A CINCH! THE IMAGES COME IN, YOUR INSTINCT NATURALLY ISOLATES THE CRIMES IN PROGRESS, AND THE PROGRAM DOES THE REST!
YOU PUT IT IN MY BRAIN?!
I WAS ALREADY IN THERE. SEEMED TO MAKE SENSE AT THE TIME.
THIS CITY'S BEING TORN APART BY CRIME. TERRORISM. FEAR. AND YOU CAN DO SOMETHING ABOUT IT. DON'T YOU WANT YOUR BABY TO SUCCEED? DON'T YOU WANT TO MAKE A DIFFERENCE?
BY SPYING ON PEOPLE?
YOU BUILT THE PROGRAM!
THAT WAS DIFFERENT!
HOW?
THIS IS IN MY *OWN HEAD!*
NOTHING HAS CHANGED ABOUT HOW THE PROGRAM WILL WORK. BESIDES, WHO'S SPYING? EVERYONE KNOWS THESE CAMERAS ARE AROUND. THE ONLY ONES WHO SHOULD BE WORRIED ARE PEOPLE WITH SOMETHING TO HIDE. WE'RE THE GOOD GUYS.
THIS IS CRAZY.
LOOK, CALM DOWN. LET'S JUST STEP OUTSIDE AND REALLY THINK ABOUT THIS. BESIDES, THERE ARE SOME PEOPLE WHO WANT TO SAY "HI" TO YOU.

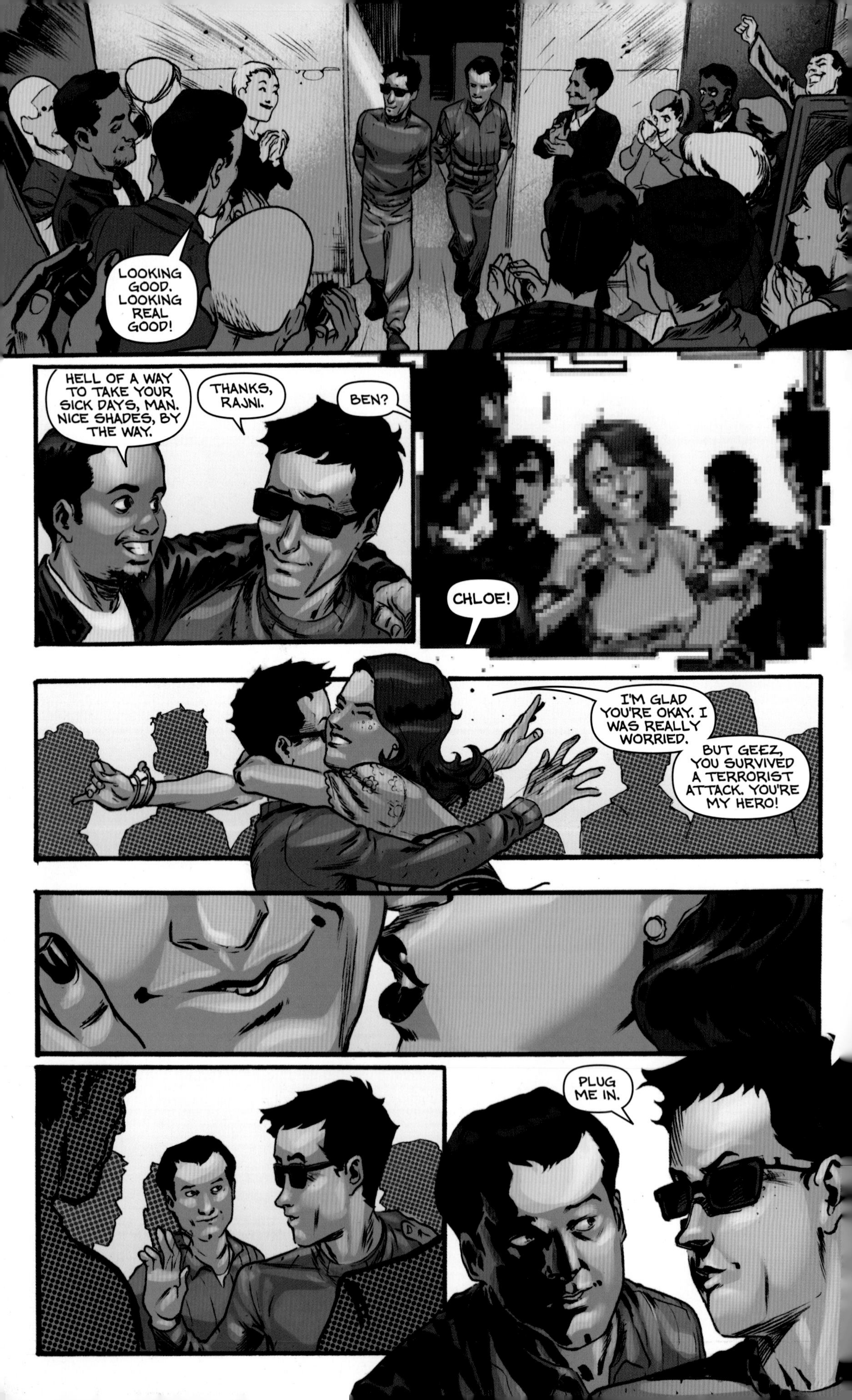
LOOKING GOOD. LOOKING REAL GOOD!
HELL OF A WAY TO TAKE YOUR SICK DAYS, MAN. NICE SHADES, BY THE WAY.
THANKS, RAJNI.
BEN?
CHLOE!
I'M GLAD YOU'RE OKAY. I WAS REALLY WORRIED.
BUT GEEZ, YOU SURVIVED A TERRORIST ATTACK. YOU'RE MY HERO!
PLUG ME IN.

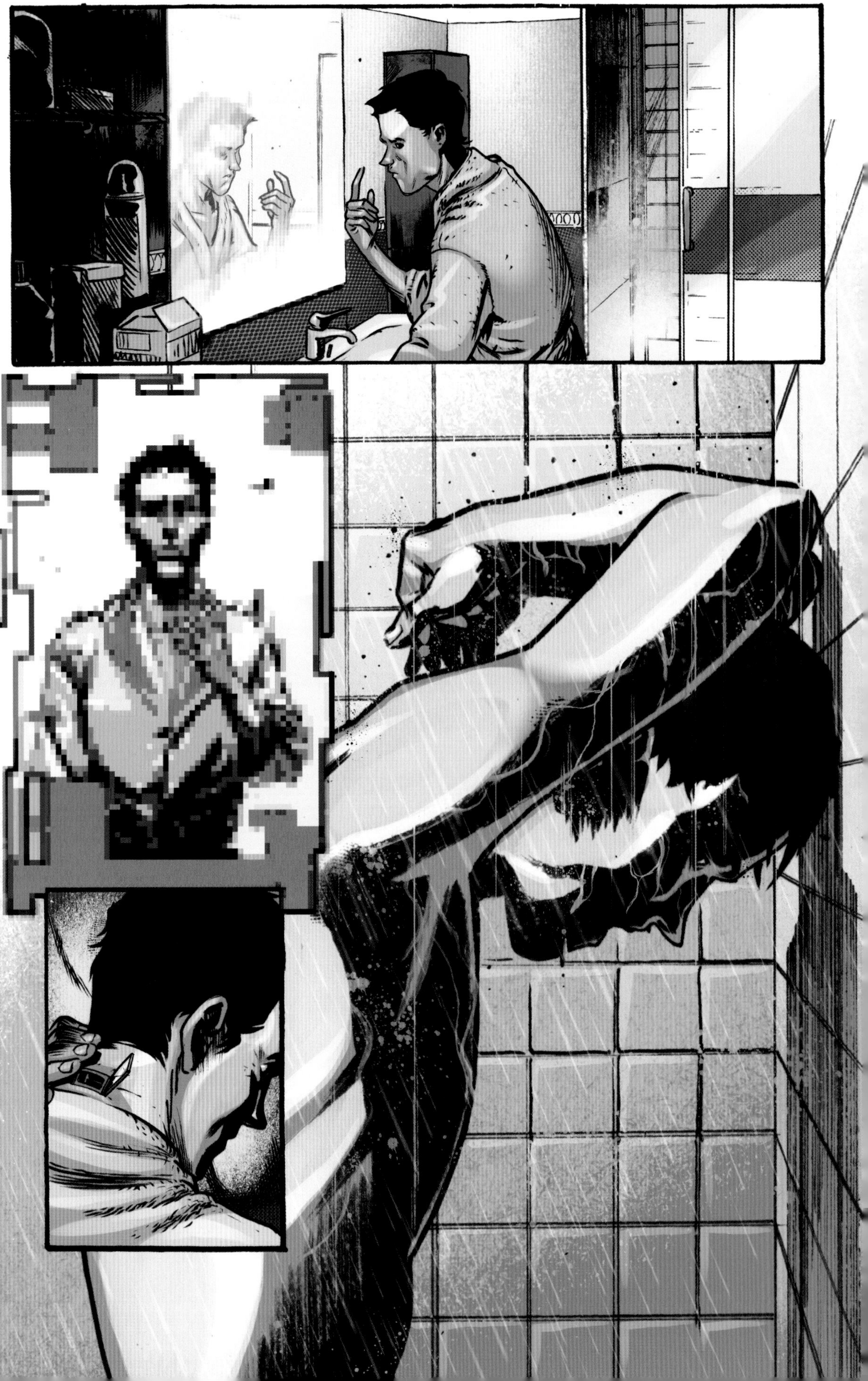

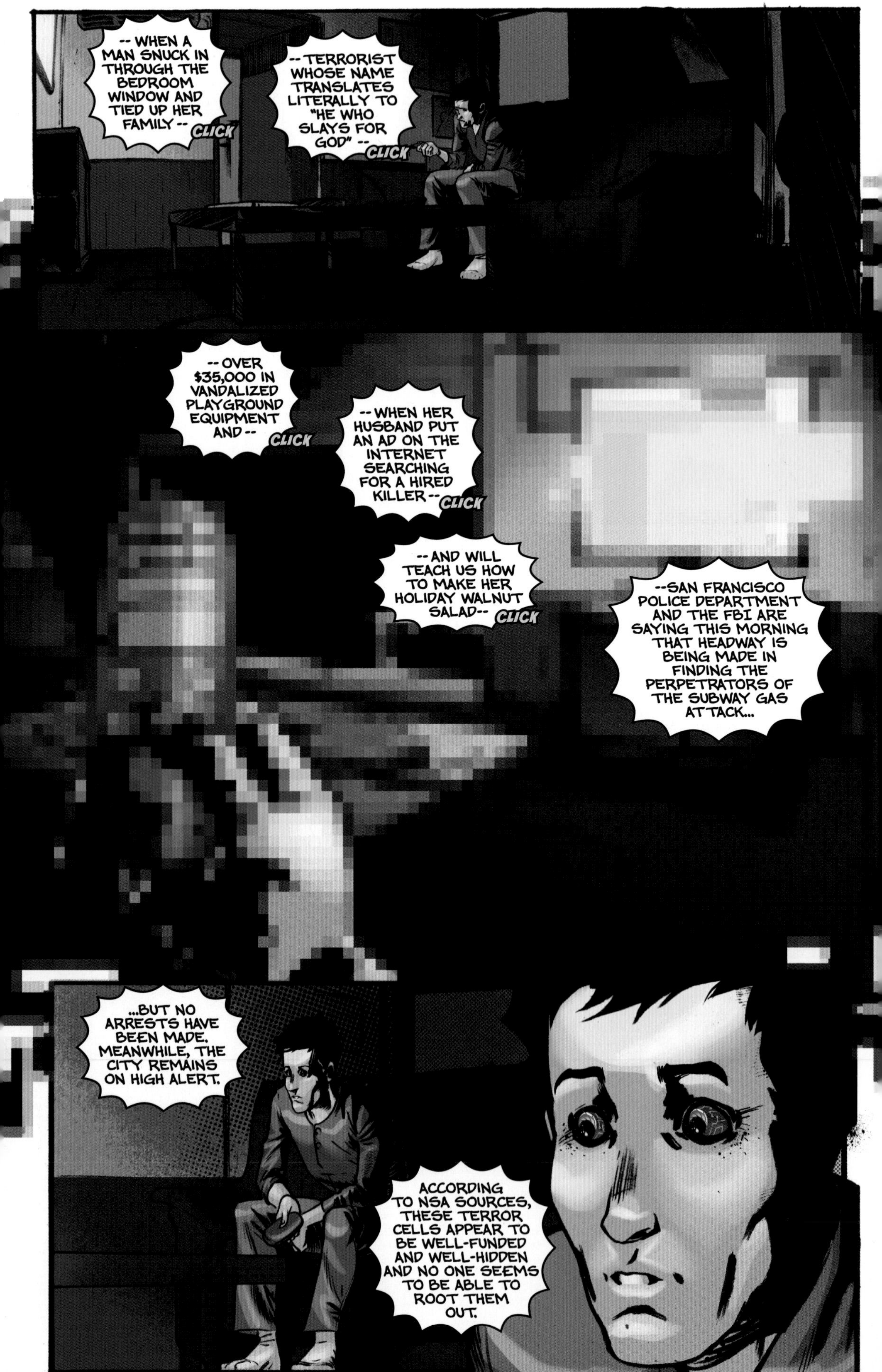
-- WHEN A MAN SNUCK IN THROUGH THE BEDROOM WINDOW AND TIED UP HER FAMILY --
CLICK
-- TERRORIST WHOSE NAME TRANSLATES LITERALLY TO "HE WHO SLAYS FOR GOD" --
CLICK
-- OVER $35,000 IN VANDALIZED PLAYGROUND EQUIPMENT AND --
CLICK
-- WHEN HER HUSBAND PUT AN AD ON THE INTERNET SEARCHING FOR A HIRED KILLER --
CLICK
-- AND WILL TEACH US HOW TO MAKE HER HOLIDAY WALNUT SALAD--
CLICK
--SAN FRANCISCO POLICE DEPARTMENT AND THE FBI ARE SAYING THIS MORNING THAT HEADWAY IS BEING MADE IN FINDING THE PERPETRATORS OF THE SUBWAY GAS ATTACK...
...BUT NO ARRESTS HAVE BEEN MADE. MEANWHILE, THE CITY REMAINS ON HIGH ALERT.
ACCORDING TO NSA SOURCES, THESE TERROR CELLS APPEAR TO BE WELL-FUNDED AND WELL-HIDDEN AND NO ONE SEEMS TO BE ABLE TO ROOT THEM OUT.

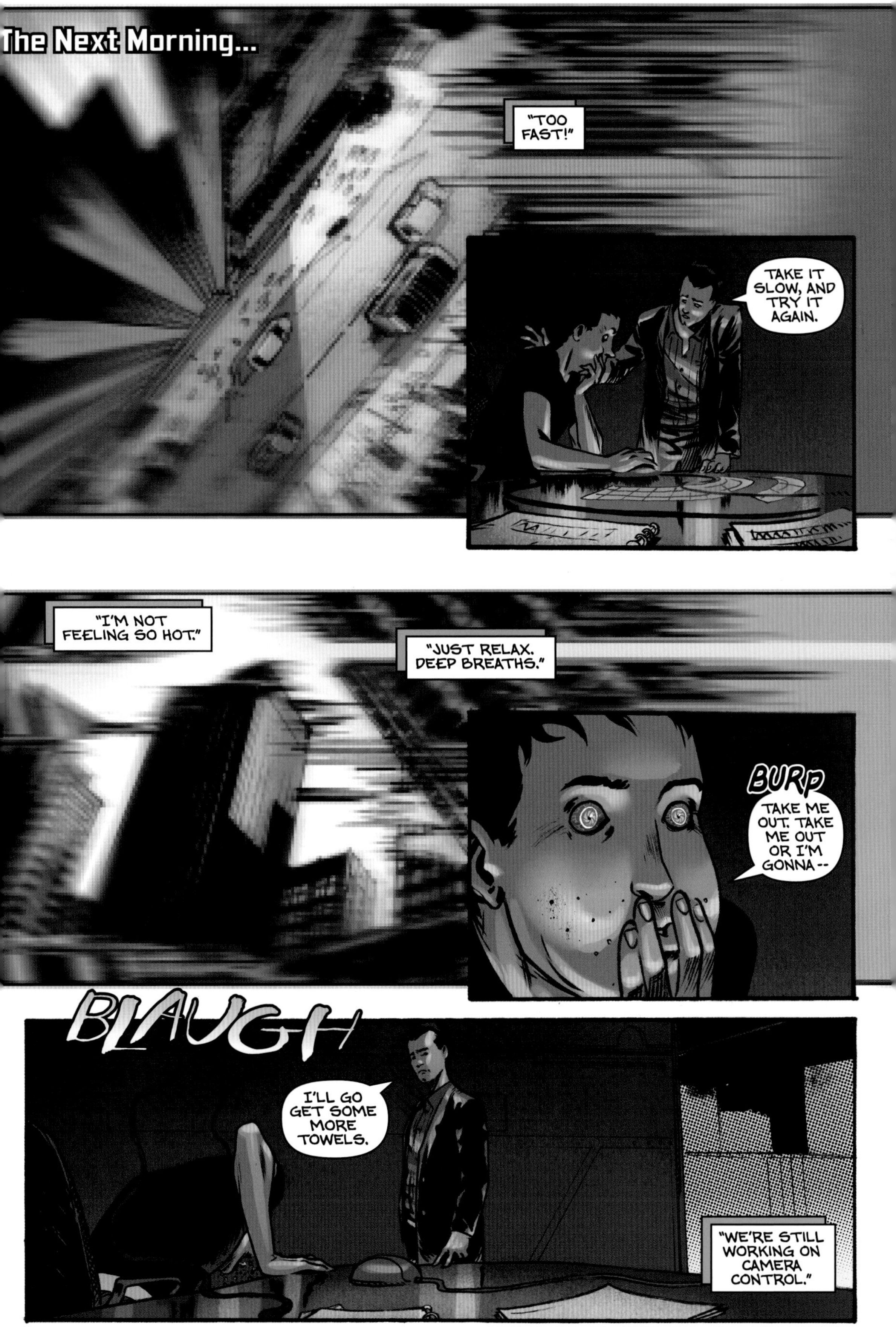
The Next Morning...
"TOO FAST!"
TAKE IT SLOW, AND TRY IT AGAIN.
"I'M NOT FEELING SO HOT."
"JUST RELAX. DEEP BREATHS."
BURP
TAKE ME OUT. TAKE ME OUT OR I'M GONNA --
BLAUGH
I'LL GO GET SOME MORE TOWELS.
"WE'RE STILL WORKING ON CAMERA CONTROL."

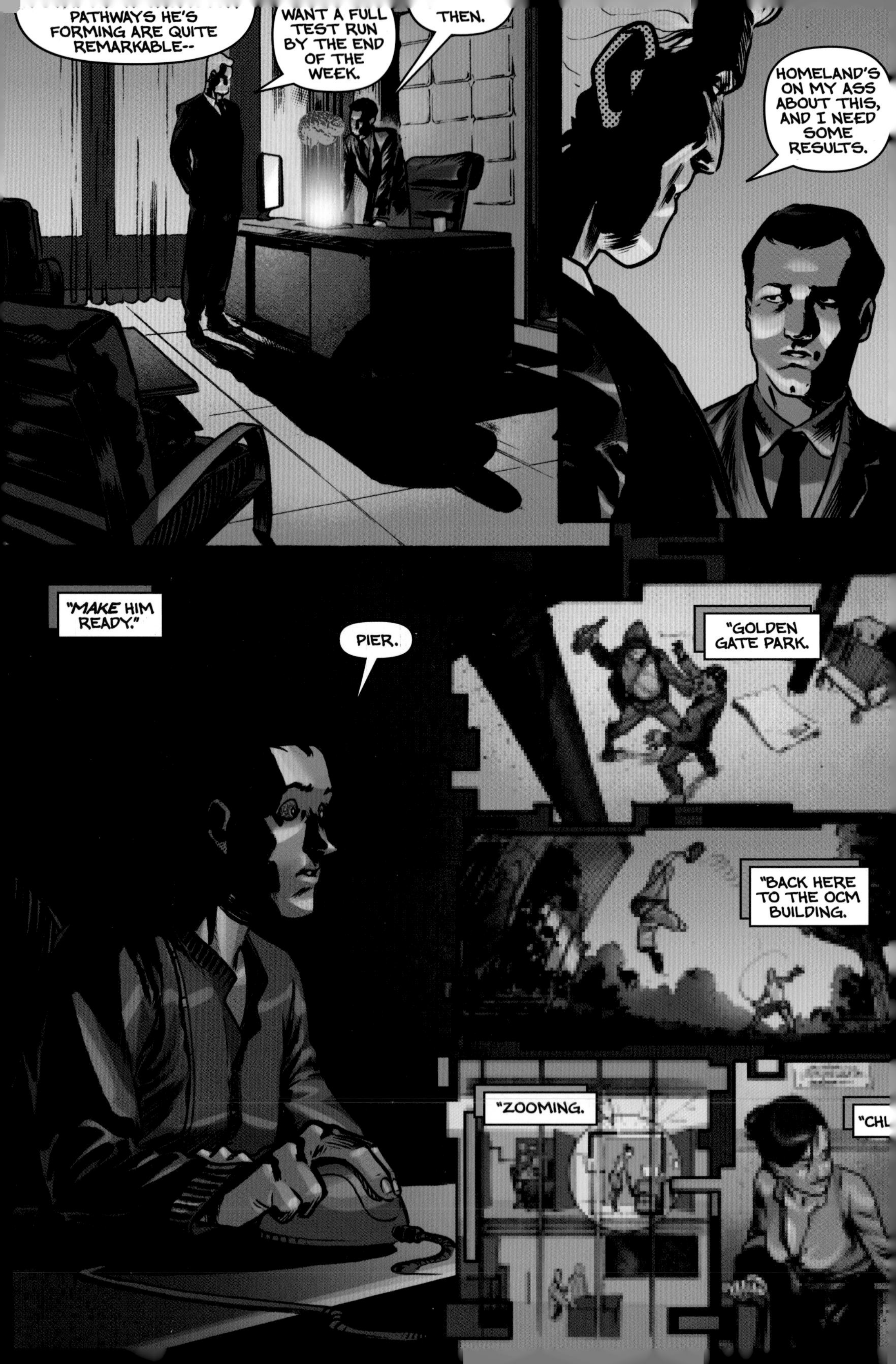
PATHWAYS HE'S FORMING ARE QUITE REMARKABLE--
WANT A FULL TEST RUN BY THE END OF THE WEEK.
THEN.
HOMELAND'S ON MY ASS ABOUT THIS, AND I NEED SOME RESULTS.
"MAKE HIM READY."
PIER.
"GOLDEN GATE PARK.
"BACK HERE TO THE OCM BUILDING.
"ZOOMING.

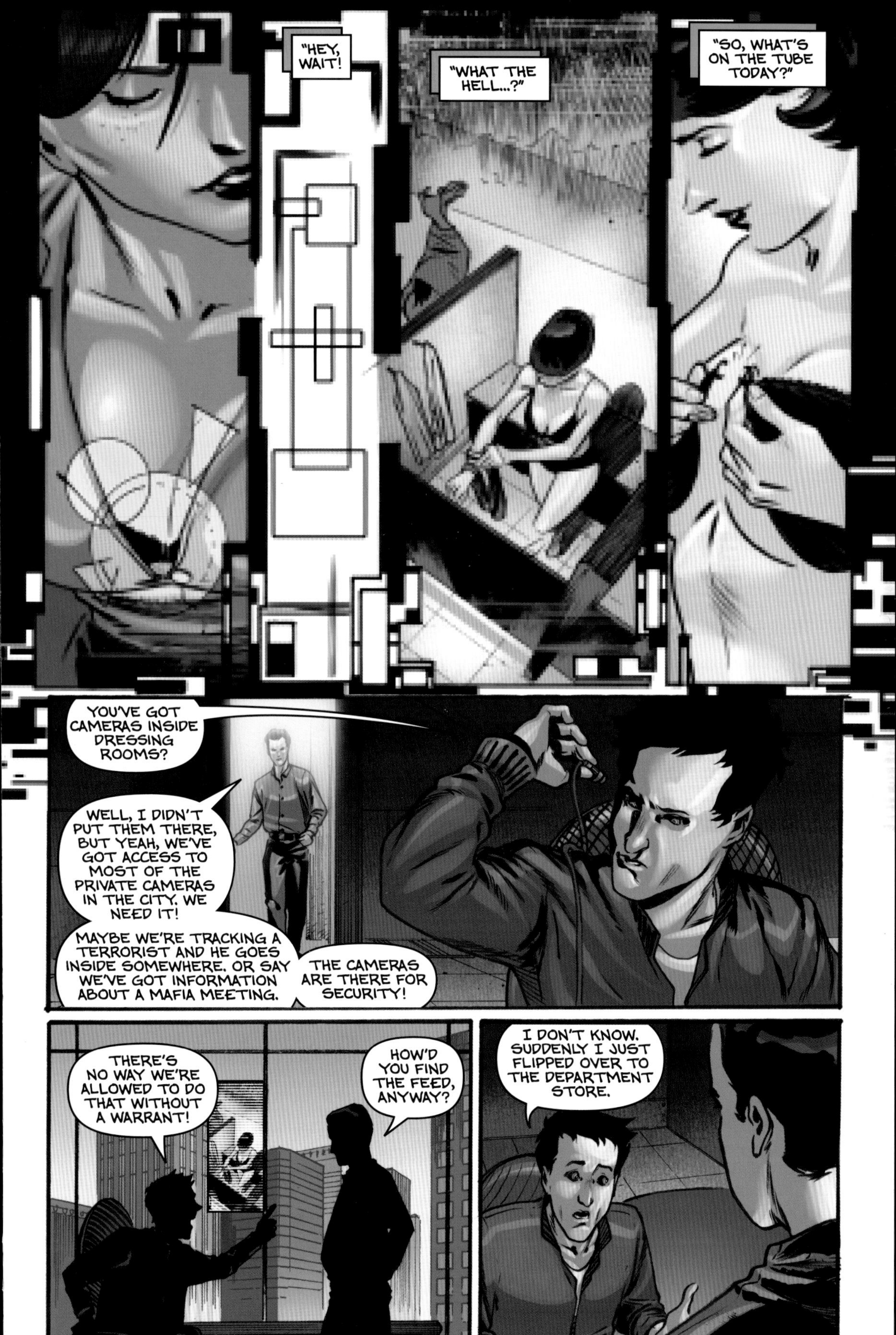
"HEY, WAIT!
"WHAT THE HELL...?"
"SO, WHAT'S ON THE TUBE TODAY?"
YOU'VE GOT CAMERAS INSIDE DRESSING ROOMS?
WELL, I DIDN'T PUT THEM THERE, BUT YEAH, WE'VE GOT ACCESS TO MOST OF THE PRIVATE CAMERAS IN THE CITY. WE NEED IT!
MAYBE WE'RE TRACKING A TERRORIST AND HE GOES INSIDE SOMEWHERE. OR SAY WE'VE GOT INFORMATION ABOUT A MAFIA MEETING.
THE CAMERAS ARE THERE FOR SECURITY!
THERE'S NO WAY WE'RE ALLOWED TO DO THAT WITHOUT A WARRANT!
HOW'D YOU FIND THE FEED, ANYWAY?
I DON'T KNOW. SUDDENLY I JUST FLIPPED OVER TO THE DEPARTMENT STORE.

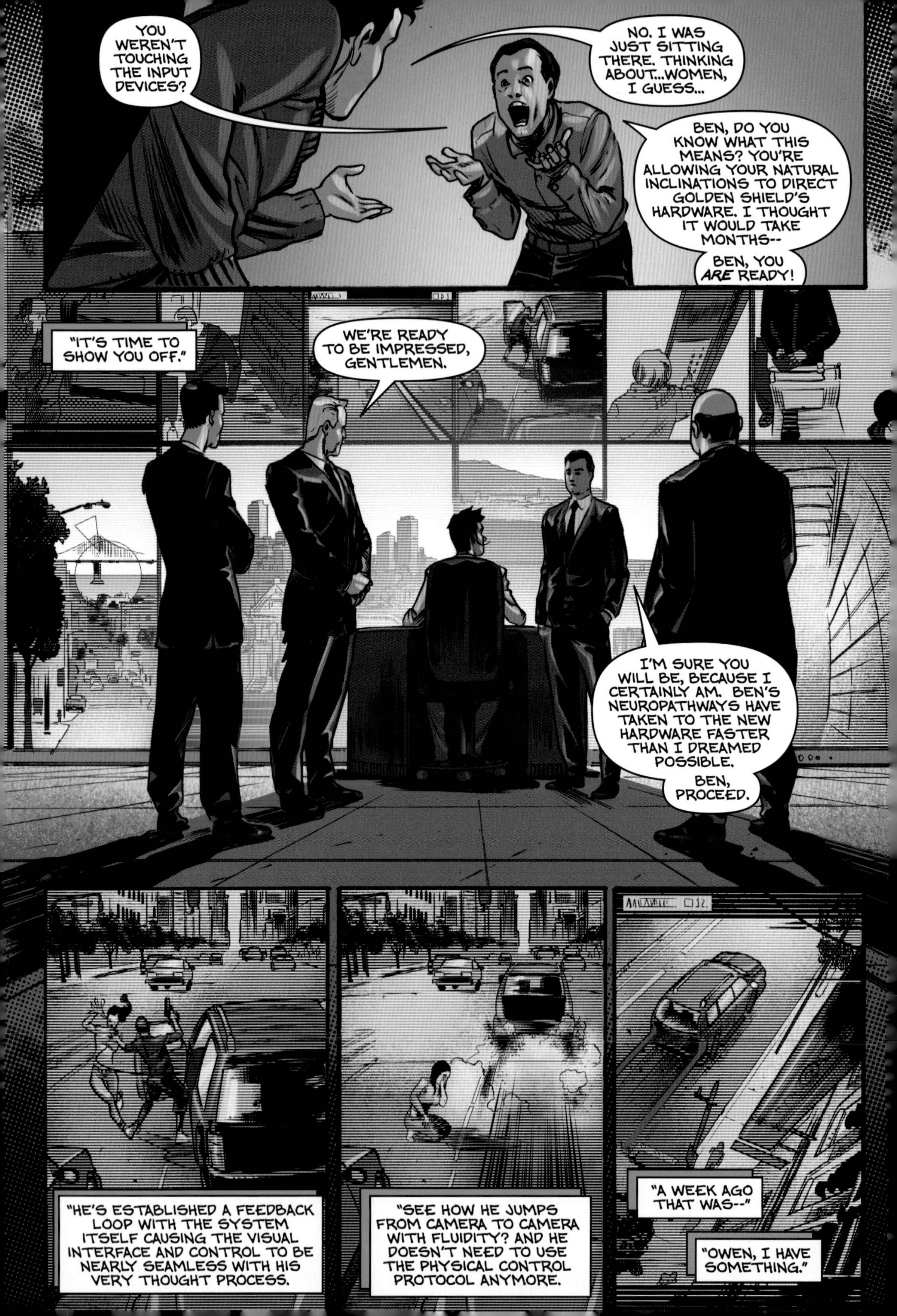
YOU WEREN'T TOUCHING THE INPUT DEVICES?
NO. I WAS JUST SITTING THERE. THINKING ABOUT...WOMEN, I GUESS...
BEN, DO YOU KNOW WHAT THIS MEANS? YOU'RE ALLOWING YOUR NATURAL INCLINATIONS TO DIRECT GOLDEN SHIELD'S HARDWARE. I THOUGHT IT WOULD TAKE MONTHS--
BEN, YOU *ARE* READY!
"IT'S TIME TO SHOW YOU OFF."
WE'RE READY TO BE IMPRESSED, GENTLEMEN.
I'M SURE YOU WILL BE, BECAUSE I CERTAINLY AM. BEN'S NEUROPATHWAYS HAVE TAKEN TO THE NEW HARDWARE FASTER THAN I DREAMED POSSIBLE.
BEN, PROCEED.
"HE'S ESTABLISHED A FEEDBACK LOOP WITH THE SYSTEM ITSELF CAUSING THE VISUAL INTERFACE AND CONTROL TO BE NEARLY SEAMLESS WITH HIS VERY THOUGHT PROCESS.
"SEE HOW HE JUMPS FROM CAMERA TO CAMERA WITH FLUIDITY? AND HE DOESN'T NEED TO USE THE PHYSICAL CONTROL PROTOCOL ANYMORE.
"A WEEK AGO THAT WAS--"
"OWEN, I HAVE SOMETHING."

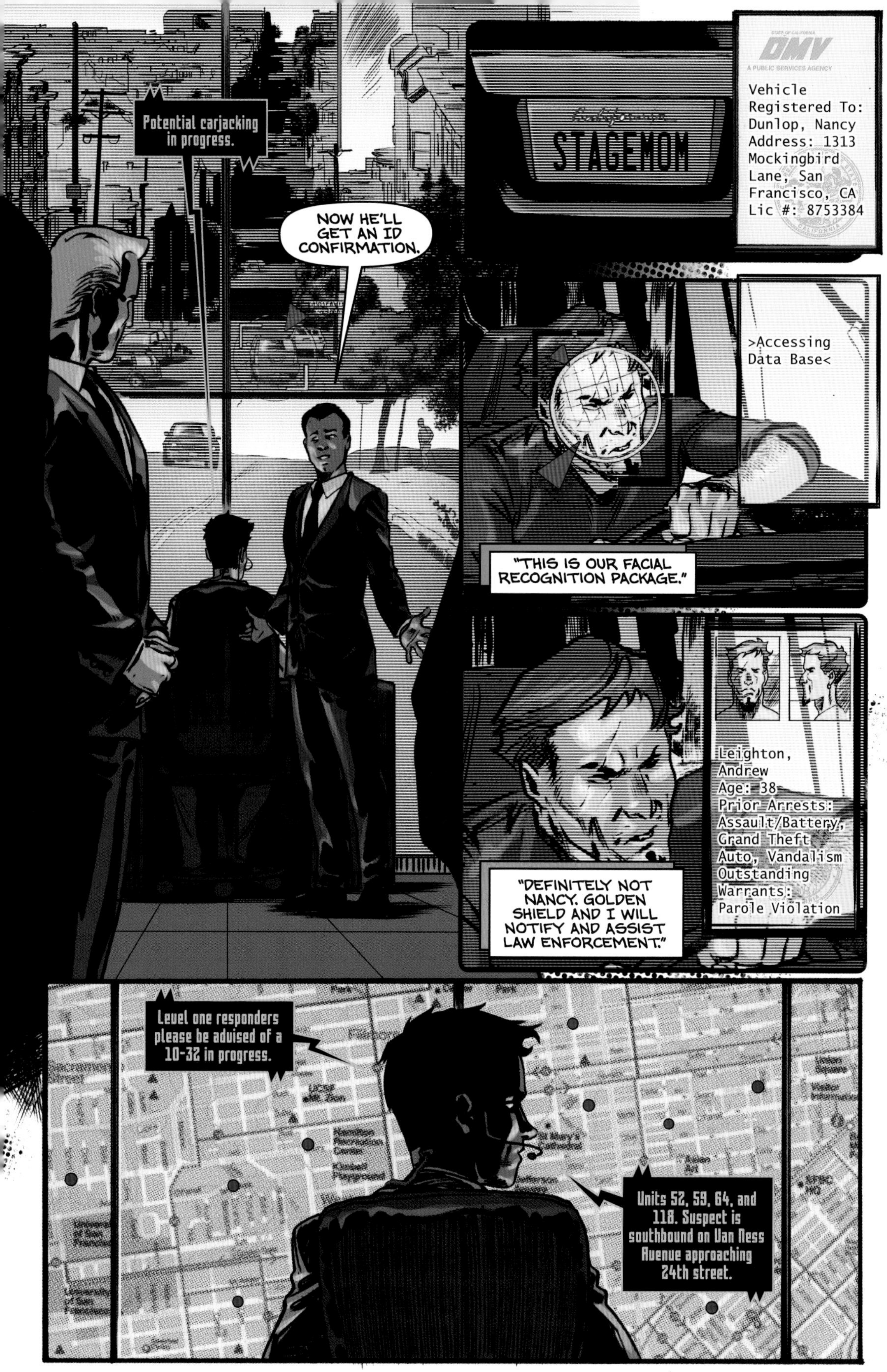
Potential carjacking in progress.
NOW HE'LL GET AN ID CONFIRMATION.
STAGEMOM
STATE OF CALIFORNIA
DMV
A PUBLIC SERVICES AGENCY
Vehicle Registered To: Dunlop, Nancy Address: 1313 Mockingbird Lane, San Francisco, CA Lic #: 8753384
>Accessing Data Base<
"THIS IS OUR FACIAL RECOGNITION PACKAGE."
Leighton, Andrew Age: 38 Prior Arrests: Assault/Battery, Grand Theft Auto, Vandalism Outstanding Warrants: Parole Violation
"DEFINITELY NOT NANCY. GOLDEN SHIELD AND I WILL NOTIFY AND ASSIST LAW ENFORCEMENT."
Level one responders please be advised of a 10-32 in progress.
Units 52, 59, 64, and 118. Suspect is southbound on Van Ness Avenue approaching 24th street.

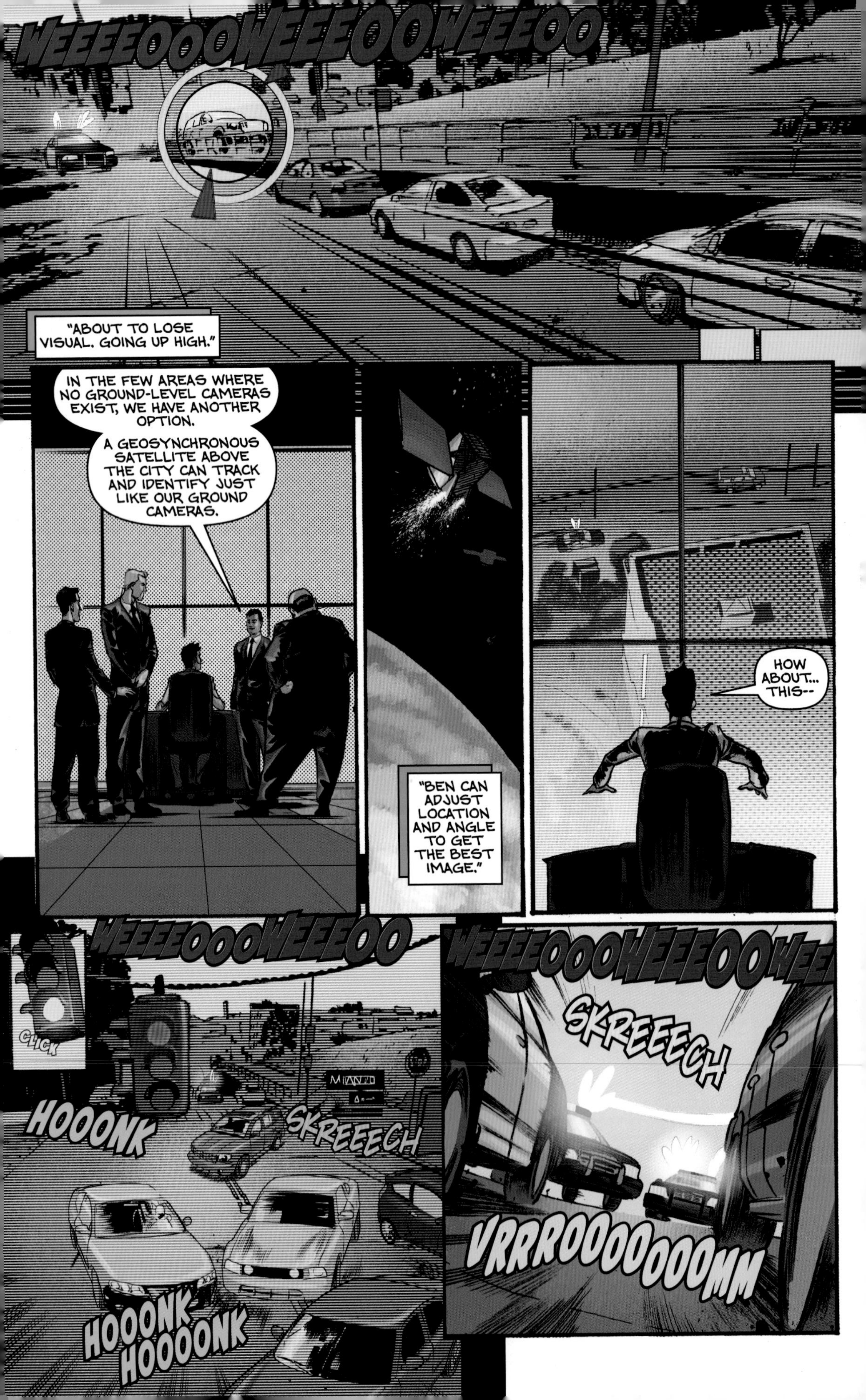
WEEEEOOOWEEEEOOWEEEEOO
"ABOUT TO LOSE VISUAL. GOING UP HIGH."
IN THE FEW AREAS WHERE NO GROUND-LEVEL CAMERAS EXIST, WE HAVE ANOTHER OPTION.
A GEOSYNCHRONOUS SATELLITE ABOVE THE CITY CAN TRACK AND IDENTIFY JUST LIKE OUR GROUND CAMERAS.
"BEN CAN ADJUST LOCATION AND ANGLE TO GET THE BEST IMAGE."
HOW ABOUT... THIS--
WEEEEOOOWEEEOO
CLICK
HOOONK
SKREEECH
HOOONK HOOOONK
SKREEECH
VRRROOOOOOOMM

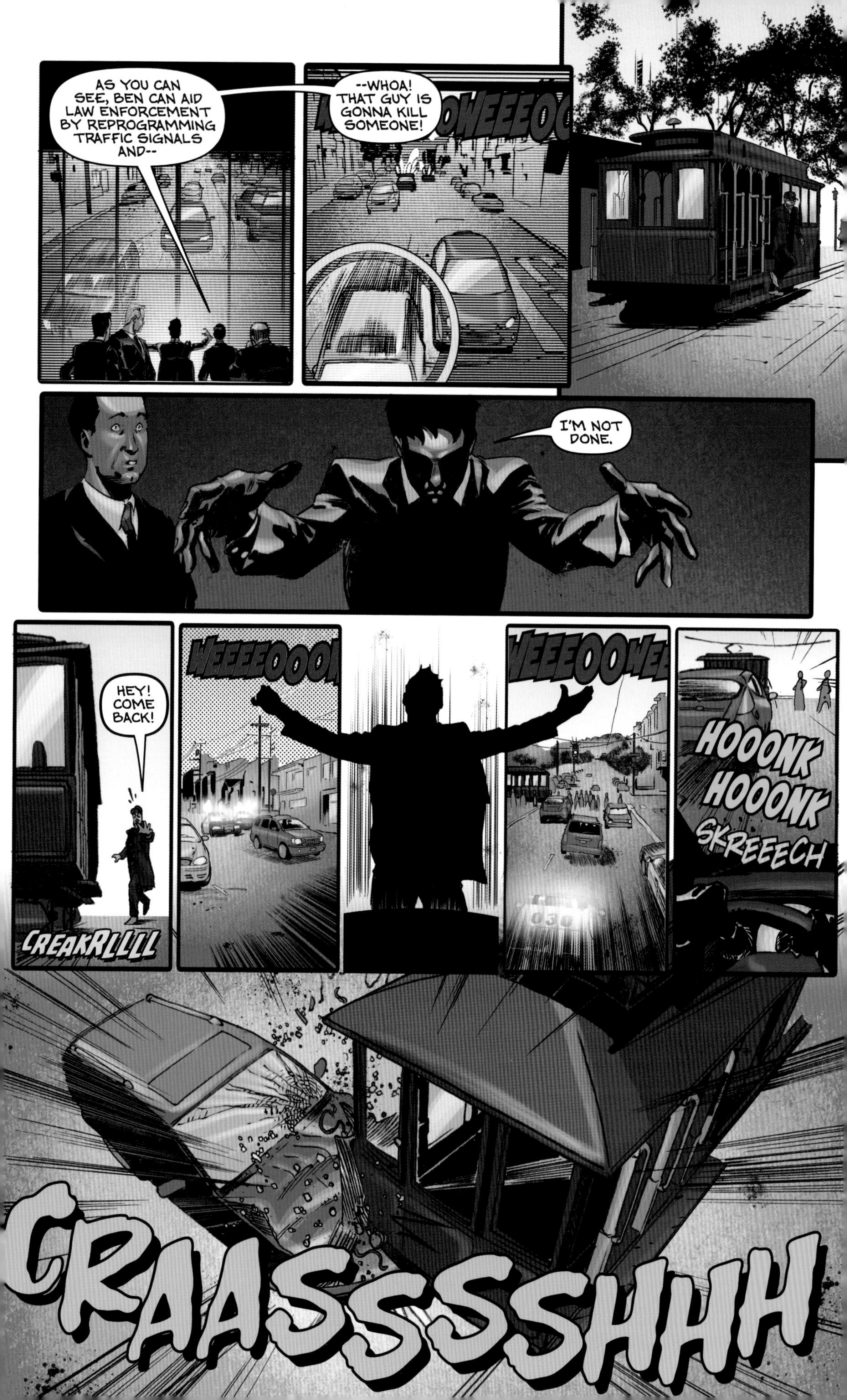
AS YOU CAN SEE, BEN CAN AID LAW ENFORCEMENT BY REPROGRAMMING TRAFFIC SIGNALS AND--
--WHOA! THAT GUY IS GONNA KILL SOMEONE!
I'M NOT DONE.
HEY! COME BACK!
CREAKRLLLL
WEEEEOOOO
WEEEOOWEE
HOOONK HOOONK
SKREEECH
CRAASSSSHHH

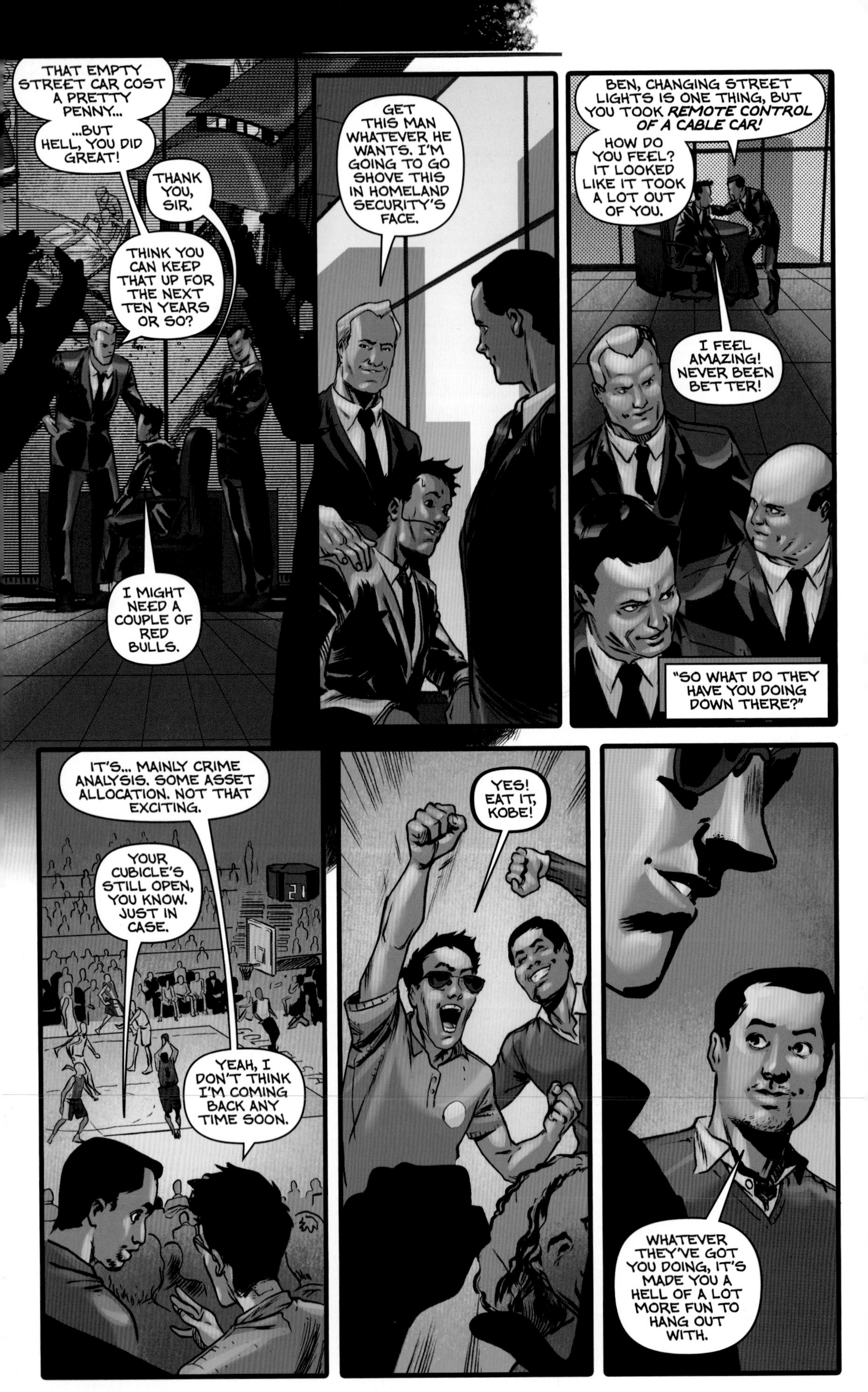
THAT EMPTY STREET CAR COST A PRETTY PENNY...
...BUT HELL, YOU DID GREAT!
THANK YOU, SIR.
THINK YOU CAN KEEP THAT UP FOR THE NEXT TEN YEARS OR SO?
I MIGHT NEED A COUPLE OF RED BULLS.
GET THIS MAN WHATEVER HE WANTS. I'M GOING TO GO SHOVE THIS IN HOMELAND SECURITY'S FACE.
BEN, CHANGING STREET LIGHTS IS ONE THING, BUT YOU TOOK *REMOTE CONTROL OF A CABLE CAR!*
HOW DO YOU FEEL? IT LOOKED LIKE IT TOOK A LOT OUT OF YOU.
I FEEL AMAZING! NEVER BEEN BETTER!
"SO WHAT DO THEY HAVE YOU DOING DOWN THERE?"
IT'S... MAINLY CRIME ANALYSIS. SOME ASSET ALLOCATION. NOT THAT EXCITING.
YOUR CUBICLE'S STILL OPEN, YOU KNOW. JUST IN CASE.
YEAH, I DON'T THINK I'M COMING BACK ANY TIME SOON.
YES! EAT IT, KOBE!
WHATEVER THEY'VE GOT YOU DOING, IT'S MADE YOU A HELL OF A LOT MORE FUN TO HANG OUT WITH.

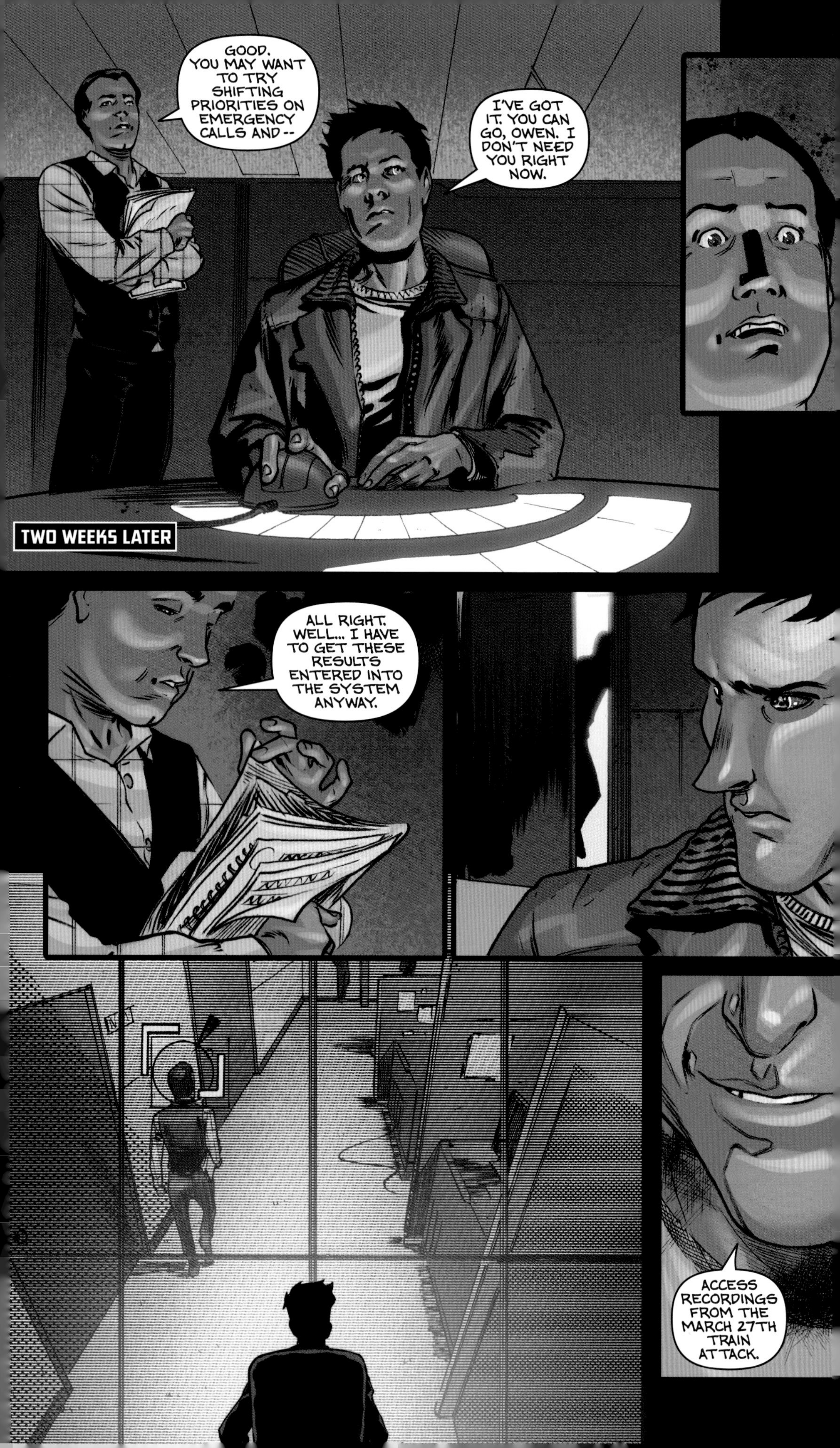
GOOD. YOU MAY WANT TO TRY SHIFTING PRIORITIES ON EMERGENCY CALLS AND --
I'VE GOT IT. YOU CAN GO, OWEN. I DON'T NEED YOU RIGHT NOW.
TWO WEEKS LATER
ALL RIGHT. WELL... I HAVE TO GET THESE RESULTS ENTERED INTO THE SYSTEM ANYWAY.
ACCESS RECORDINGS FROM THE MARCH 27TH TRAIN ATTACK.

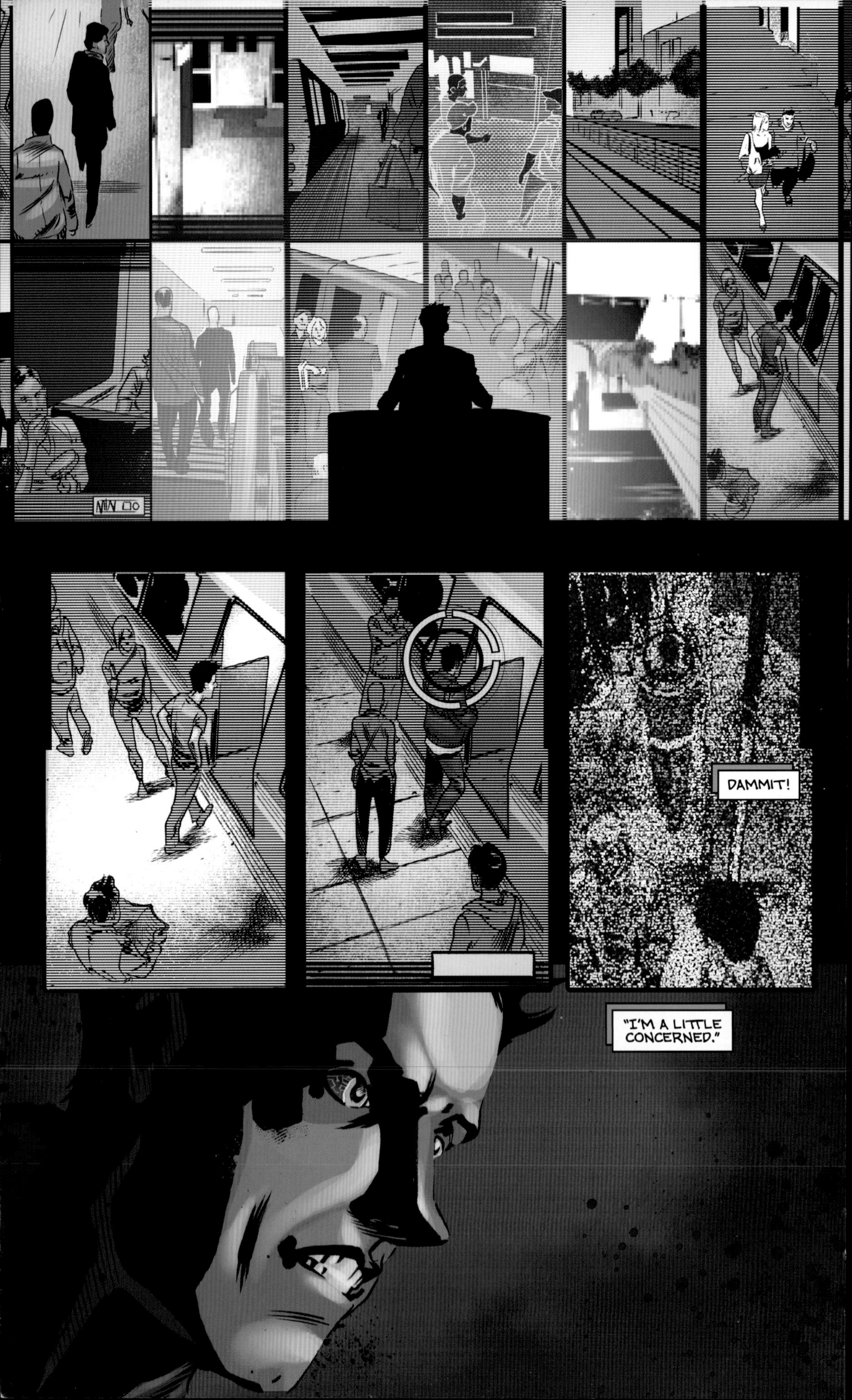
DAMMIT!
"I'M A LITTLE CONCERNED."

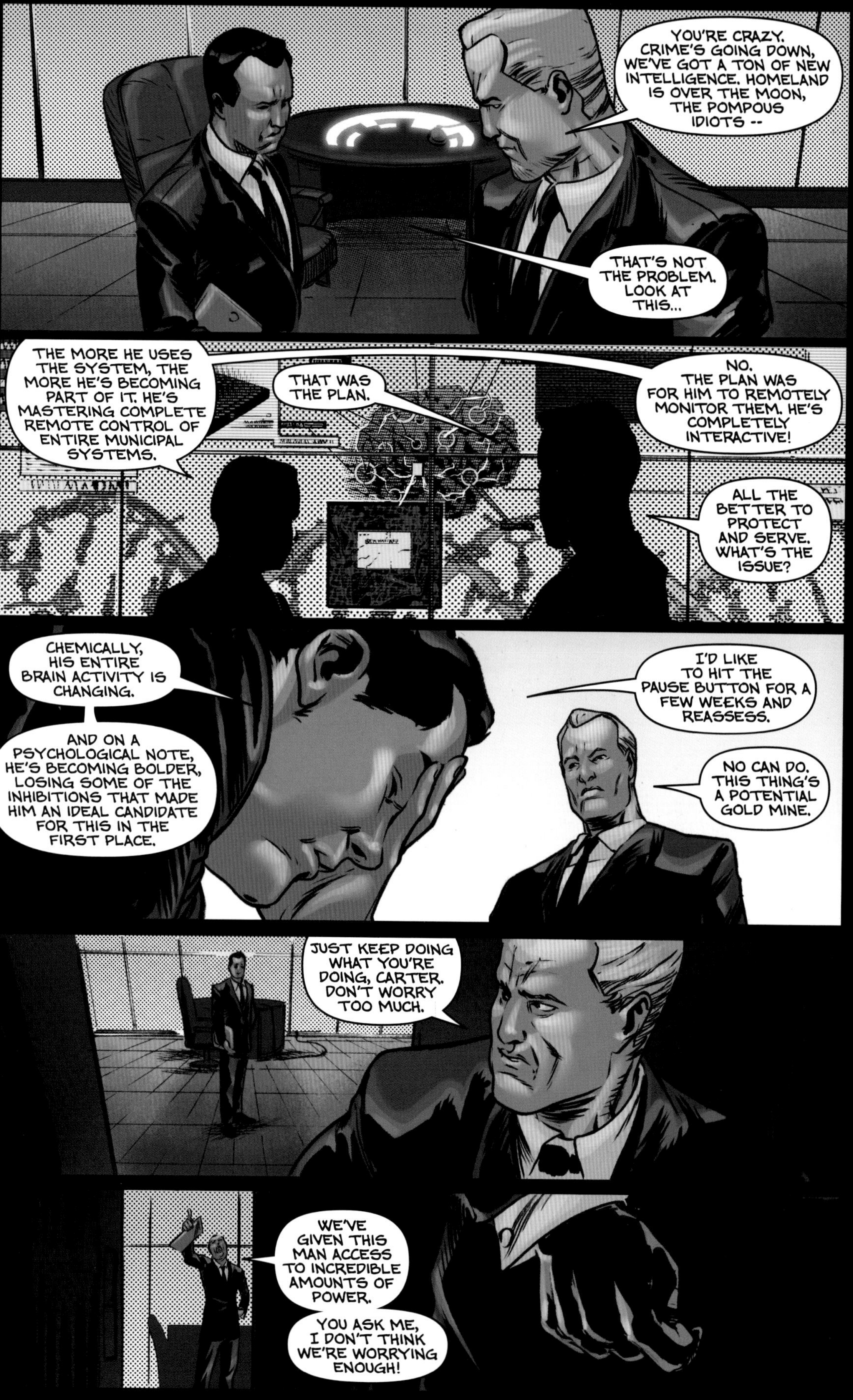
YOU'RE CRAZY. CRIME'S GOING DOWN, WE'VE GOT A TON OF NEW INTELLIGENCE. HOMELAND IS OVER THE MOON, THE POMPOUS IDIOTS --
THAT'S NOT THE PROBLEM. LOOK AT THIS...
THE MORE HE USES THE SYSTEM, THE MORE HE'S BECOMING PART OF IT. HE'S MASTERING COMPLETE REMOTE CONTROL OF ENTIRE MUNICIPAL SYSTEMS.
THAT WAS THE PLAN.
NO. THE PLAN WAS FOR HIM TO REMOTELY MONITOR THEM. HE'S COMPLETELY INTERACTIVE!
ALL THE BETTER TO PROTECT AND SERVE. WHAT'S THE ISSUE?
CHEMICALLY, HIS ENTIRE BRAIN ACTIVITY IS CHANGING.
AND ON A PSYCHOLOGICAL NOTE, HE'S BECOMING BOLDER, LOSING SOME OF THE INHIBITIONS THAT MADE HIM AN IDEAL CANDIDATE FOR THIS IN THE FIRST PLACE.
I'D LIKE TO HIT THE PAUSE BUTTON FOR A FEW WEEKS AND REASSESS.
NO CAN DO. THIS THING'S A POTENTIAL GOLD MINE.
JUST KEEP DOING WHAT YOU'RE DOING, CARTER. DON'T WORRY TOO MUCH.
WE'VE GIVEN THIS MAN ACCESS TO INCREDIBLE AMOUNTS OF POWER.
YOU ASK ME, I DON'T THINK WE'RE WORRYING ENOUGH!

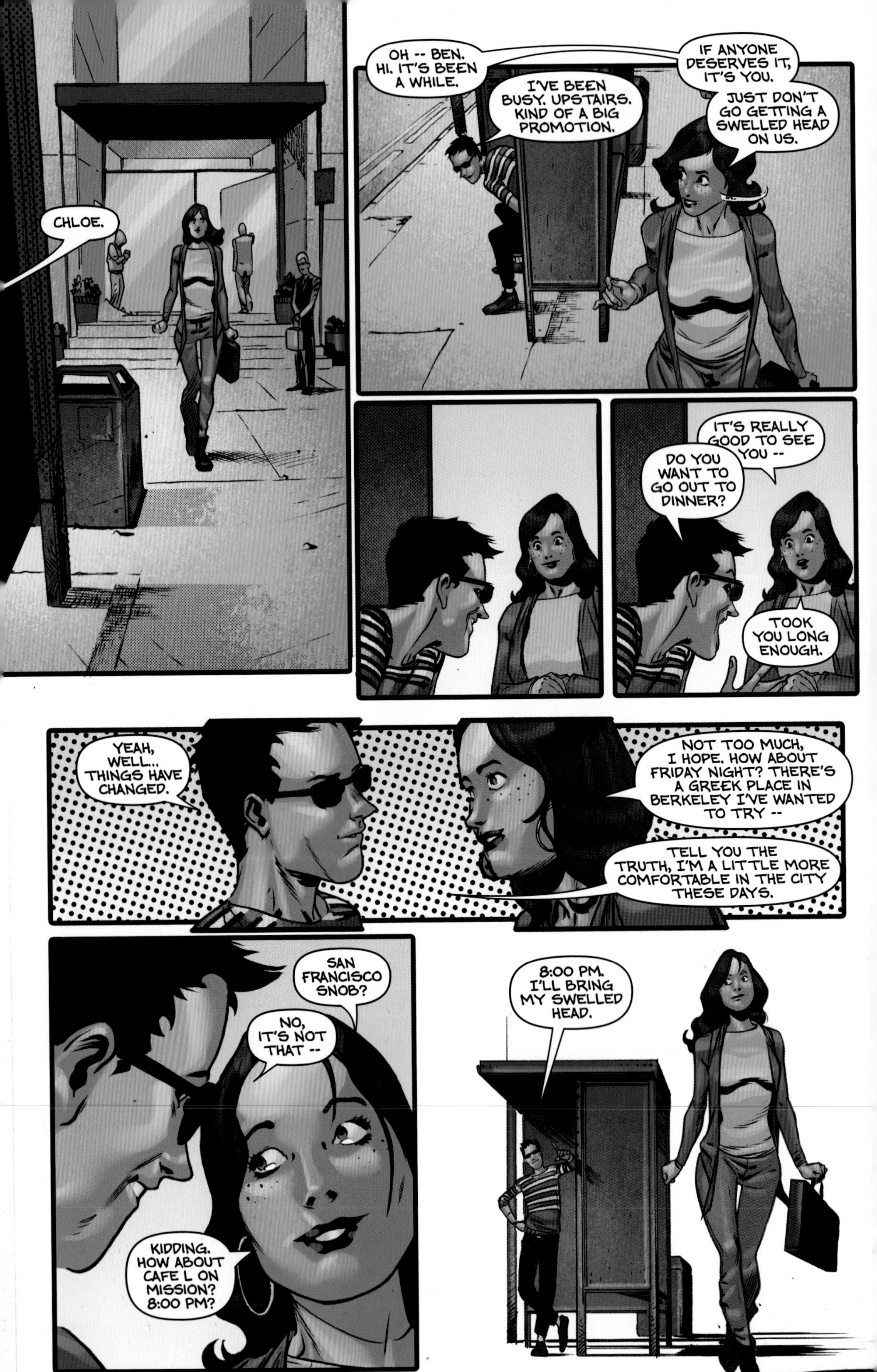
CHLOE.
OH -- BEN. HI. IT'S BEEN A WHILE.
I'VE BEEN BUSY. UPSTAIRS. KIND OF A BIG PROMOTION.
IF ANYONE DESERVES IT, IT'S YOU.
JUST DON'T GO GETTING A SWELLED HEAD ON US.
IT'S REALLY GOOD TO SEE YOU --
DO YOU WANT TO GO OUT TO DINNER?
TOOK YOU LONG ENOUGH.
YEAH, WELL... THINGS HAVE CHANGED.
NOT TOO MUCH, I HOPE. HOW ABOUT FRIDAY NIGHT? THERE'S A GREEK PLACE IN BERKELEY I'VE WANTED TO TRY --
TELL YOU THE TRUTH, I'M A LITTLE MORE COMFORTABLE IN THE CITY THESE DAYS.
SAN FRANCISCO SNOB?
NO, IT'S NOT THAT --
KIDDING. HOW ABOUT CAFE L ON MISSION? 8:00 PM?
8:00 PM. I'LL BRING MY SWELLED HEAD.

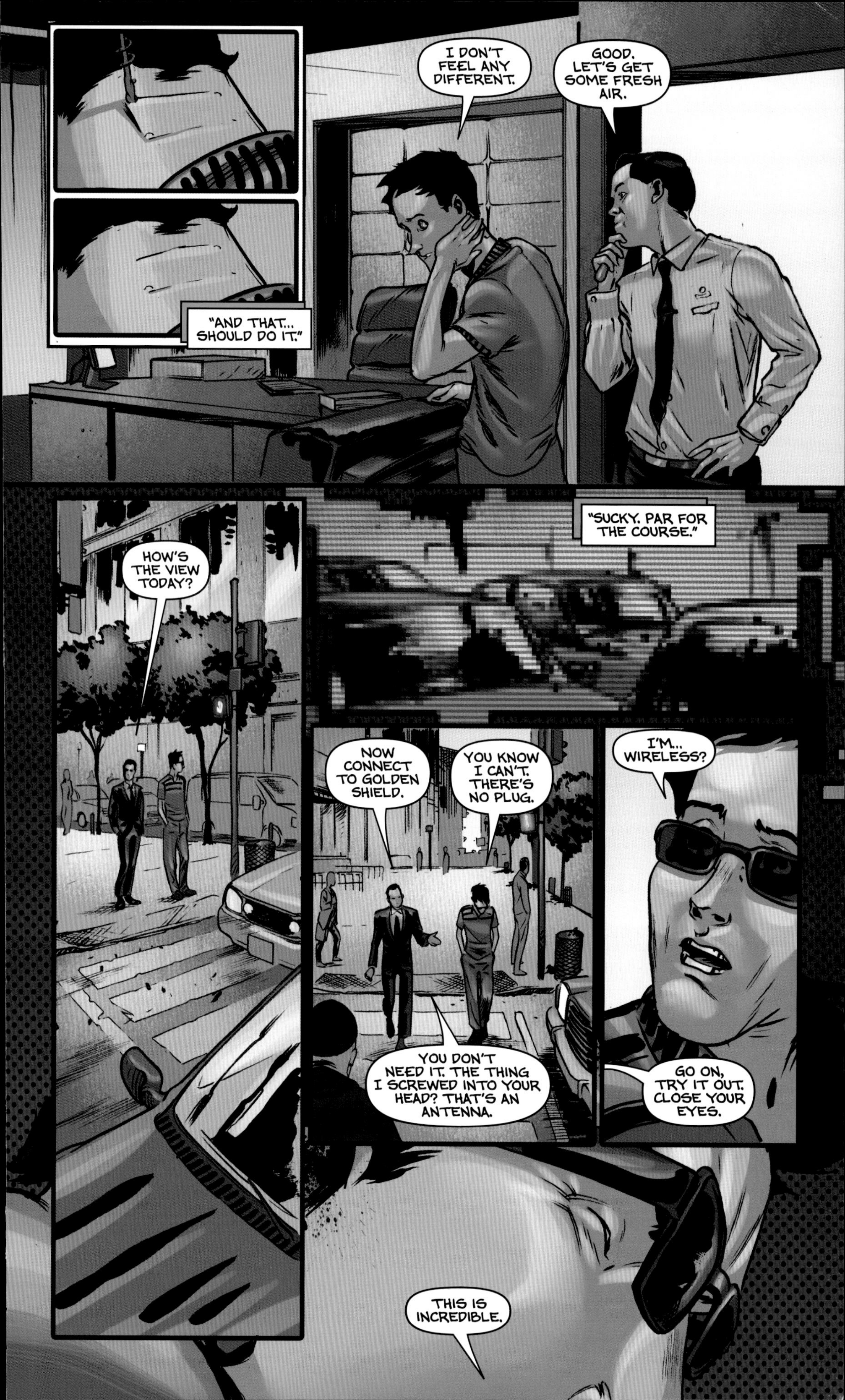
"AND THAT... SHOULD DO IT."
I DON'T FEEL ANY DIFFERENT.
GOOD. LET'S GET SOME FRESH AIR.
HOW'S THE VIEW TODAY?
"SUCKY. PAR FOR THE COURSE."
NOW CONNECT TO GOLDEN SHIELD.
YOU KNOW I CAN'T. THERE'S NO PLUG.
YOU DON'T NEED IT. THE THING I SCREWED INTO YOUR HEAD? THAT'S AN ANTENNA.
I'M... WIRELESS?
GO ON, TRY IT OUT. CLOSE YOUR EYES.
THIS IS INCREDIBLE.

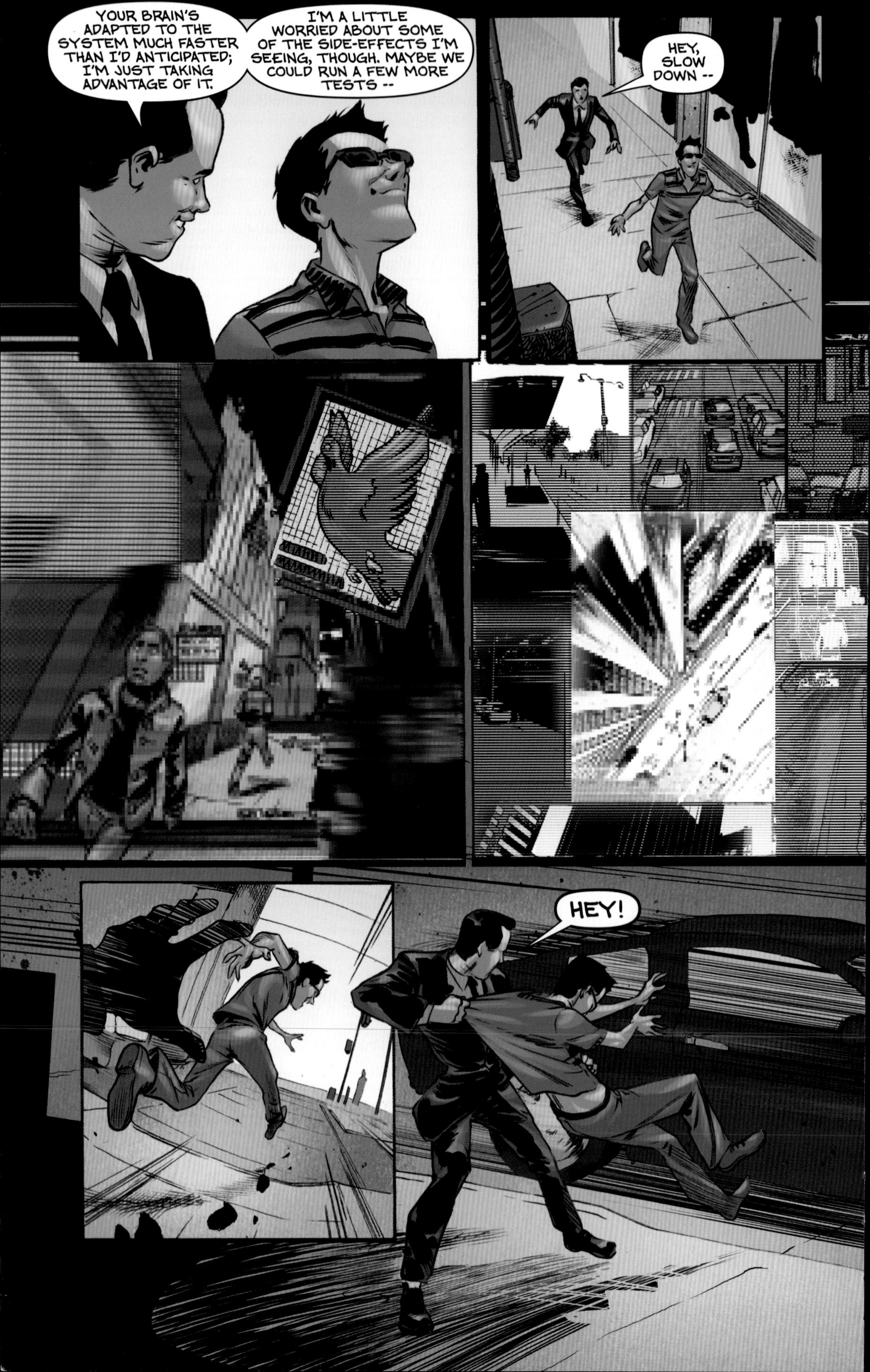
YOUR BRAIN'S ADAPTED TO THE SYSTEM MUCH FASTER THAN I'D ANTICIPATED; I'M JUST TAKING ADVANTAGE OF IT.
I'M A LITTLE WORRIED ABOUT SOME OF THE SIDE-EFFECTS I'M SEEING, THOUGH. MAYBE WE COULD RUN A FEW MORE TESTS --
HEY, SLOW DOWN --
HEY!

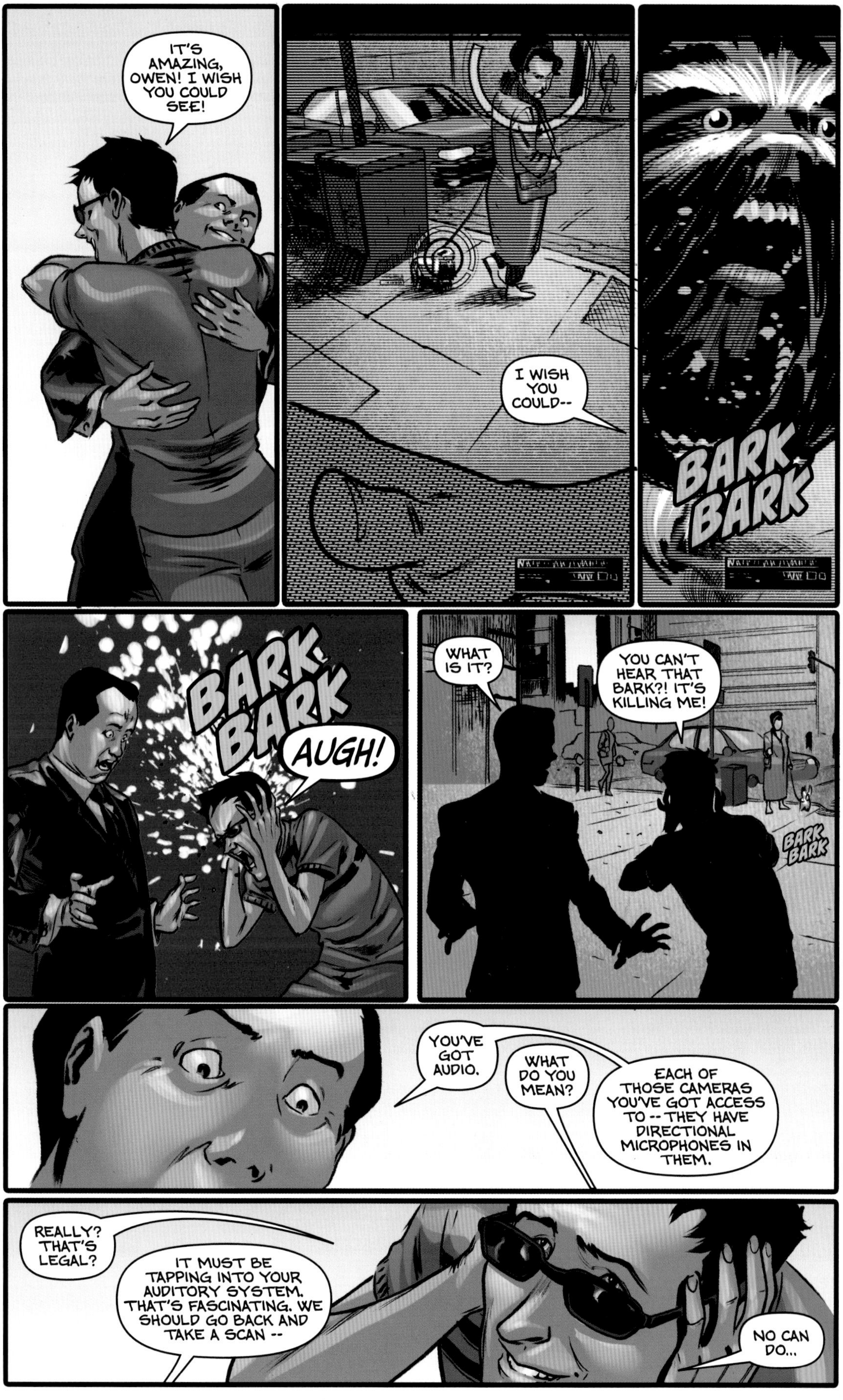
IT'S AMAZING, OWEN! I WISH YOU COULD SEE!
I WISH YOU COULD--
BARK BARK
BARK BARK
AUGH!
WHAT IS IT?
YOU CAN'T HEAR THAT BARK?! IT'S KILLING ME!
BARK BARK
YOU'VE GOT AUDIO.
WHAT DO YOU MEAN?
EACH OF THOSE CAMERAS YOU'VE GOT ACCESS TO -- THEY HAVE DIRECTIONAL MICROPHONES IN THEM.
REALLY? THAT'S LEGAL?
IT MUST BE TAPPING INTO YOUR AUDITORY SYSTEM. THAT'S FASCINATING. WE SHOULD GO BACK AND TAKE A SCAN --
NO CAN DO...

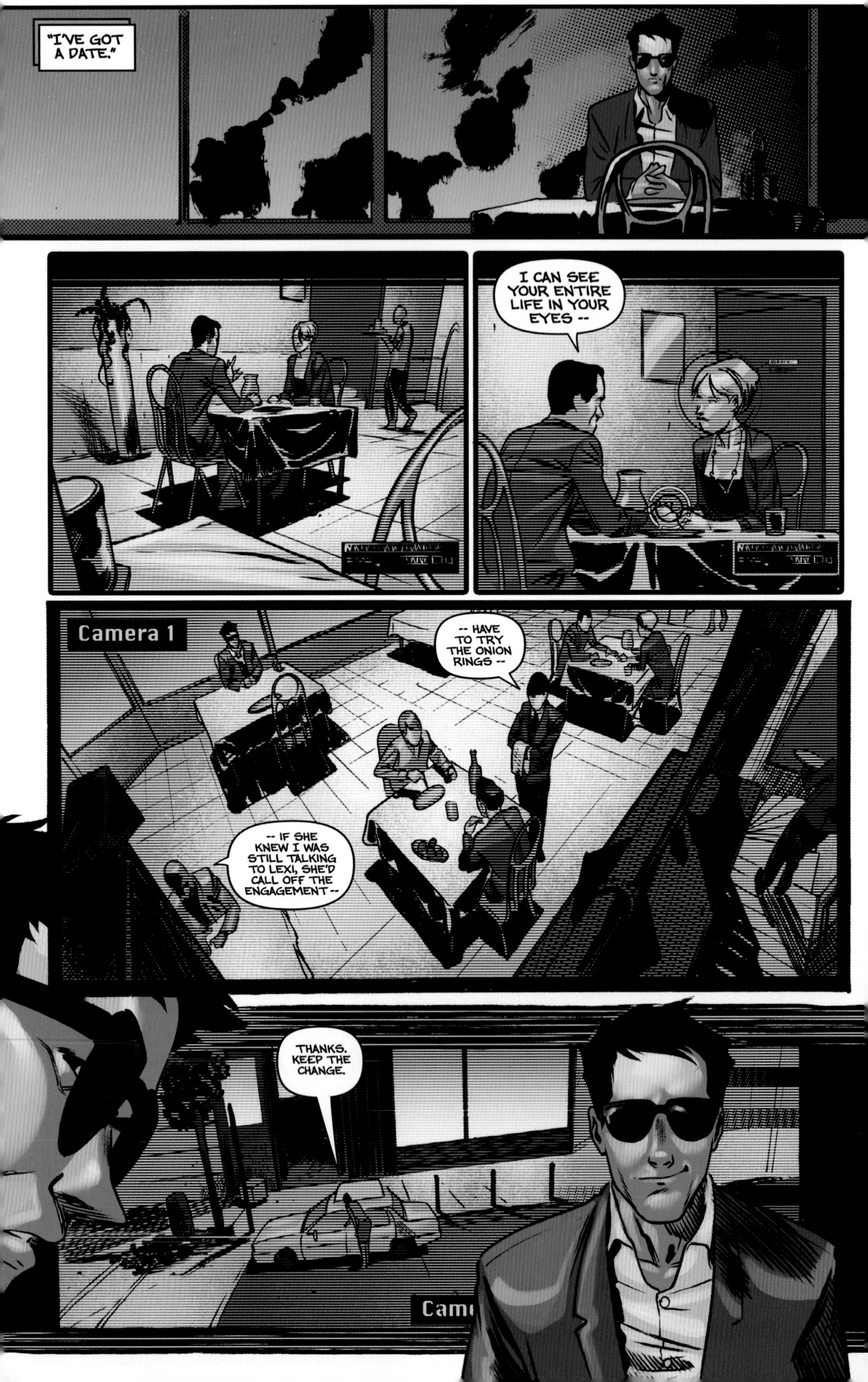
"I'VE GOT A DATE."
I CAN SEE YOUR ENTIRE LIFE IN YOUR EYES --
Camera 1
-- HAVE TO TRY THE ONION RINGS --
-- IF SHE KNEW I WAS STILL TALKING TO LEXI, SHE'D CALL OFF THE ENGAGEMENT --
THANKS. KEEP THE CHANGE.

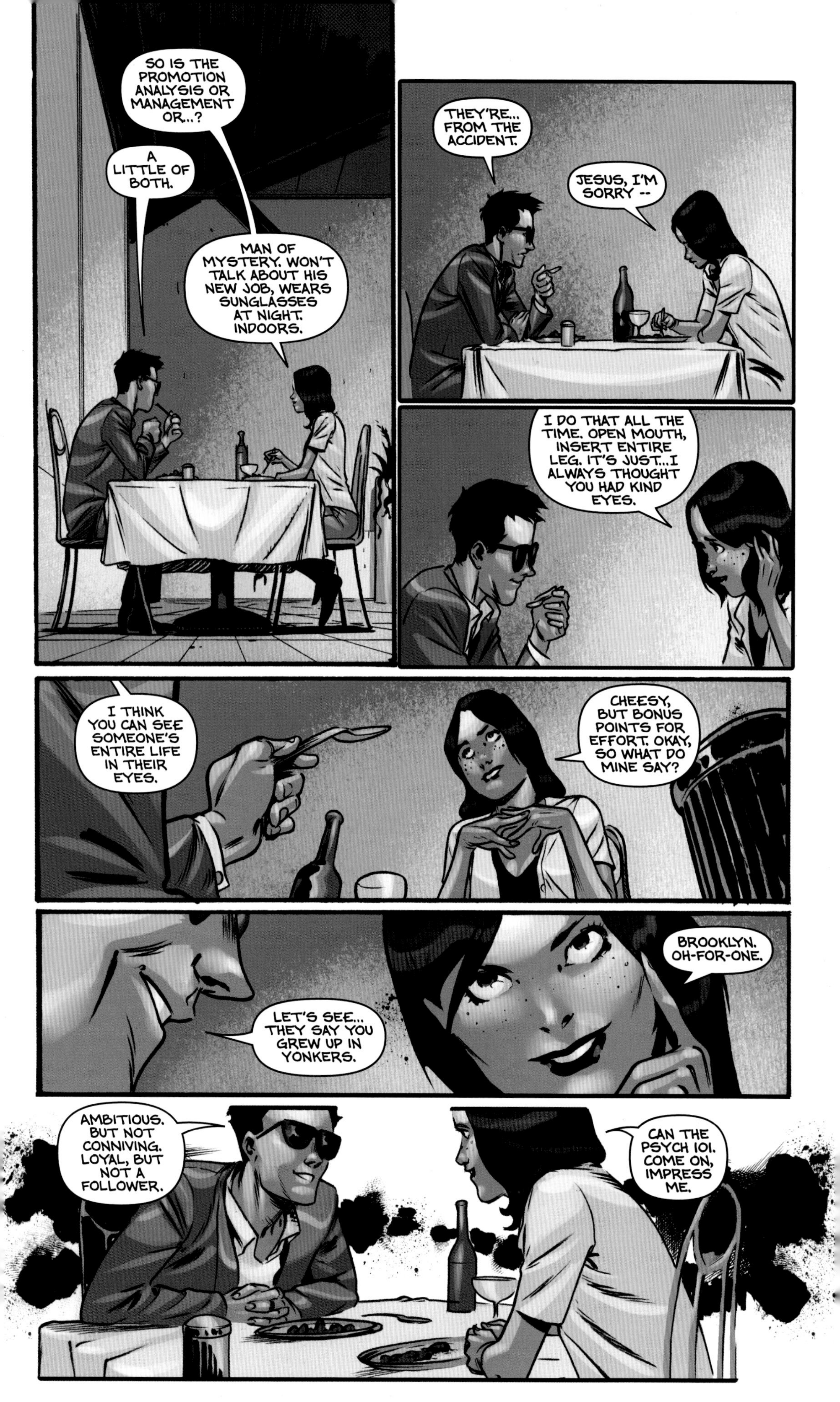

SO IS THE PROMOTION ANALYSIS OR MANAGEMENT OR...?
A LITTLE OF BOTH.
MAN OF MYSTERY. WON'T TALK ABOUT HIS NEW JOB, WEARS SUNGLASSES AT NIGHT. INDOORS.
THEY'RE... FROM THE ACCIDENT.
JESUS, I'M SORRY --
I DO THAT ALL THE TIME. OPEN MOUTH, INSERT ENTIRE LEG. IT'S JUST...I ALWAYS THOUGHT YOU HAD KIND EYES.
I THINK YOU CAN SEE SOMEONE'S ENTIRE LIFE IN THEIR EYES.
CHEESY, BUT BONUS POINTS FOR EFFORT. OKAY, SO WHAT DO MINE SAY?
LET'S SEE... THEY SAY YOU GREW UP IN YONKERS.
BROOKLYN. OH-FOR-ONE.
AMBITIOUS. BUT NOT CONNIVING. LOYAL, BUT NOT A FOLLOWER.
CAN THE PSYCH 101. COME ON, IMPRESS ME.

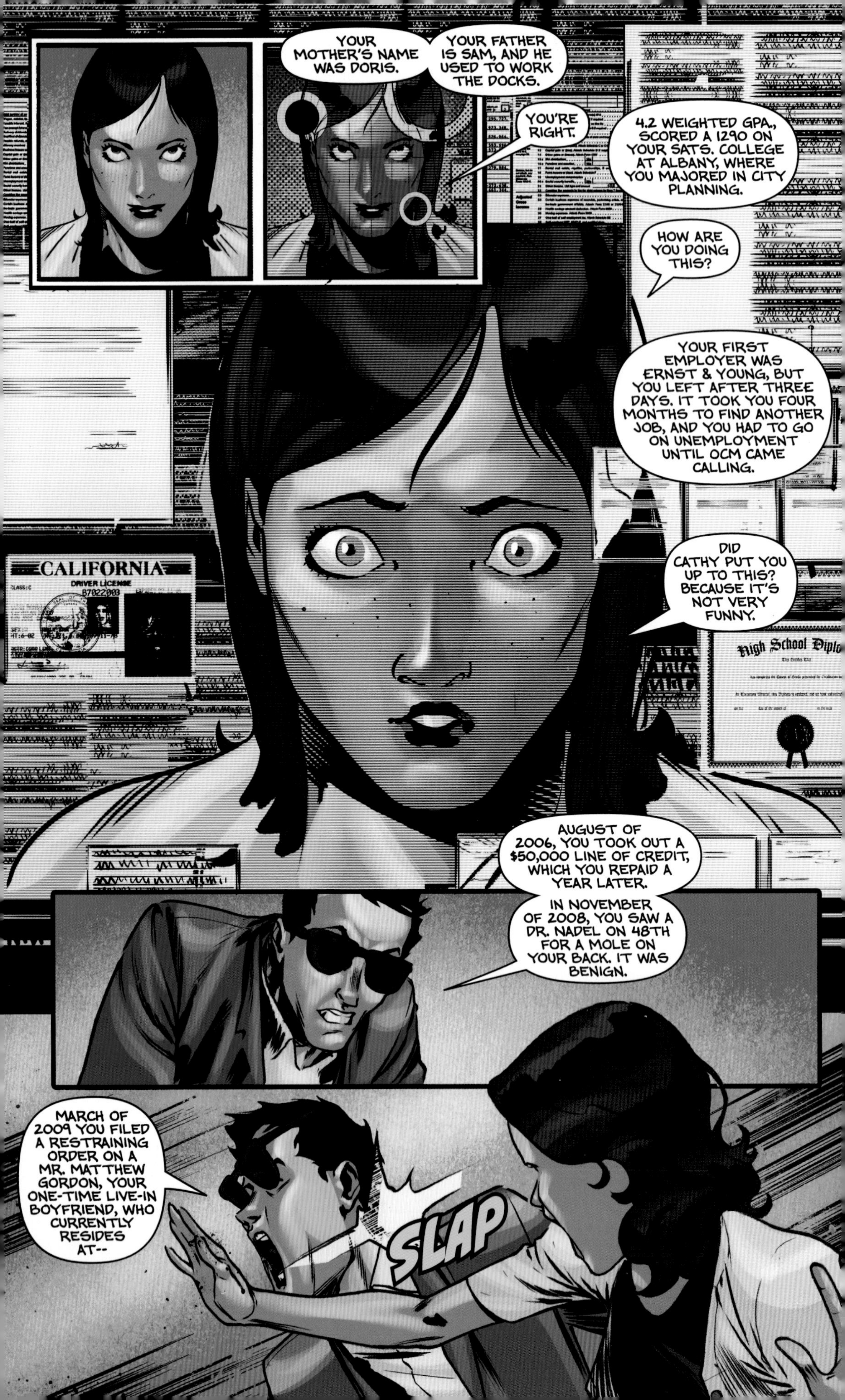
YOUR MOTHER'S NAME WAS DORIS.
YOUR FATHER IS SAM, AND HE USED TO WORK THE DOCKS.
YOU'RE RIGHT.
4.2 WEIGHTED GPA., SCORED A 1290 ON YOUR SATS. COLLEGE AT ALBANY, WHERE YOU MAJORED IN CITY PLANNING.
HOW ARE YOU DOING THIS?
YOUR FIRST EMPLOYER WAS ERNST & YOUNG, BUT YOU LEFT AFTER THREE DAYS. IT TOOK YOU FOUR MONTHS TO FIND ANOTHER JOB, AND YOU HAD TO GO ON UNEMPLOYMENT UNTIL OCM CAME CALLING.
CALIFORNIA
DRIVER LICENSE
DID CATHY PUT YOU UP TO THIS? BECAUSE IT'S NOT VERY FUNNY.
High School Diplo
AUGUST OF 2006, YOU TOOK OUT A $50,000 LINE OF CREDIT, WHICH YOU REPAID A YEAR LATER.
IN NOVEMBER OF 2008, YOU SAW A DR. NADEL ON 48TH FOR A MOLE ON YOUR BACK. IT WAS BENIGN.
MARCH OF 2009 YOU FILED A RESTRAINING ORDER ON A MR. MATTHEW GORDON, YOUR ONE-TIME LIVE-IN BOYFRIEND, WHO CURRENTLY RESIDES AT--
SLAP

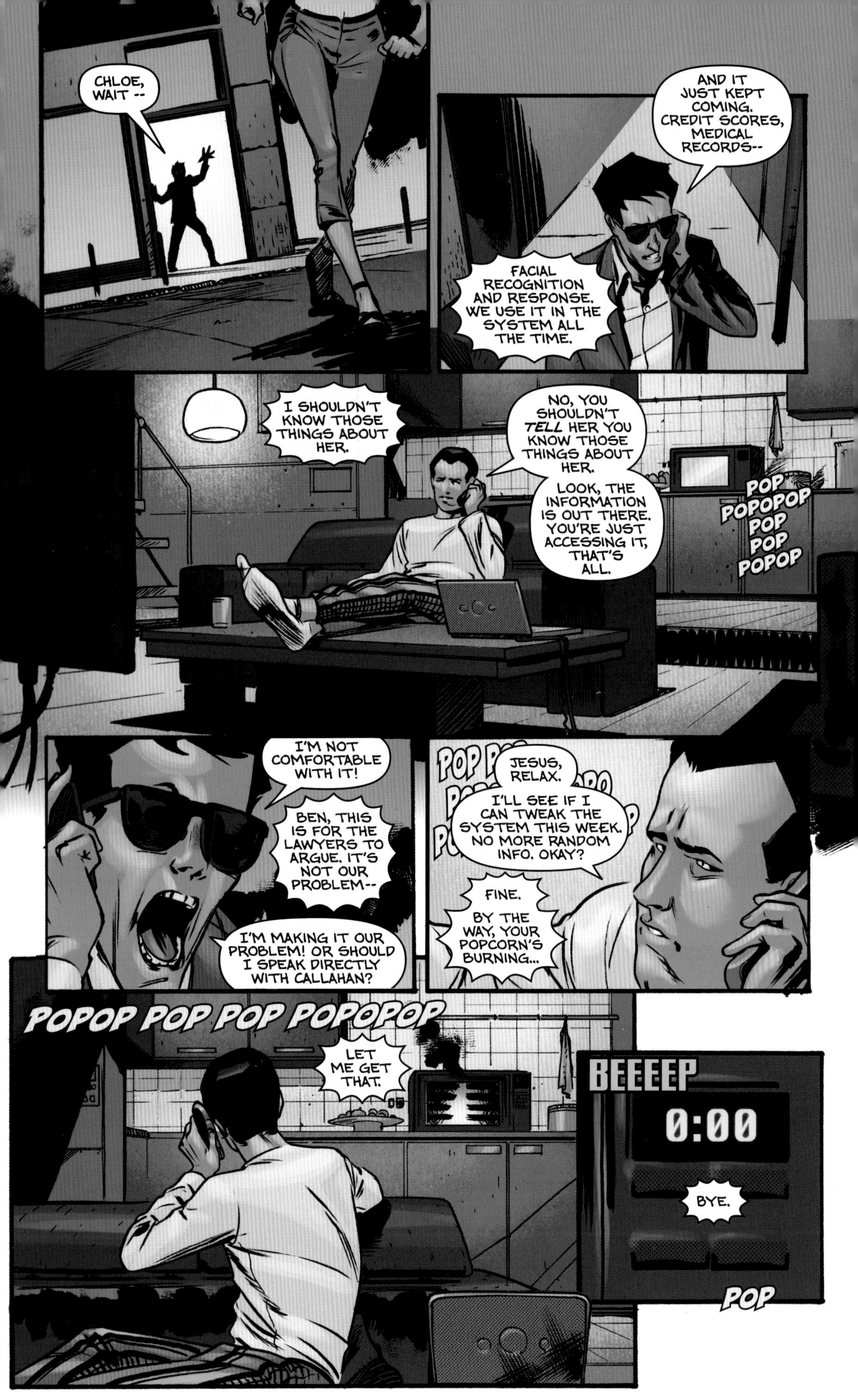
CHLOE, WAIT --
AND IT JUST KEPT COMING. CREDIT SCORES, MEDICAL RECORDS--
FACIAL RECOGNITION AND RESPONSE. WE USE IT IN THE SYSTEM ALL THE TIME.
I SHOULDN'T KNOW THOSE THINGS ABOUT HER.
NO, YOU SHOULDN'T *TELL* HER YOU KNOW THOSE THINGS ABOUT HER.
LOOK, THE INFORMATION IS OUT THERE. YOU'RE JUST ACCESSING IT, THAT'S ALL.
POP POPOPOP POP POP POPOP
I'M NOT COMFORTABLE WITH IT!
BEN, THIS IS FOR THE LAWYERS TO ARGUE. IT'S NOT OUR PROBLEM--
I'M MAKING IT OUR PROBLEM! OR SHOULD I SPEAK DIRECTLY WITH CALLAHAN?
JESUS, RELAX.
I'LL SEE IF I CAN TWEAK THE SYSTEM THIS WEEK. NO MORE RANDOM INFO. OKAY?
FINE.
BY THE WAY, YOUR POPCORN'S BURNING...
POPOP POP POP POPOPOP
LET ME GET THAT.
BEEEEP
0:00
BYE.
POP

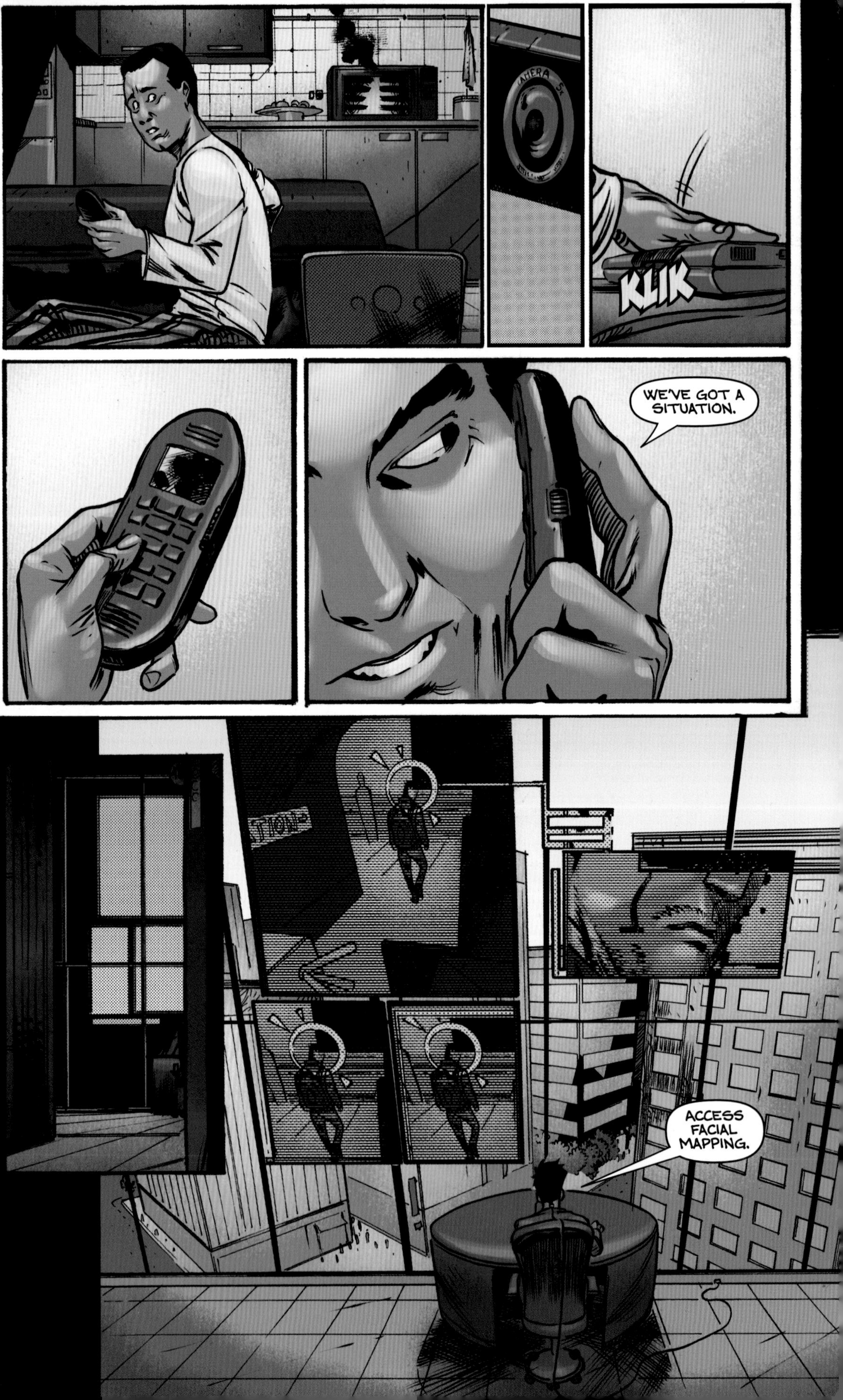
CAMERA 5
KLIK
WE'VE GOT A SITUATION.
ACCESS FACIAL MAPPING.

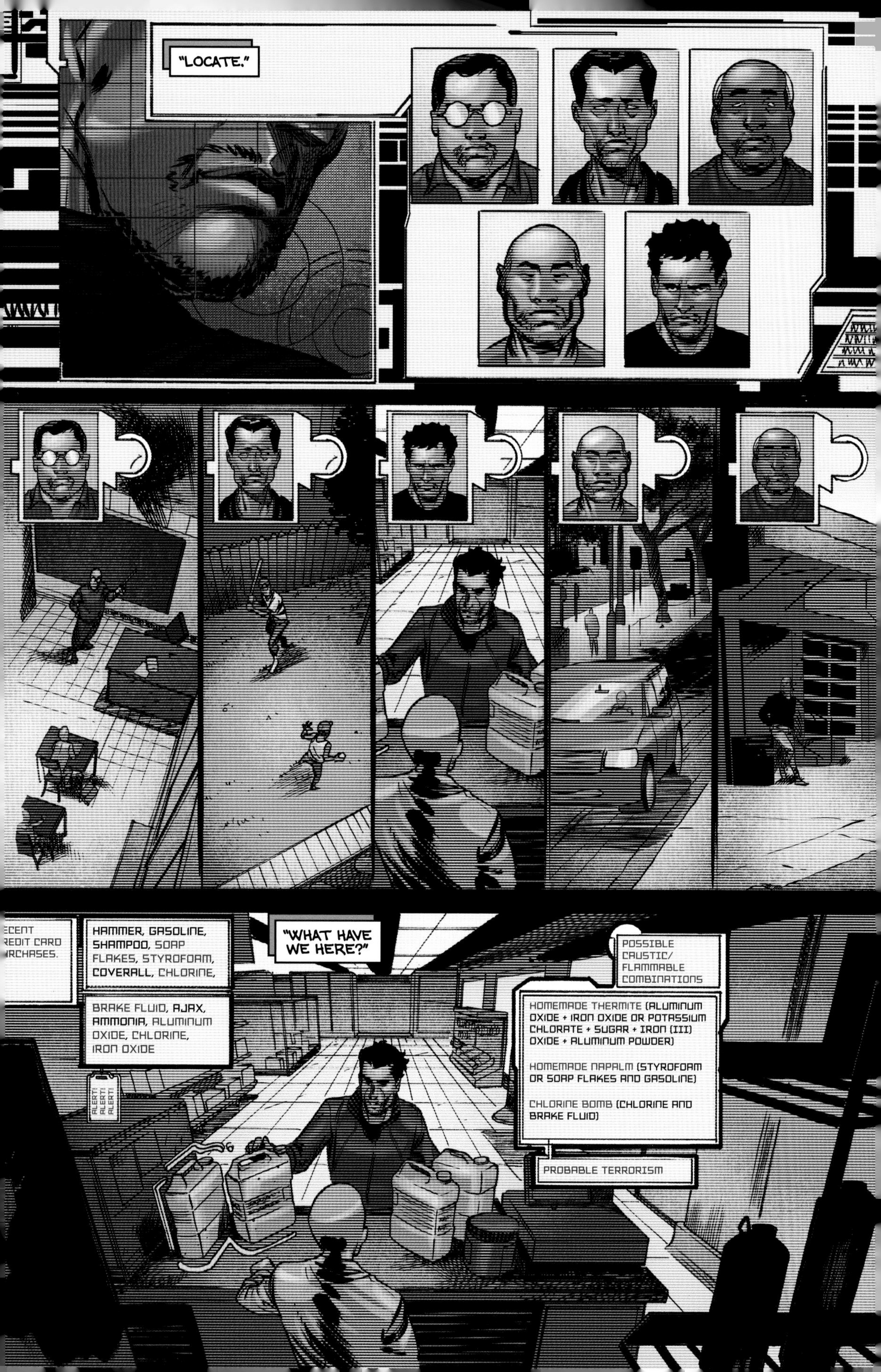

"LOCATE."
RECENT CREDIT CARD PURCHASES.
HAMMER, GASOLINE, SHAMPOO, SOAP FLAKES, STYROFOAM, COVERALL, CHLORINE,
BRAKE FLUID, AJAX, AMMONIA, ALUMINUM OXIDE, CHLORINE, IRON OXIDE
ALERT! ALERT! ALERT!
"WHAT HAVE WE HERE?"
POSSIBLE CAUSTIC/ FLAMMABLE COMBINATIONS
HOMEMADE THERMITE (ALUMINUM OXIDE + IRON OXIDE OR POTASSIUM CHLORATE + SUGAR + IRON (III) OXIDE + ALUMINUM POWDER)
HOMEMADE NAPALM (STYROFOAM OR SOAP FLAKES AND GASOLINE)
CHLORINE BOMB (CHLORINE AND BRAKE FLUID)
PROBABLE TERRORISM

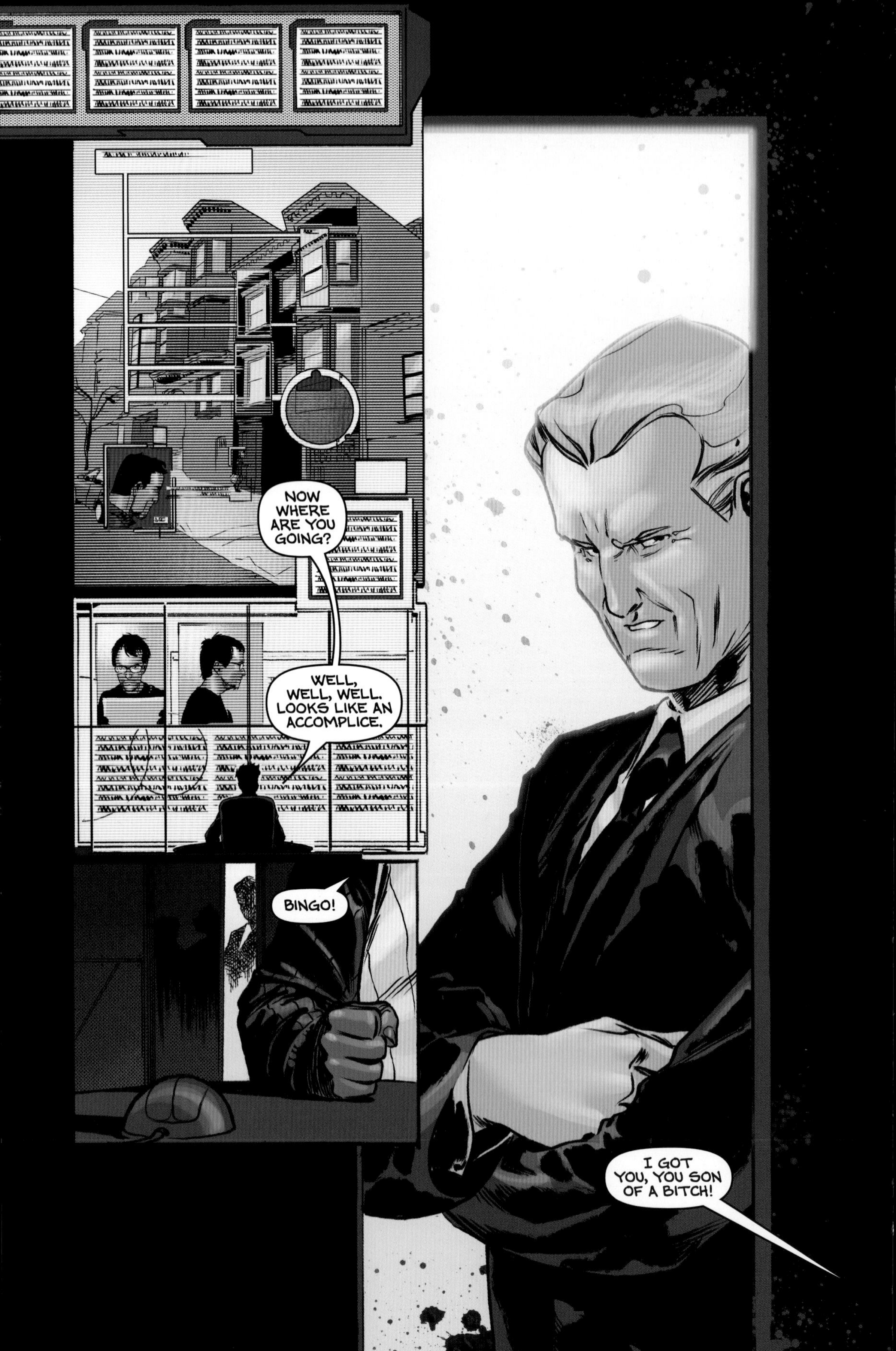
NOW WHERE ARE YOU GOING?
WELL, WELL, WELL. LOOKS LIKE AN ACCOMPLICE.
BINGO!
I GOT YOU, YOU SON OF A BITCH!

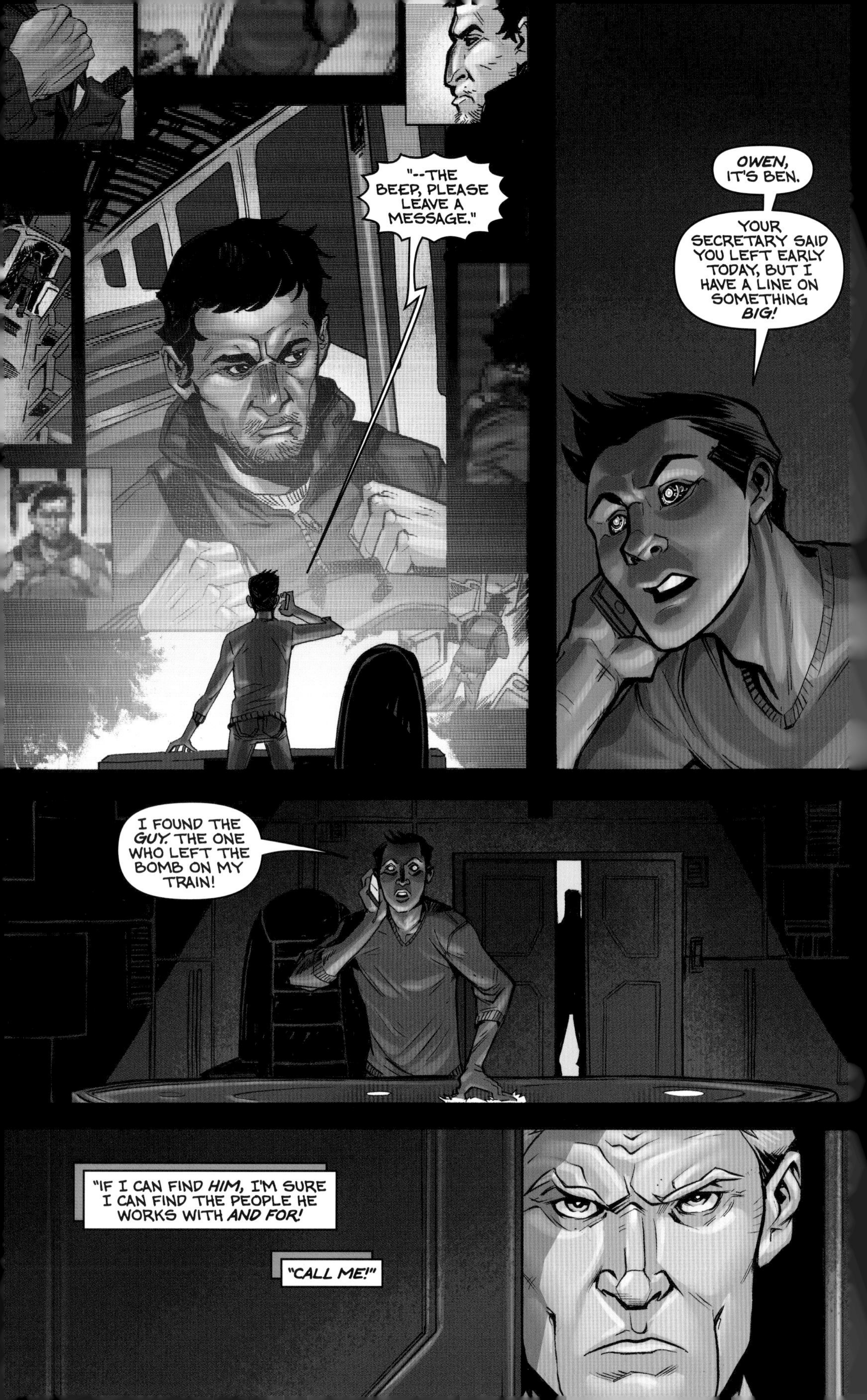
"--THE BEEP, PLEASE LEAVE A MESSAGE."
OWEN, IT'S BEN.
YOUR SECRETARY SAID YOU LEFT EARLY TODAY, BUT I HAVE A LINE ON SOMETHING BIG!
I FOUND THE GUY. THE ONE WHO LEFT THE BOMB ON MY TRAIN!
"IF I CAN FIND HIM, I'M SURE I CAN FIND THE PEOPLE HE WORKS WITH AND FOR!
"CALL ME!"

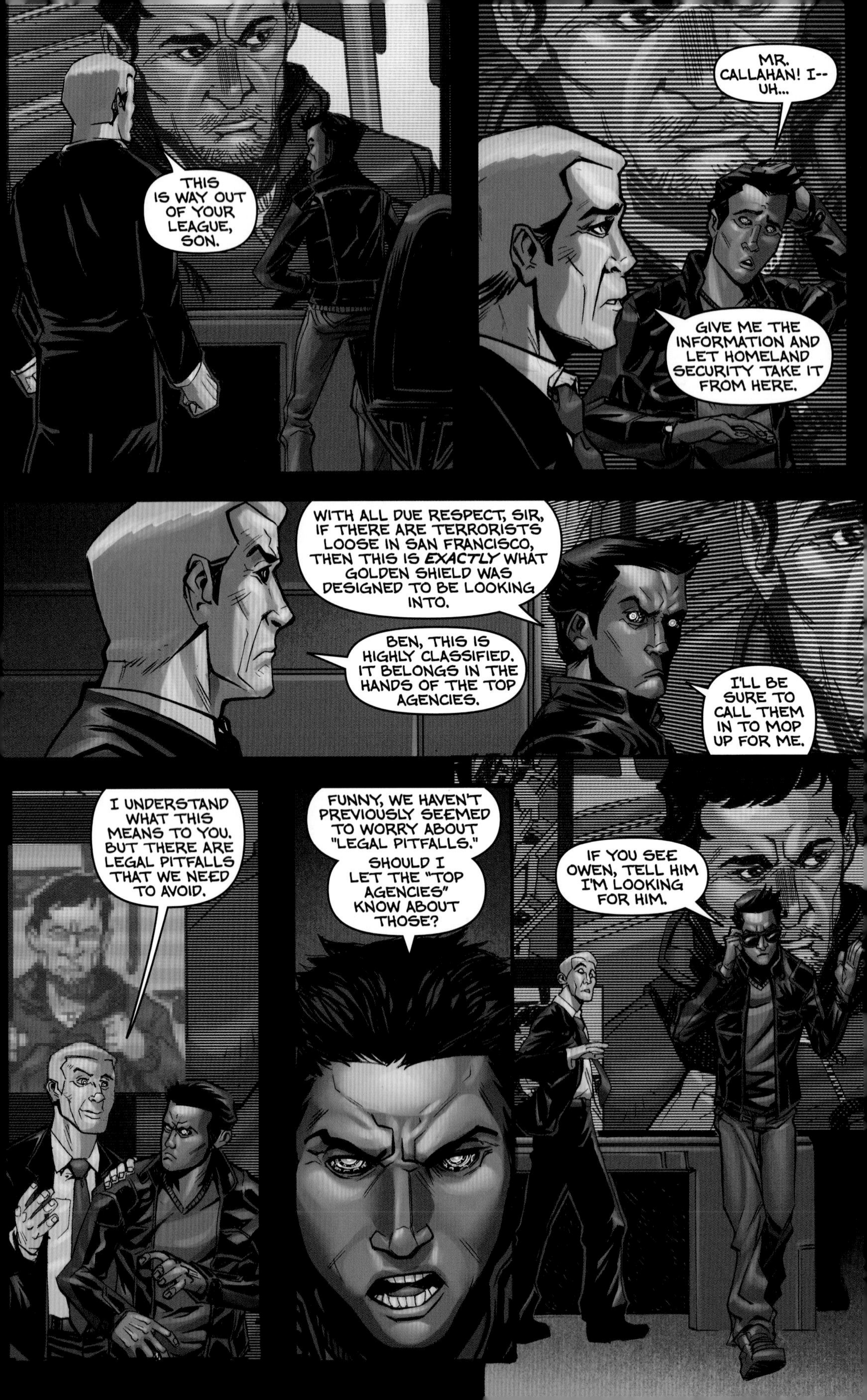
THIS IS WAY OUT OF YOUR LEAGUE, SON.
MR. CALLAHAN! I-- UH...
GIVE ME THE INFORMATION AND LET HOMELAND SECURITY TAKE IT FROM HERE.
WITH ALL DUE RESPECT, SIR, IF THERE ARE TERRORISTS LOOSE IN SAN FRANCISCO, THEN THIS IS *EXACTLY* WHAT GOLDEN SHIELD WAS DESIGNED TO BE LOOKING INTO.
BEN, THIS IS HIGHLY CLASSIFIED. IT BELONGS IN THE HANDS OF THE TOP AGENCIES.
I'LL BE SURE TO CALL THEM IN TO MOP UP FOR ME.
I UNDERSTAND WHAT THIS MEANS TO YOU. BUT THERE ARE LEGAL PITFALLS THAT WE NEED TO AVOID.
FUNNY, WE HAVEN'T PREVIOUSLY SEEMED TO WORRY ABOUT "LEGAL PITFALLS."
SHOULD I LET THE "TOP AGENCIES" KNOW ABOUT THOSE?
IF YOU SEE OWEN, TELL HIM I'M LOOKING FOR HIM.

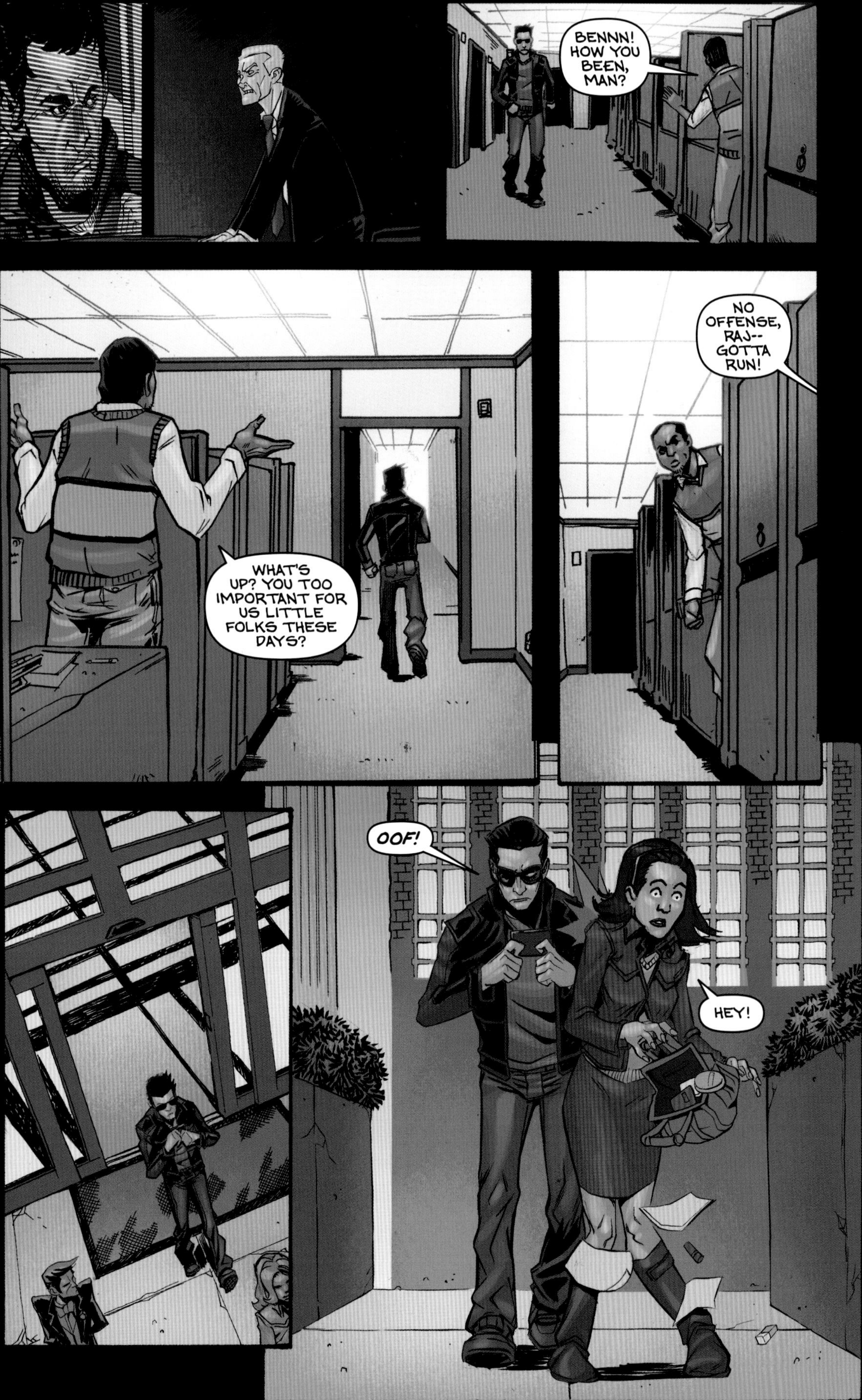
BENNN! HOW YOU BEEN, MAN?
WHAT'S UP? YOU TOO IMPORTANT FOR US LITTLE FOLKS THESE DAYS?
NO OFFENSE, RAJ-- GOTTA RUN!
OOF!
HEY!

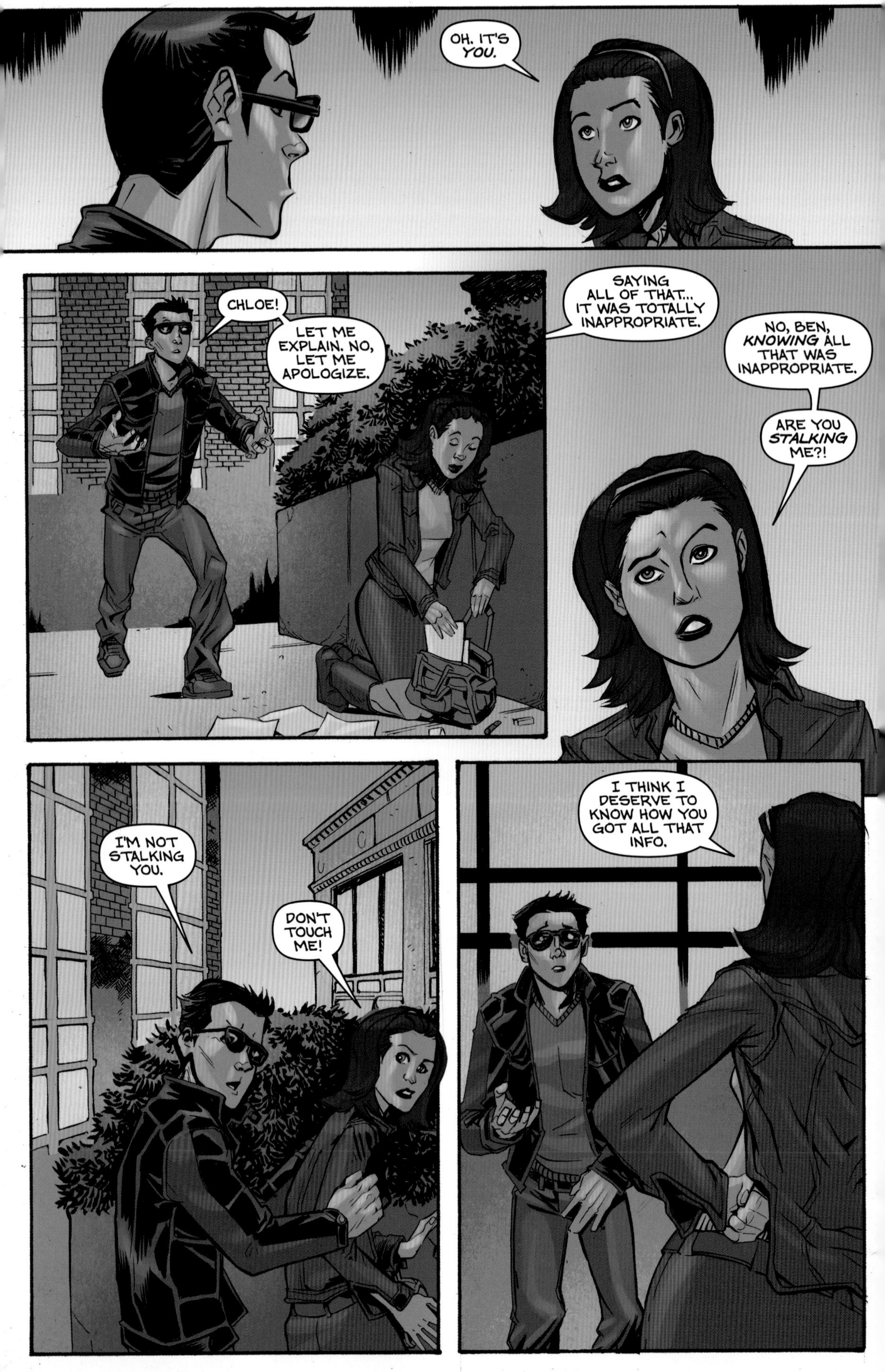

OH. IT'S YOU.
CHLOE!
LET ME EXPLAIN. NO, LET ME APOLOGIZE.
SAYING ALL OF THAT... IT WAS TOTALLY INAPPROPRIATE.
NO, BEN, KNOWING ALL THAT WAS INAPPROPRIATE.
ARE YOU STALKING ME?!
I'M NOT STALKING YOU.
DON'T TOUCH ME!
I THINK I DESERVE TO KNOW HOW YOU GOT ALL THAT INFO.

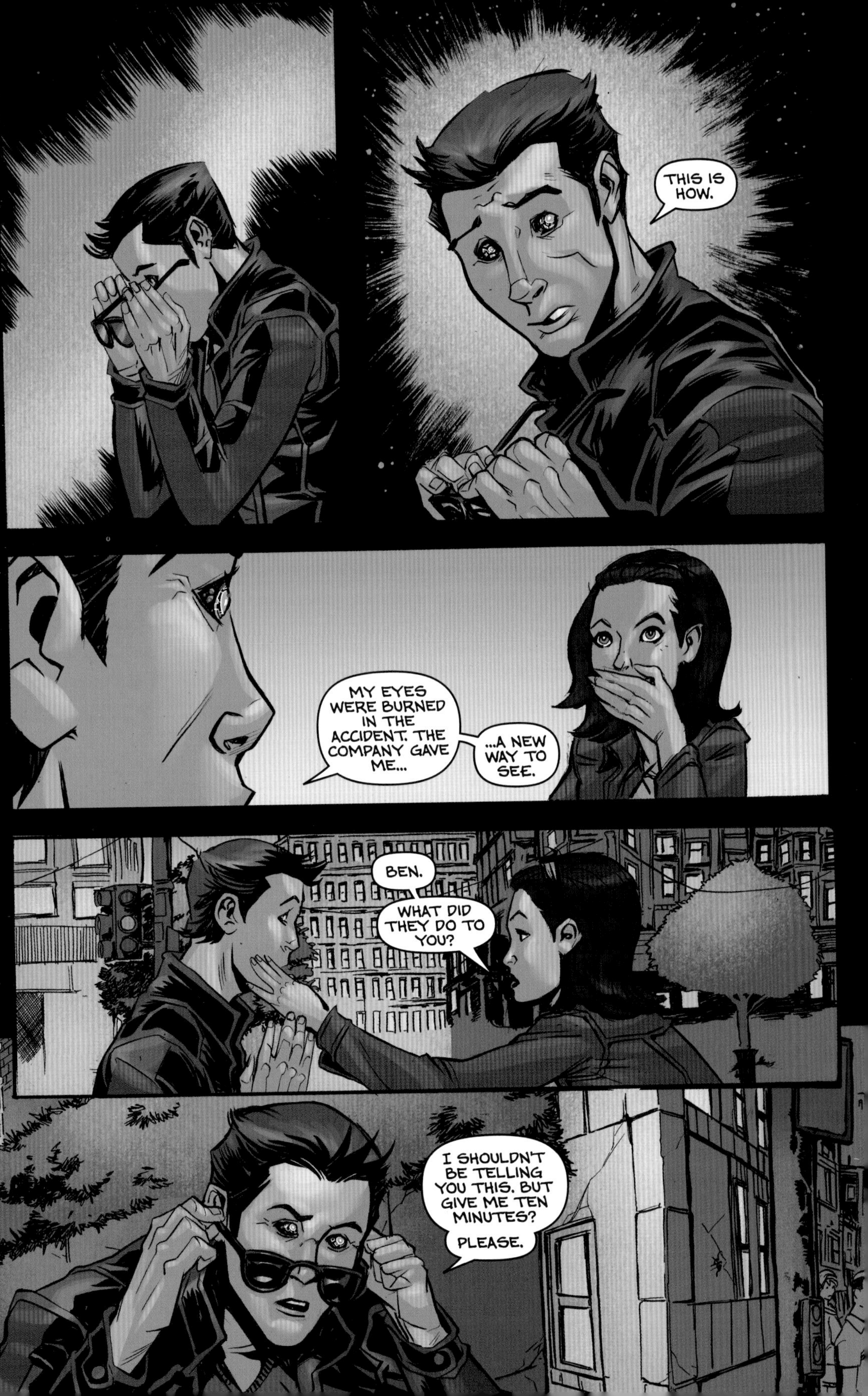
THIS IS HOW.
MY EYES WERE BURNED IN THE ACCIDENT. THE COMPANY GAVE ME...
...A NEW WAY TO SEE.
BEN.
WHAT DID THEY DO TO YOU?
I SHOULDN'T BE TELLING YOU THIS. BUT GIVE ME TEN MINUTES?
PLEASE.

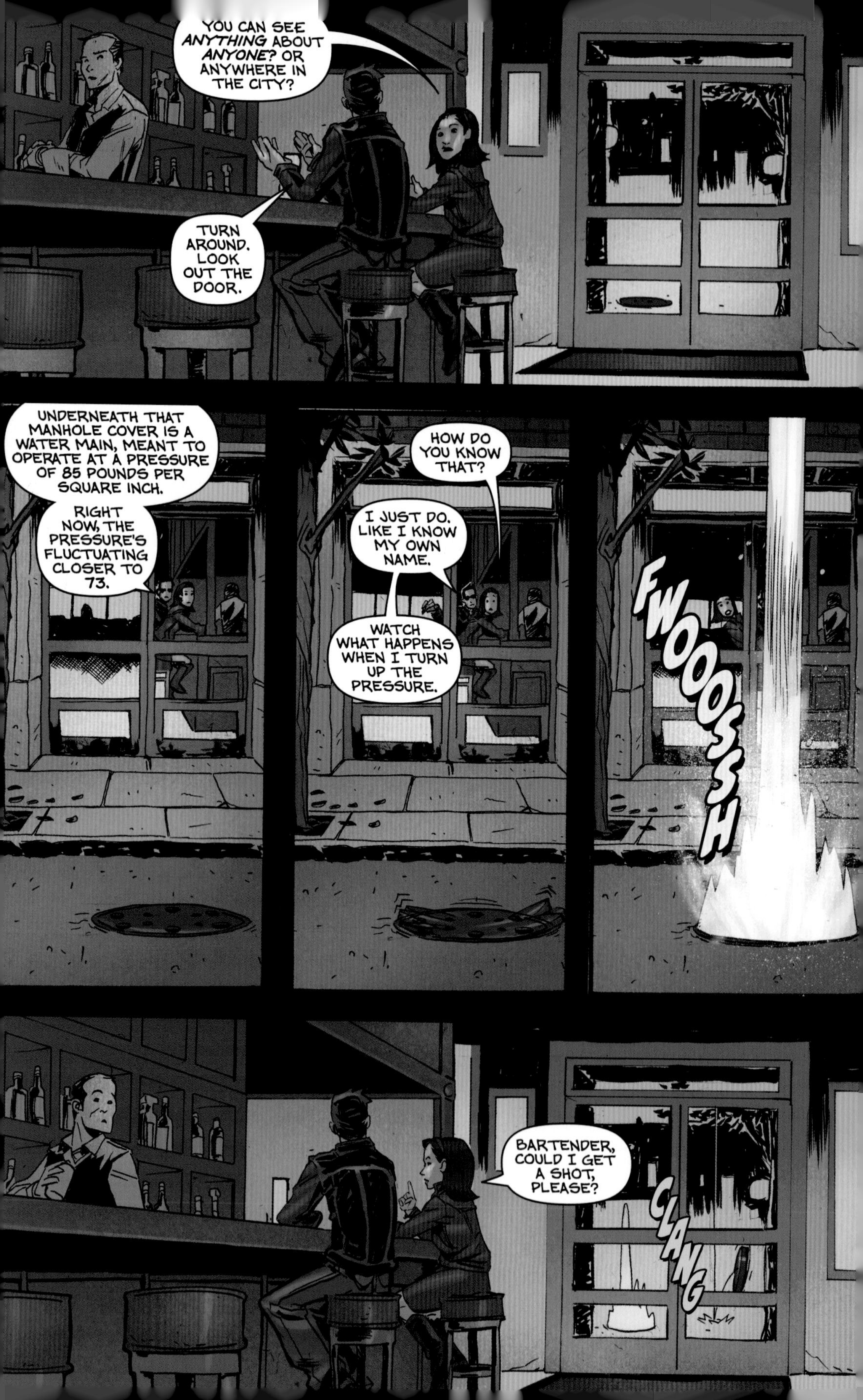
YOU CAN SEE *ANYTHING* ABOUT *ANYONE*? OR ANYWHERE IN THE CITY?
TURN AROUND. LOOK OUT THE DOOR.
UNDERNEATH THAT MANHOLE COVER IS A WATER MAIN, MEANT TO OPERATE AT A PRESSURE OF 85 POUNDS PER SQUARE INCH.
RIGHT NOW, THE PRESSURE'S FLUCTUATING CLOSER TO 73.
HOW DO YOU KNOW THAT?
I JUST DO. LIKE I KNOW MY OWN NAME.
WATCH WHAT HAPPENS WHEN I TURN UP THE PRESSURE.
FWOOOOSSH
BARTENDER, COULD I GET A SHOT, PLEASE?
CLANG

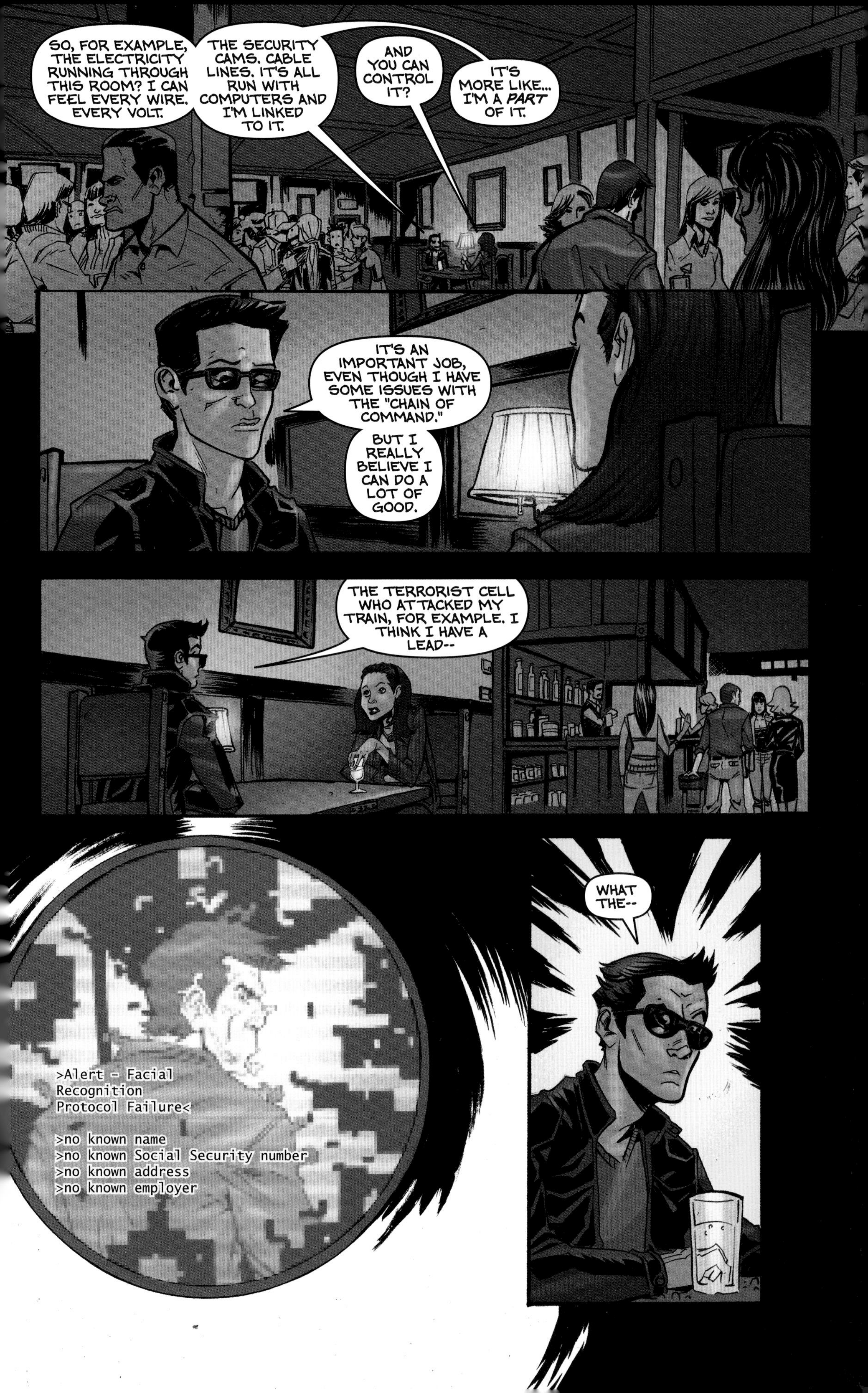
SO, FOR EXAMPLE, THE ELECTRICITY RUNNING THROUGH THIS ROOM? I CAN FEEL EVERY WIRE. EVERY VOLT.
THE SECURITY CAMS. CABLE LINES. IT'S ALL RUN WITH COMPUTERS AND I'M LINKED TO IT.
AND YOU CAN CONTROL IT?
IT'S MORE LIKE... I'M A *PART* OF IT.
IT'S AN IMPORTANT JOB, EVEN THOUGH I HAVE SOME ISSUES WITH THE "CHAIN OF COMMAND."
BUT I REALLY BELIEVE I CAN DO A LOT OF GOOD.
THE TERRORIST CELL WHO ATTACKED MY TRAIN, FOR EXAMPLE. I THINK I HAVE A LEAD--
>Alert - Facial Recognition Protocol Failure<
>no known name
>no known Social Security number
>no known address
>no known employer
WHAT THE--

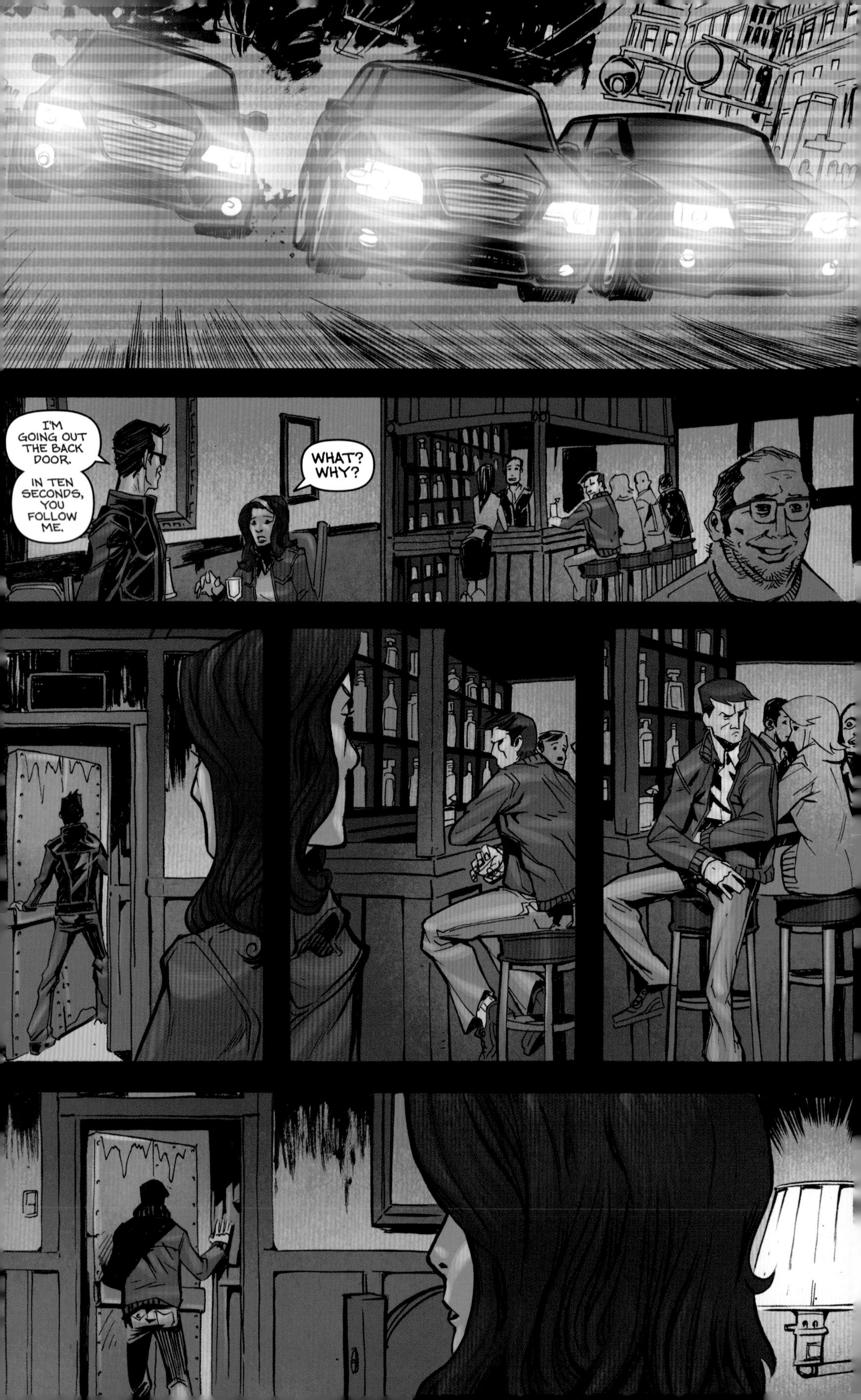
I'M GOING OUT THE BACK DOOR.
IN TEN SECONDS, YOU FOLLOW ME.
WHAT? WHY?

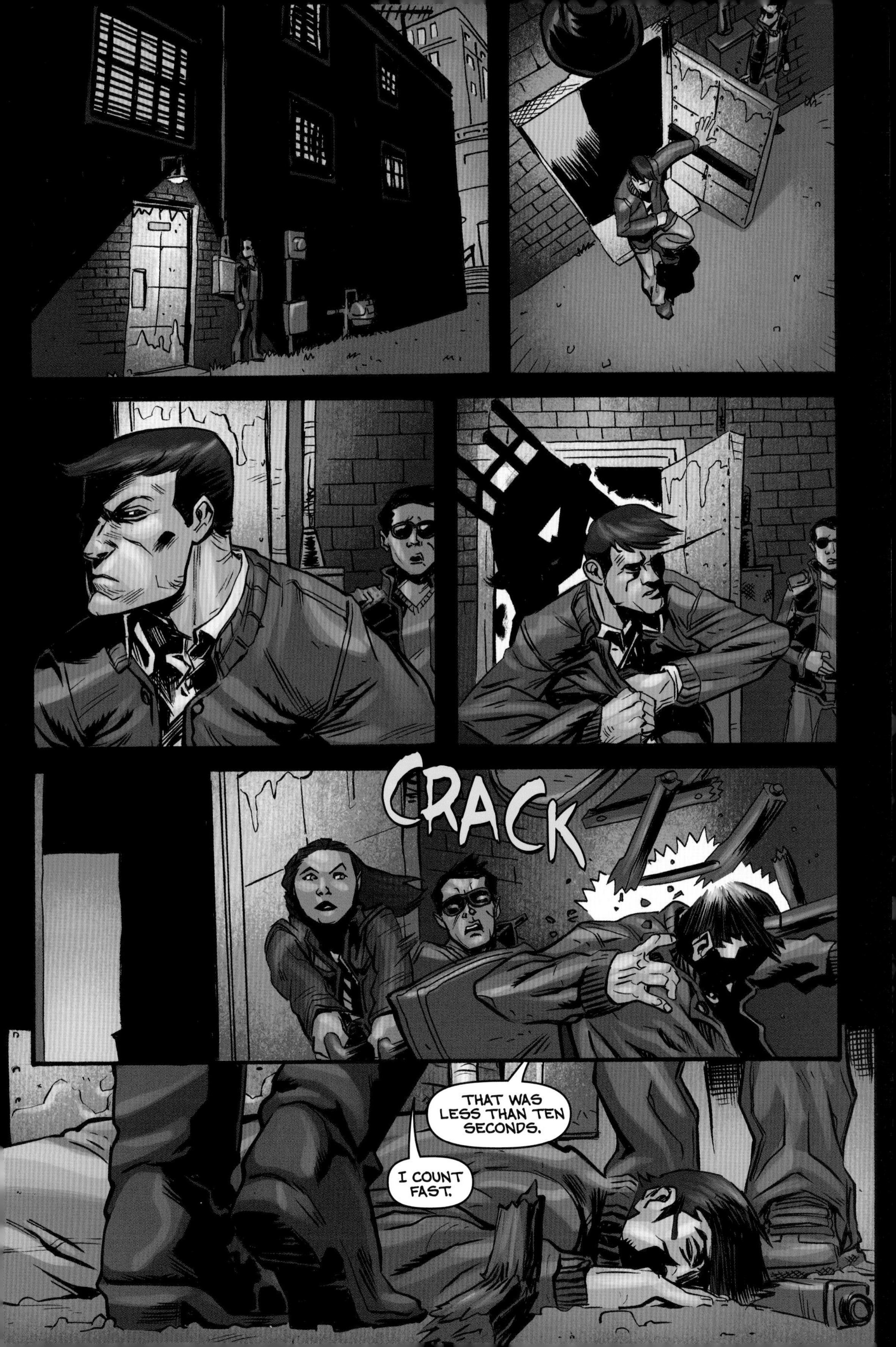
CRACK
THAT WAS LESS THAN TEN SECONDS.
I COUNT FAST.

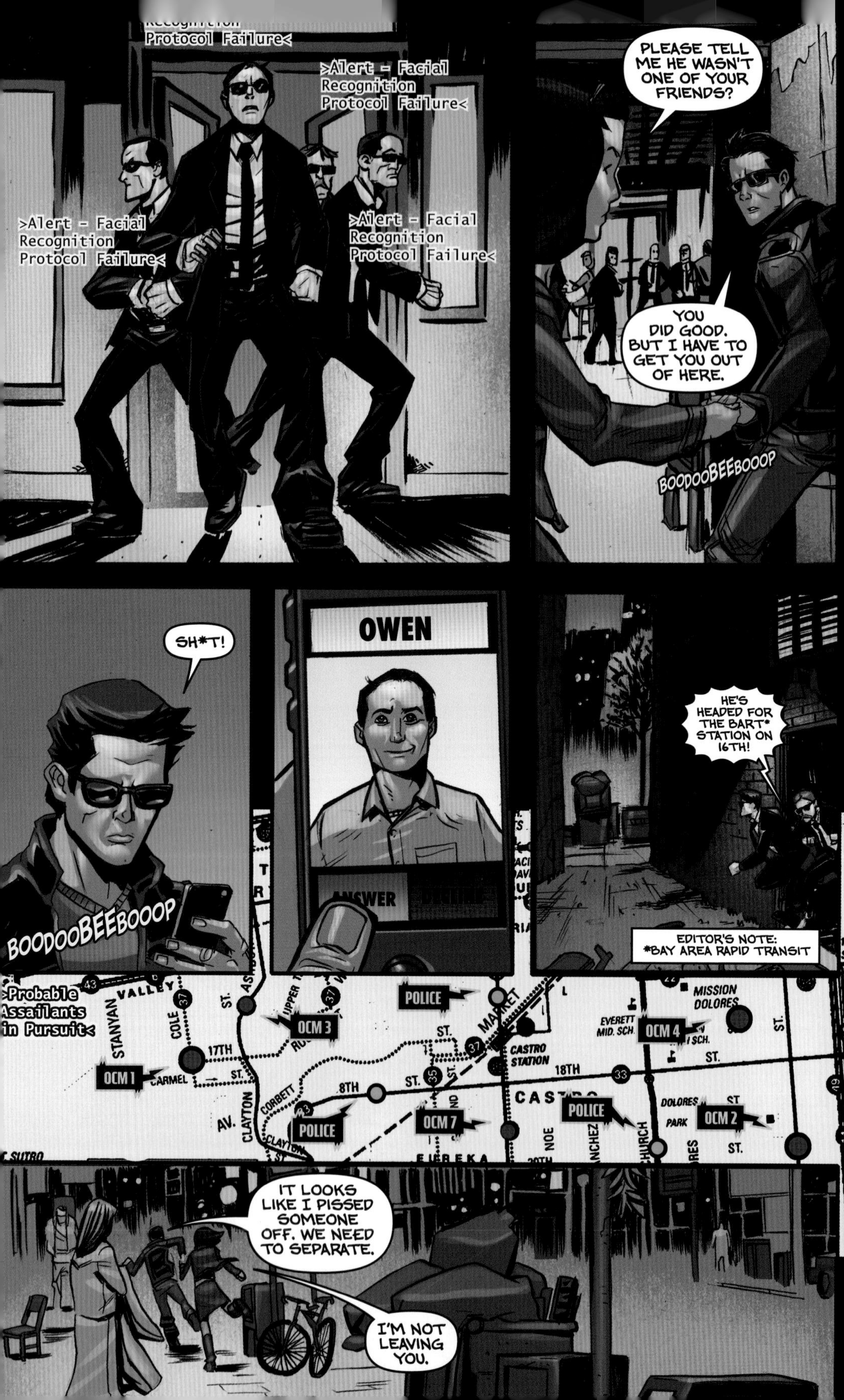

Protocol Failure<
>Alert - Facial Recognition Protocol Failure<
>Alert - Facial Recognition Protocol Failure<
>Alert - Facial Recognition Protocol Failure<
PLEASE TELL ME HE WASN'T ONE OF YOUR FRIENDS?
YOU DID GOOD. BUT I HAVE TO GET YOU OUT OF HERE.
BOODOOBEEBOOOP
SH*T!
BOODOOBEEBOOOP
OWEN
HE'S HEADED FOR THE BART* STATION ON 16TH!
EDITOR'S NOTE: *BAY AREA RAPID TRANSIT
>Probable Assailants in Pursuit<
OCM 1
OCM 3
POLICE
OCM 4
MISSION DOLORES
EVERETT MID. SCH.
CASTRO STATION
17TH
18TH
POLICE
OCM 7
POLICE
OCM 2
DOLORES PARK
STANYAN
COLE
CLAYTON
CARMEL
CORBETT
MARKET
NOE
CHURCH
IT LOOKS LIKE I PISSED SOMEONE OFF. WE NEED TO SEPARATE.
I'M NOT LEAVING YOU.

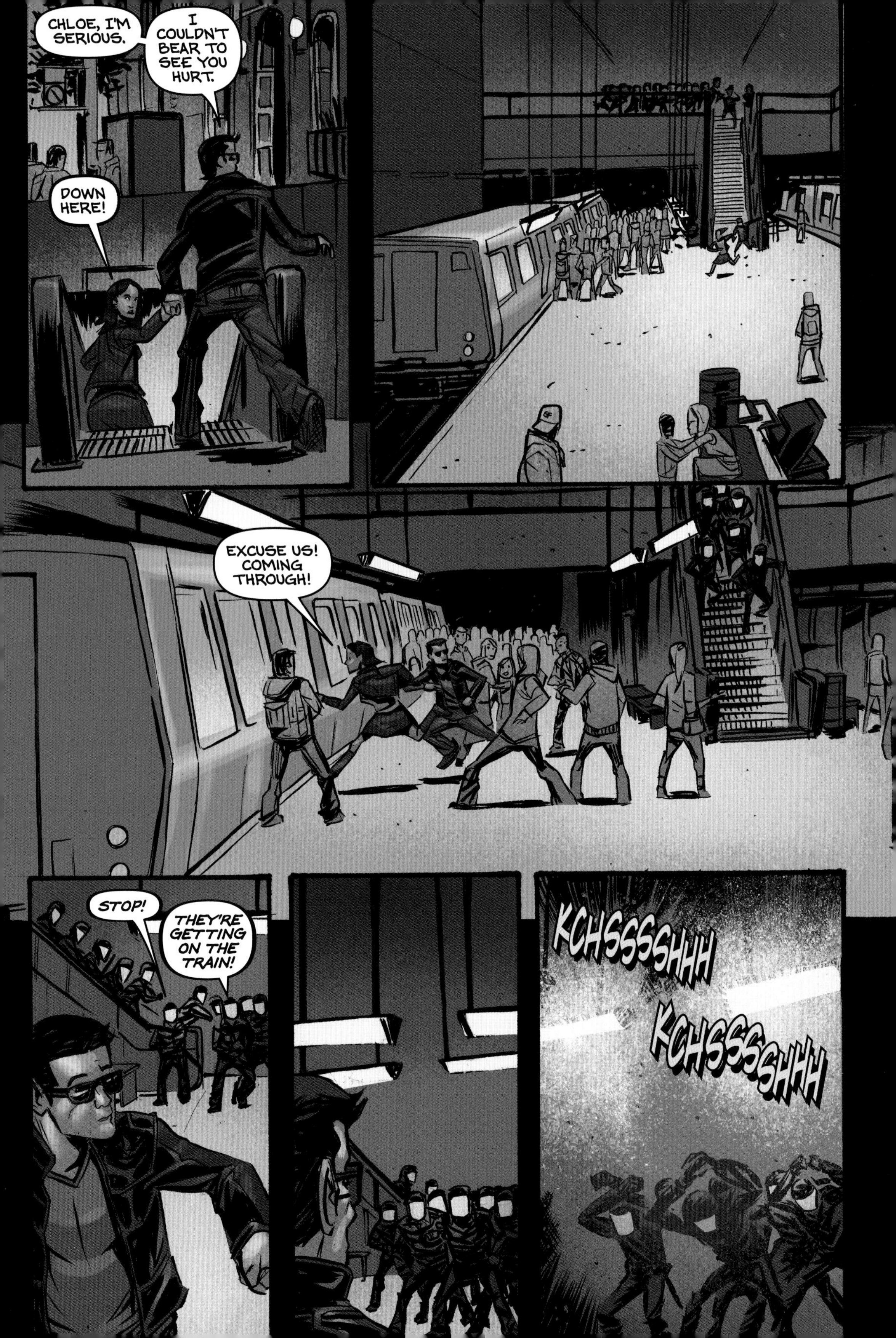
CHLOE, I'M SERIOUS.
I COULDN'T BEAR TO SEE YOU HURT.
DOWN HERE!
EXCUSE US! COMING THROUGH!
STOP!
THEY'RE GETTING ON THE TRAIN!
KCHSSSSHHH
KCHSSSSHHH

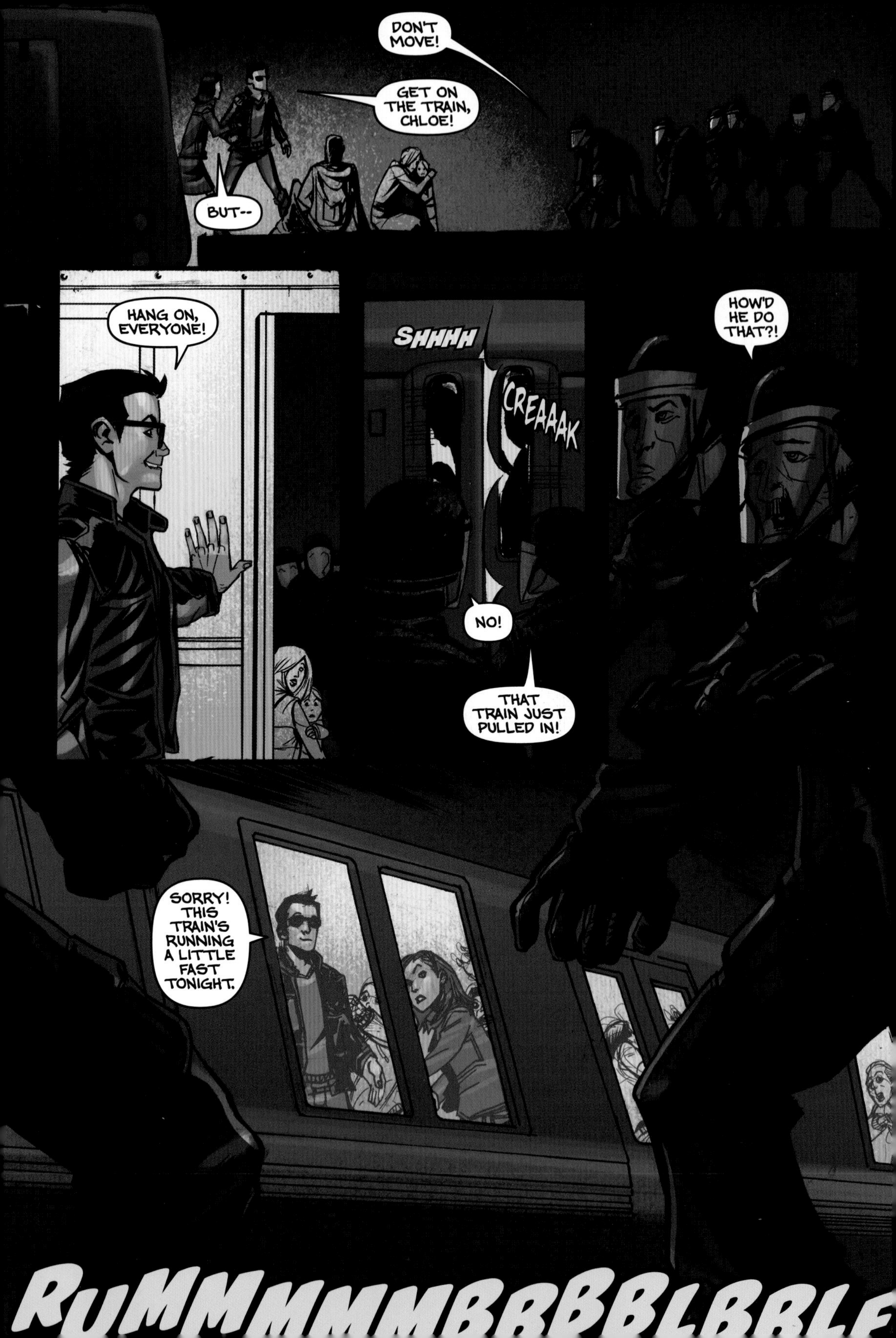
DON'T MOVE!
GET ON THE TRAIN, CHLOE!
BUT--
HANG ON, EVERYONE!
SHHHH
CREAAAK
HOW'D HE DO THAT?!
NO!
THAT TRAIN JUST PULLED IN!
SORRY! THIS TRAIN'S RUNNING A LITTLE FAST TONIGHT.
RUMMMMMBBBBLBBLE

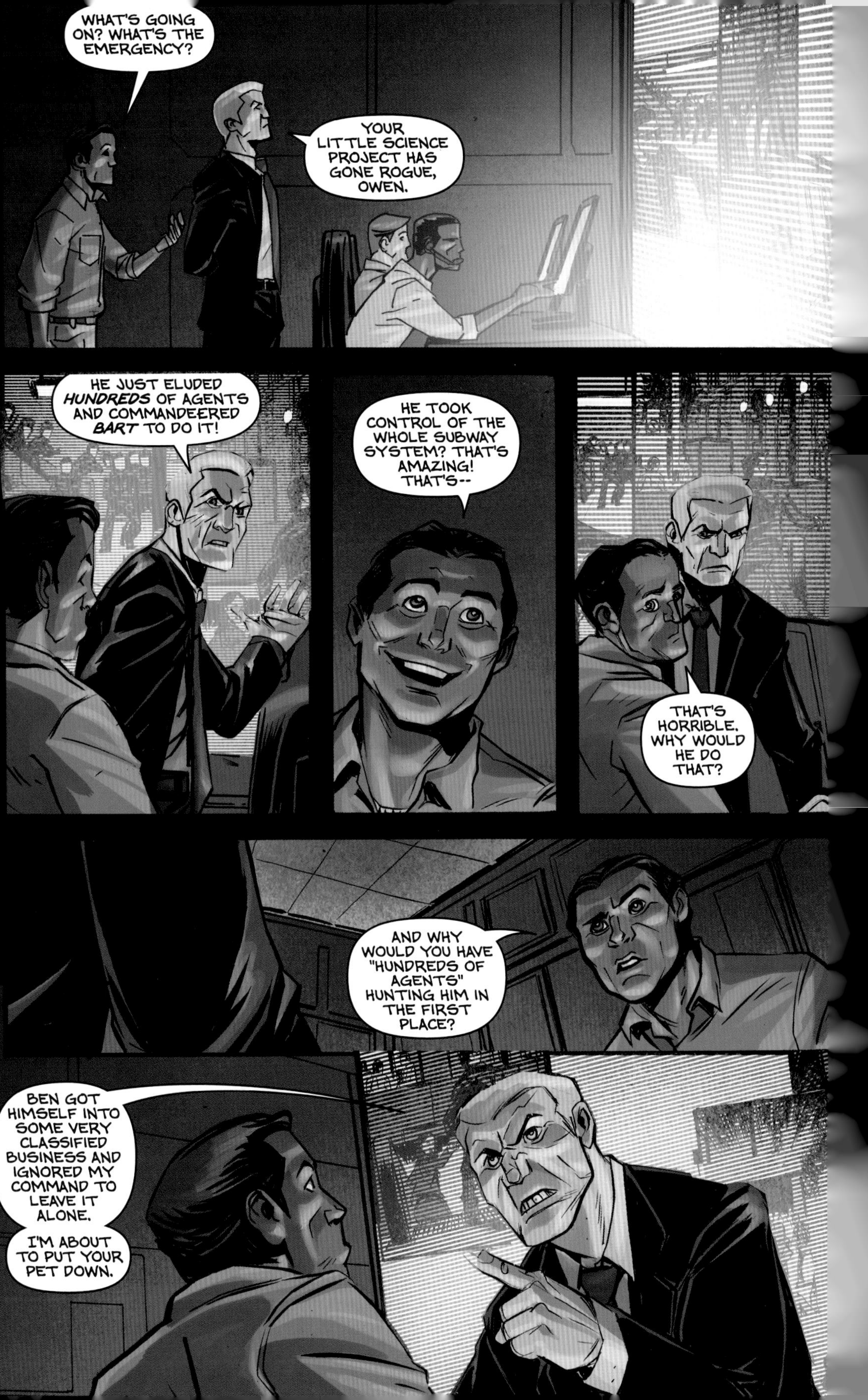
WHAT'S GOING ON? WHAT'S THE EMERGENCY?
YOUR LITTLE SCIENCE PROJECT HAS GONE ROGUE, OWEN.
HE JUST ELUDED *HUNDREDS* OF AGENTS AND COMMANDEERED *BART* TO DO IT!
HE TOOK CONTROL OF THE WHOLE SUBWAY SYSTEM? THAT'S AMAZING! THAT'S--
THAT'S HORRIBLE. WHY WOULD HE DO THAT?
AND WHY WOULD YOU HAVE "HUNDREDS OF AGENTS" HUNTING HIM IN THE FIRST PLACE?
BEN GOT HIMSELF INTO SOME VERY CLASSIFIED BUSINESS AND IGNORED MY COMMAND TO LEAVE IT ALONE.
I'M ABOUT TO PUT YOUR PET DOWN.

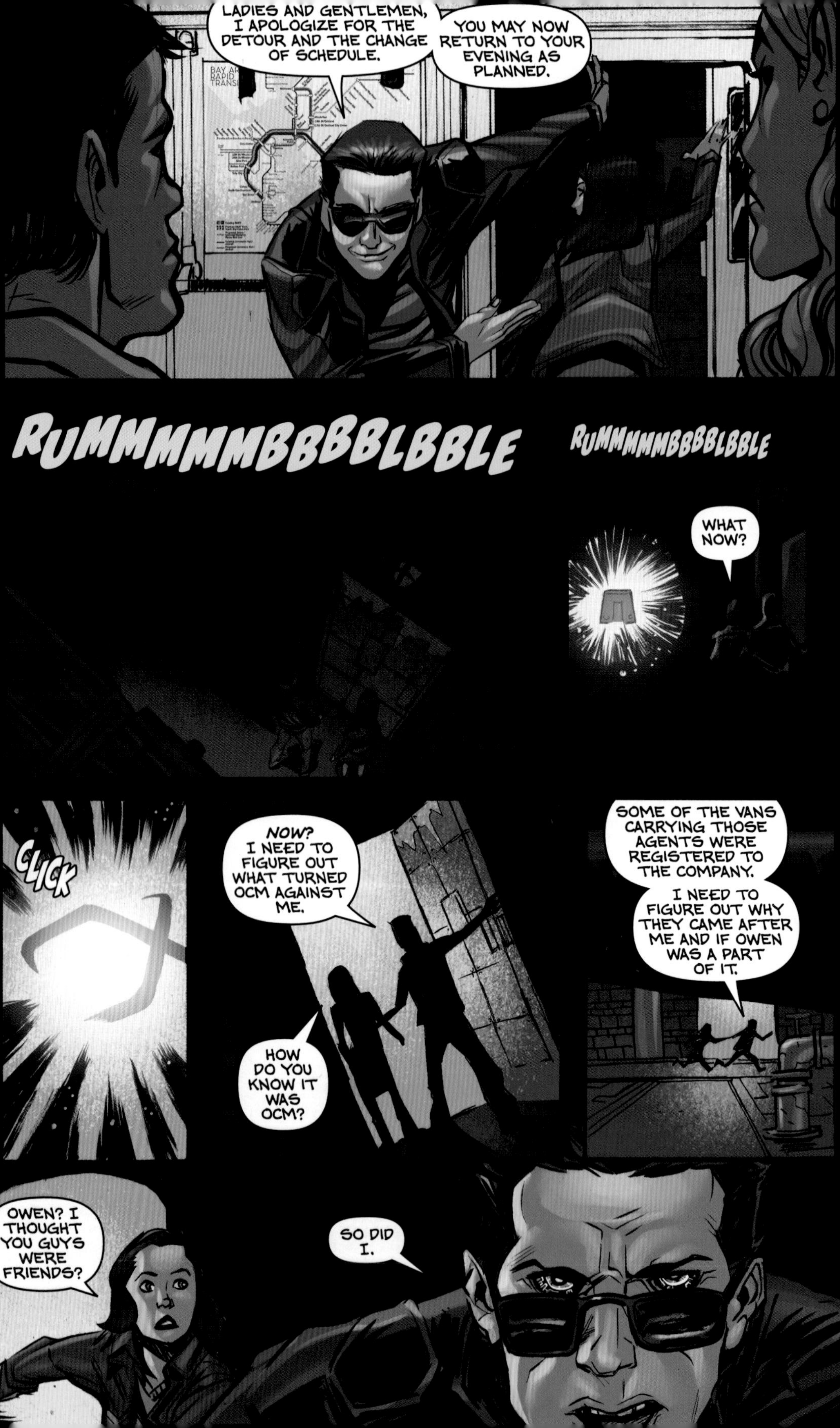
LADIES AND GENTLEMEN, I APOLOGIZE FOR THE DETOUR AND THE CHANGE OF SCHEDULE.
YOU MAY NOW RETURN TO YOUR EVENING AS PLANNED.
BAY AREA RAPID TRANSIT
RUMMMMMMBBBBLBBLE
RUMMMMMMBBBBLBBLE
WHAT NOW?
CLICK
NOW? I NEED TO FIGURE OUT WHAT TURNED OCM AGAINST ME.
HOW DO YOU KNOW IT WAS OCM?
SOME OF THE VANS CARRYING THOSE AGENTS WERE REGISTERED TO THE COMPANY.
I NEED TO FIGURE OUT WHY THEY CAME AFTER ME AND IF OWEN WAS A PART OF IT.
OWEN? I THOUGHT YOU GUYS WERE FRIENDS?
SO DID I.

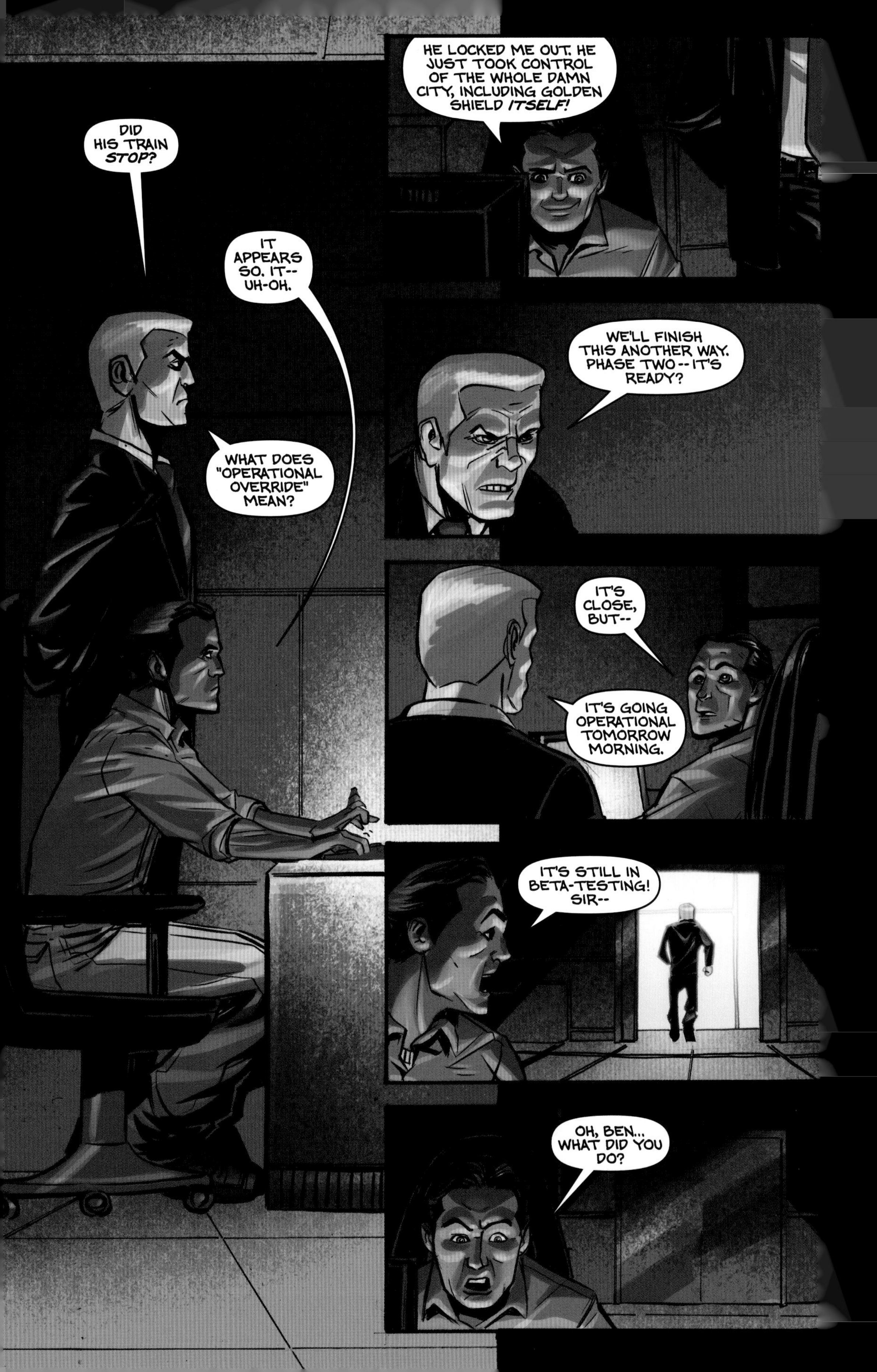
DID HIS TRAIN *STOP?*
HE LOCKED ME OUT. HE JUST TOOK CONTROL OF THE WHOLE DAMN CITY, INCLUDING GOLDEN SHIELD *ITSELF!*
IT APPEARS SO. IT-- UH-OH.
WHAT DOES "OPERATIONAL OVERRIDE" MEAN?
WE'LL FINISH THIS ANOTHER WAY. PHASE TWO -- IT'S READY?
IT'S CLOSE, BUT--
IT'S GOING OPERATIONAL TOMORROW MORNING.
IT'S STILL IN BETA-TESTING! SIR--
OH, BEN... WHAT DID YOU DO?

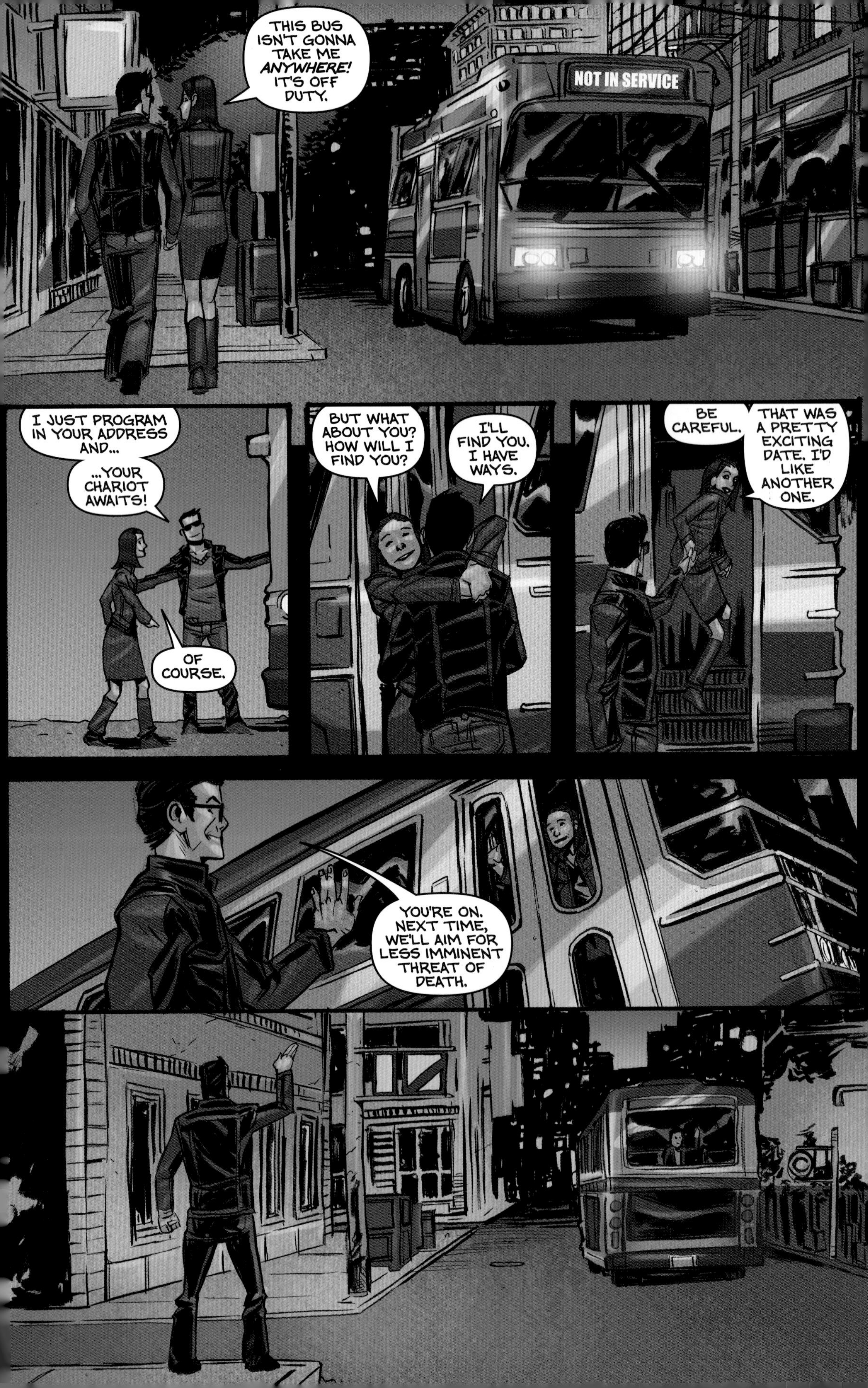
THIS BUS ISN'T GONNA TAKE ME *ANYWHERE!* IT'S OFF DUTY.
NOT IN SERVICE
I JUST PROGRAM IN YOUR ADDRESS AND...
...YOUR CHARIOT AWAITS!
OF COURSE.
BUT WHAT ABOUT YOU? HOW WILL I FIND YOU?
I'LL FIND YOU. I HAVE WAYS.
BE CAREFUL.
THAT WAS A PRETTY EXCITING DATE. I'D LIKE ANOTHER ONE.
YOU'RE ON. NEXT TIME, WE'LL AIM FOR LESS IMMINENT THREAT OF DEATH.

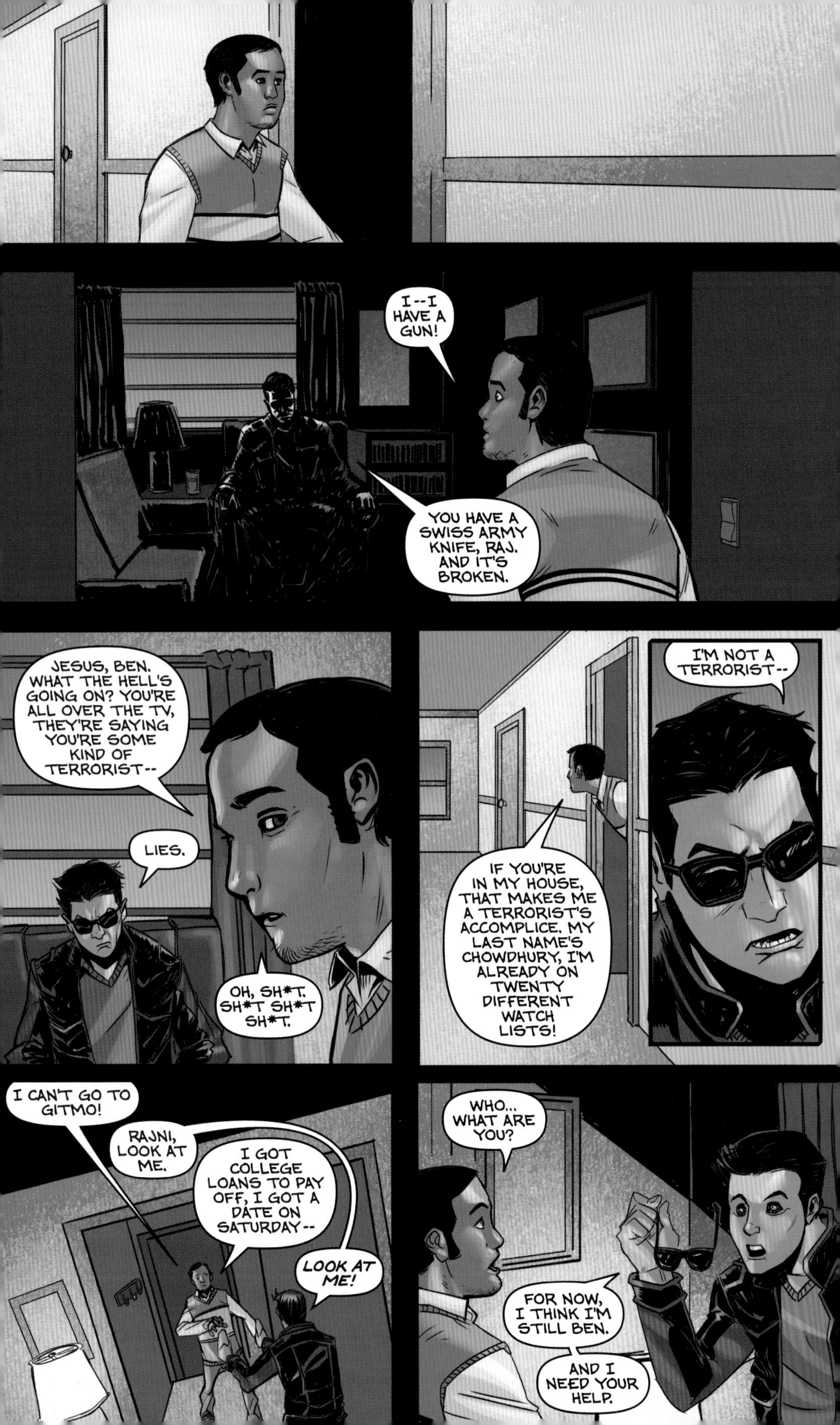

I--I HAVE A GUN!
YOU HAVE A SWISS ARMY KNIFE, RAJ. AND IT'S BROKEN.
JESUS, BEN. WHAT THE HELL'S GOING ON? YOU'RE ALL OVER THE TV, THEY'RE SAYING YOU'RE SOME KIND OF TERRORIST--
LIES.
OH, SH*T. SH*T SH*T SH*T.
IF YOU'RE IN MY HOUSE, THAT MAKES ME A TERRORIST'S ACCOMPLICE. MY LAST NAME'S CHOWDHURY, I'M ALREADY ON TWENTY DIFFERENT WATCH LISTS!
I'M NOT A TERRORIST--
I CAN'T GO TO GITMO!
RAJNI, LOOK AT ME.
I GOT COLLEGE LOANS TO PAY OFF, I GOT A DATE ON SATURDAY--
LOOK AT ME!
WHO... WHAT ARE YOU?
FOR NOW, I THINK I'M STILL BEN.
AND I NEED YOUR HELP.

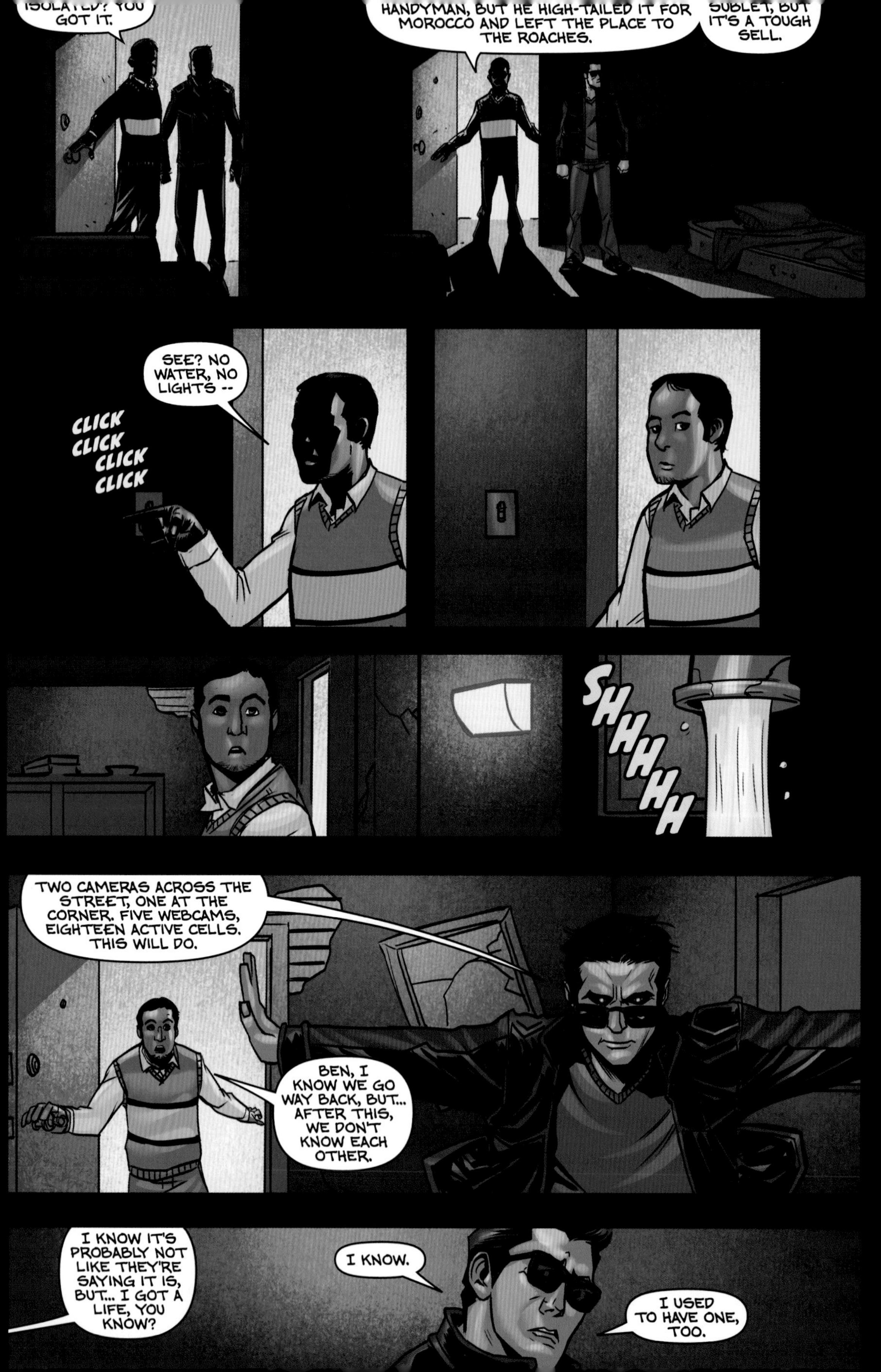
ISOLATED? YOU GOT IT.
HANDYMAN, BUT HE HIGH-TAILED IT FOR MOROCCO AND LEFT THE PLACE TO THE ROACHES.
SUBLET, BUT IT'S A TOUGH SELL.
SEE? NO WATER, NO LIGHTS --
CLICK CLICK CLICK CLICK
SHHHHH
TWO CAMERAS ACROSS THE STREET, ONE AT THE CORNER. FIVE WEBCAMS, EIGHTEEN ACTIVE CELLS. THIS WILL DO.
BEN, I KNOW WE GO WAY BACK, BUT... AFTER THIS, WE DON'T KNOW EACH OTHER.
I KNOW IT'S PROBABLY NOT LIKE THEY'RE SAYING IT IS, BUT... I GOT A LIFE, YOU KNOW?
I KNOW.
I USED TO HAVE ONE, TOO.

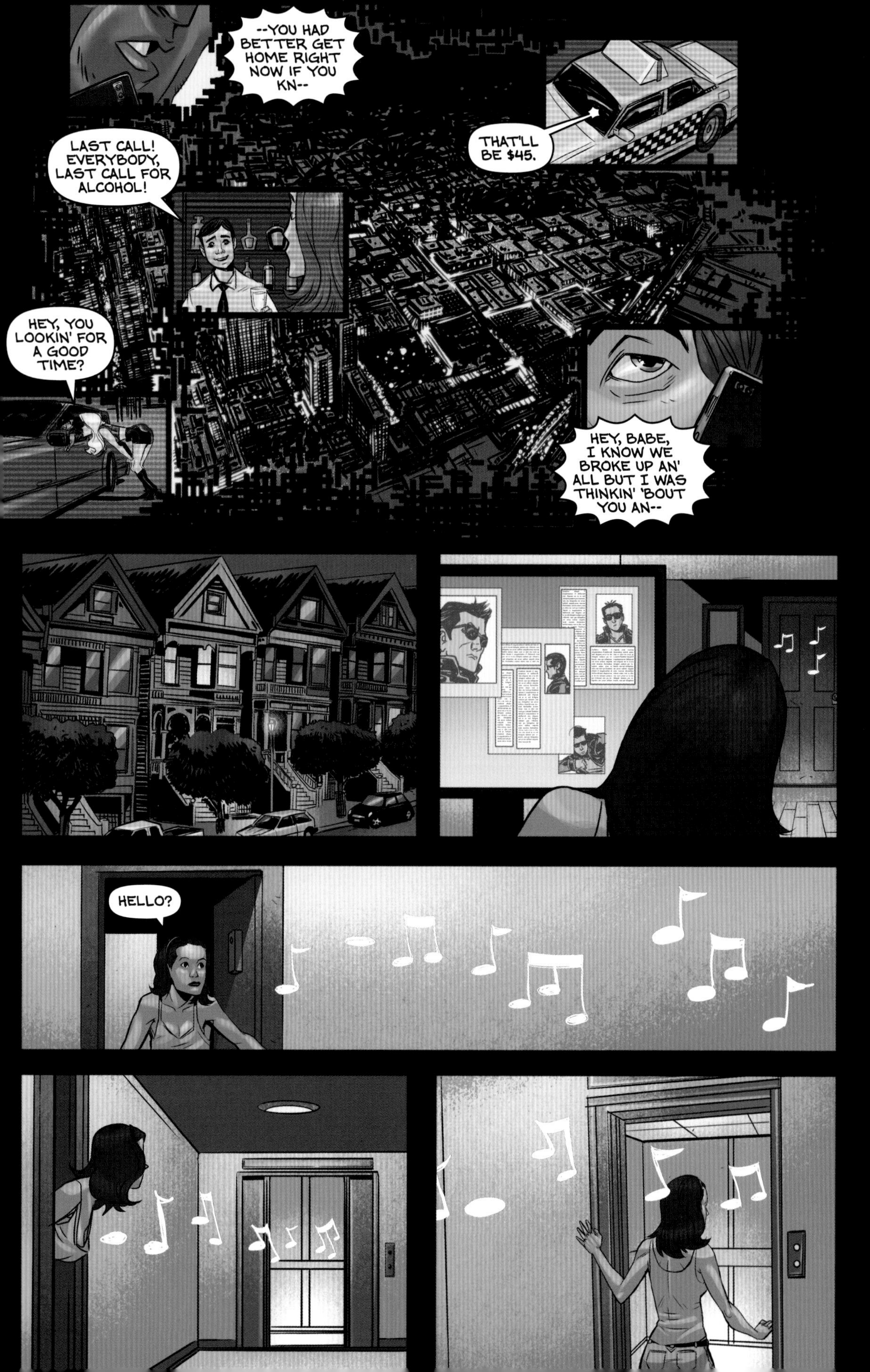

--YOU HAD BETTER GET HOME RIGHT NOW IF YOU KN--
THAT'LL BE $45.
LAST CALL! EVERYBODY, LAST CALL FOR ALCOHOL!
HEY, YOU LOOKIN' FOR A GOOD TIME?
HEY, BABE, I KNOW WE BROKE UP AN' ALL BUT I WAS THINKIN' 'BOUT YOU AN--
HELLO?

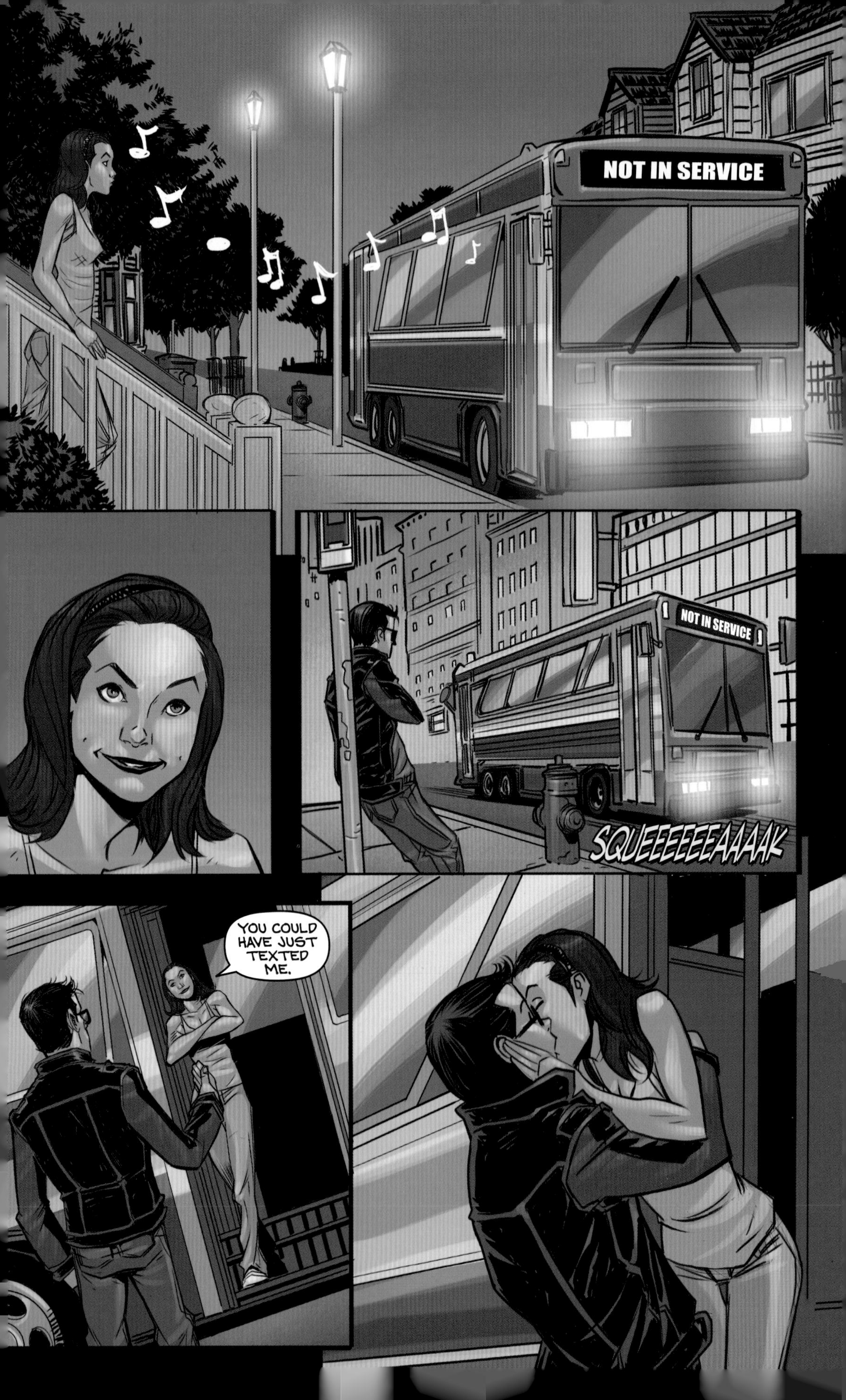
NOT IN SERVICE
NOT IN SERVICE
SQUEEEEEEEAAAAK
YOU COULD HAVE JUST TEXTED ME.

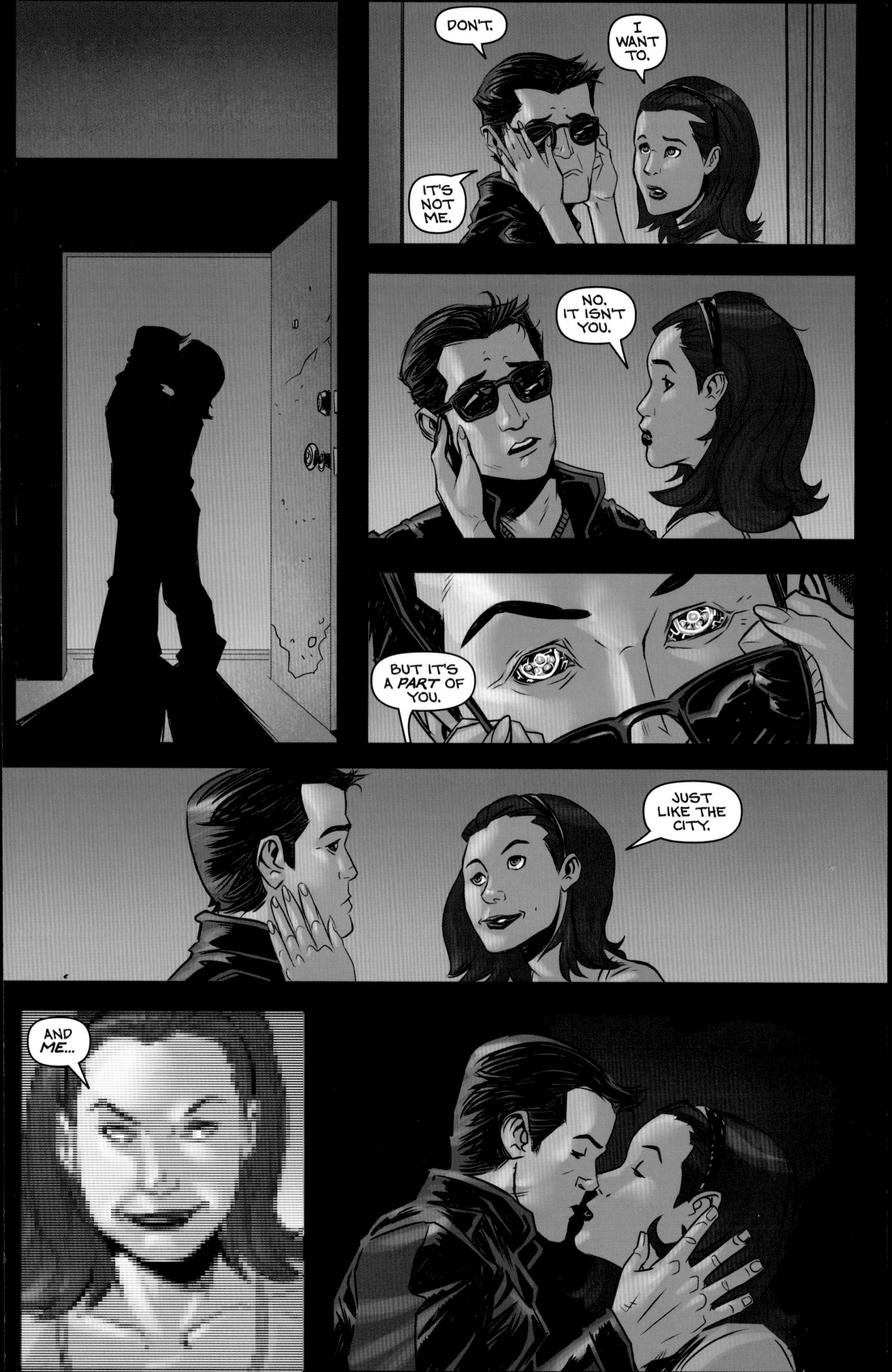
DON'T.
I WANT TO.
IT'S NOT ME.
NO. IT ISN'T YOU.
BUT IT'S A *PART* OF YOU.
JUST LIKE THE CITY.
AND *ME*...

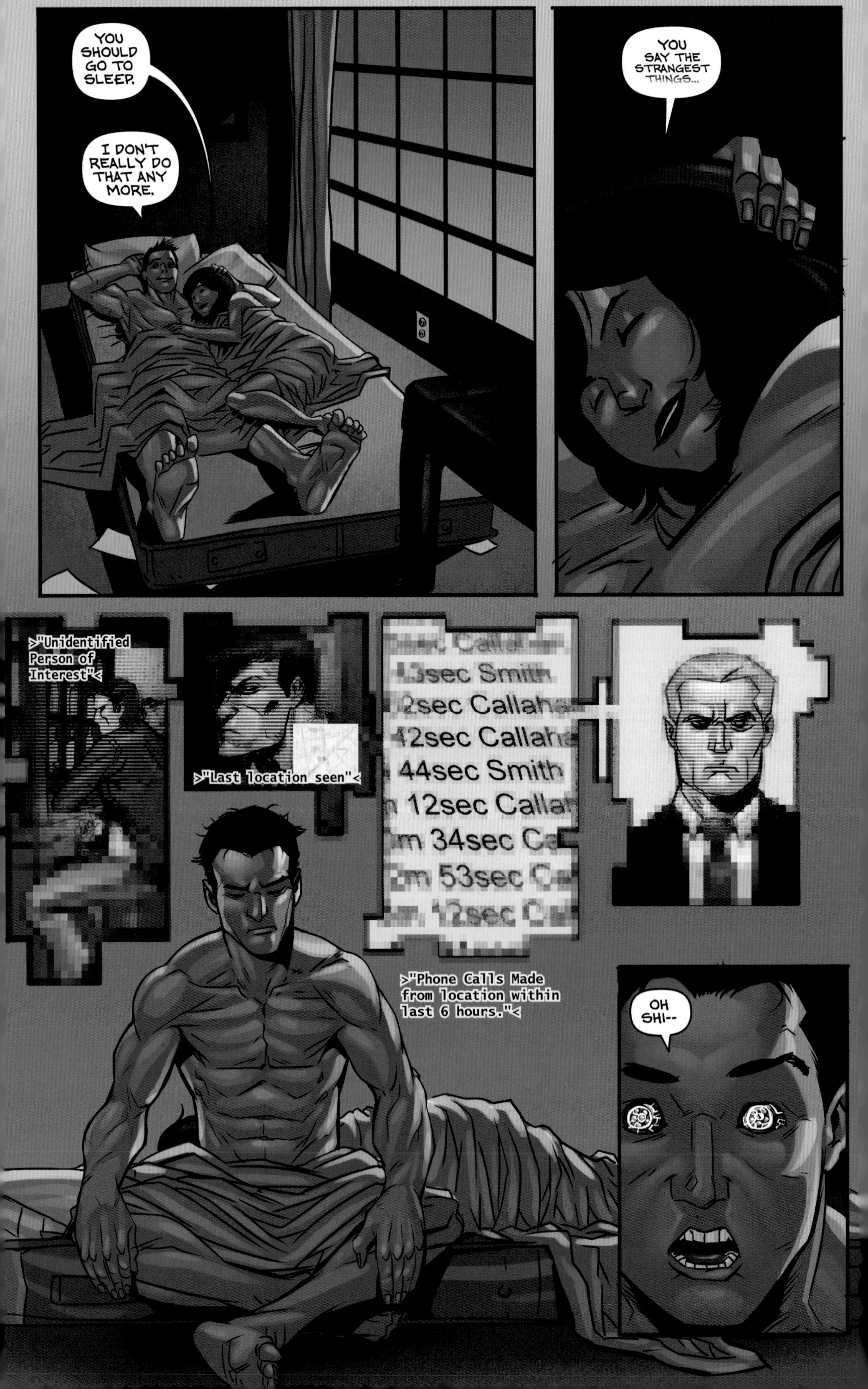
YOU SHOULD GO TO SLEEP.
I DON'T REALLY DO THAT ANY MORE.
YOU SAY THE STRANGEST THINGS...
>"Unidentified Person of Interest"<
>"Last location seen"<
3sec Smith
2sec Callaha
42sec Callaha
44sec Smith
12sec Callal
m 34sec Ca
m 53sec C
>"Phone Calls Made from location within last 6 hours."<
OH SHI--

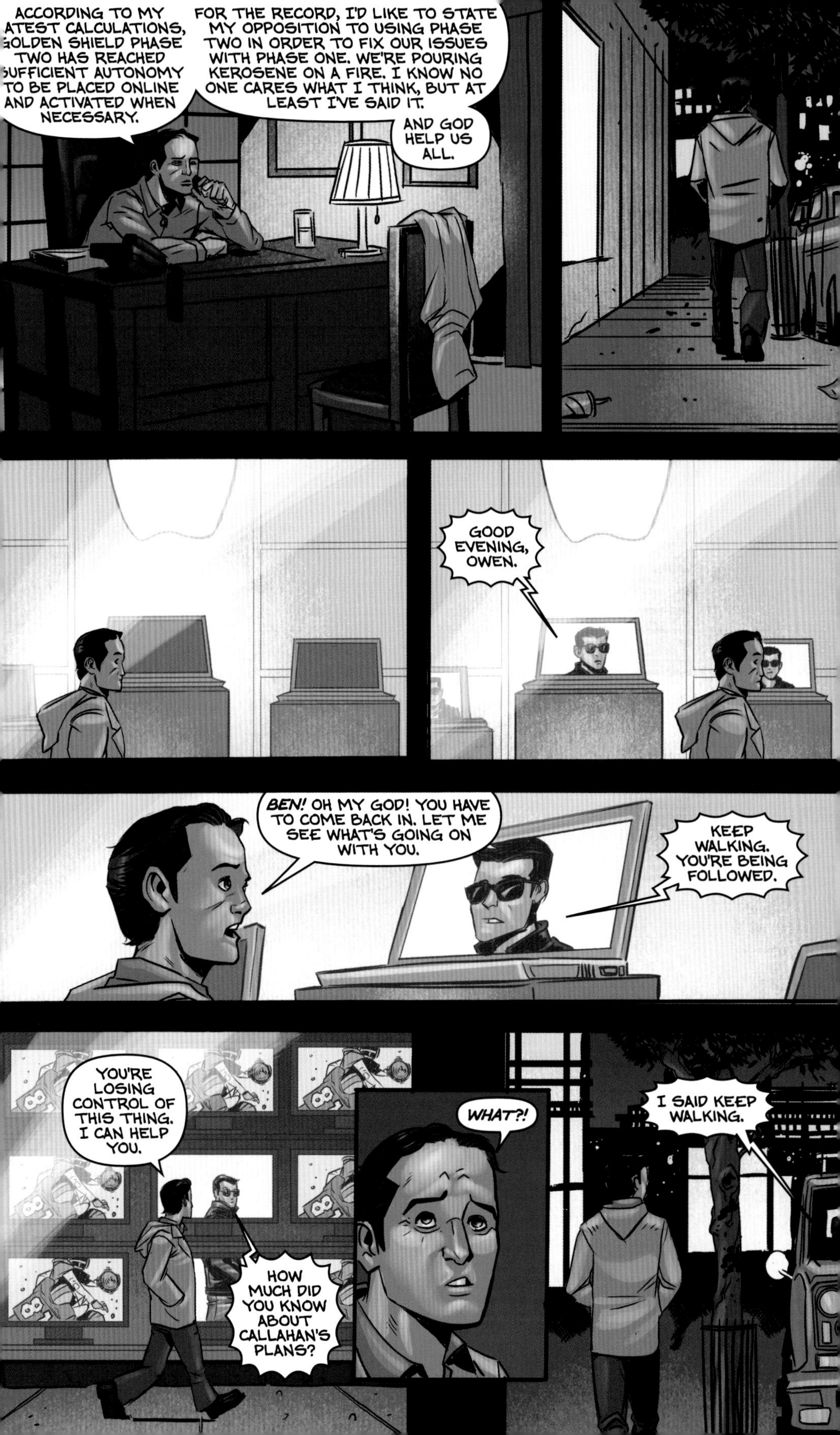
ACCORDING TO MY LATEST CALCULATIONS, GOLDEN SHIELD PHASE TWO HAS REACHED SUFFICIENT AUTONOMY TO BE PLACED ONLINE AND ACTIVATED WHEN NECESSARY.
FOR THE RECORD, I'D LIKE TO STATE MY OPPOSITION TO USING PHASE TWO IN ORDER TO FIX OUR ISSUES WITH PHASE ONE. WE'RE POURING KEROSENE ON A FIRE. I KNOW NO ONE CARES WHAT I THINK, BUT AT LEAST I'VE SAID IT.
AND GOD HELP US ALL.
GOOD EVENING, OWEN.
BEN! OH MY GOD! YOU HAVE TO COME BACK IN. LET ME SEE WHAT'S GOING ON WITH YOU.
KEEP WALKING. YOU'RE BEING FOLLOWED.
YOU'RE LOSING CONTROL OF THIS THING. I CAN HELP YOU.
HOW MUCH DID YOU KNOW ABOUT CALLAHAN'S PLANS?
WHAT?!
I SAID KEEP WALKING.

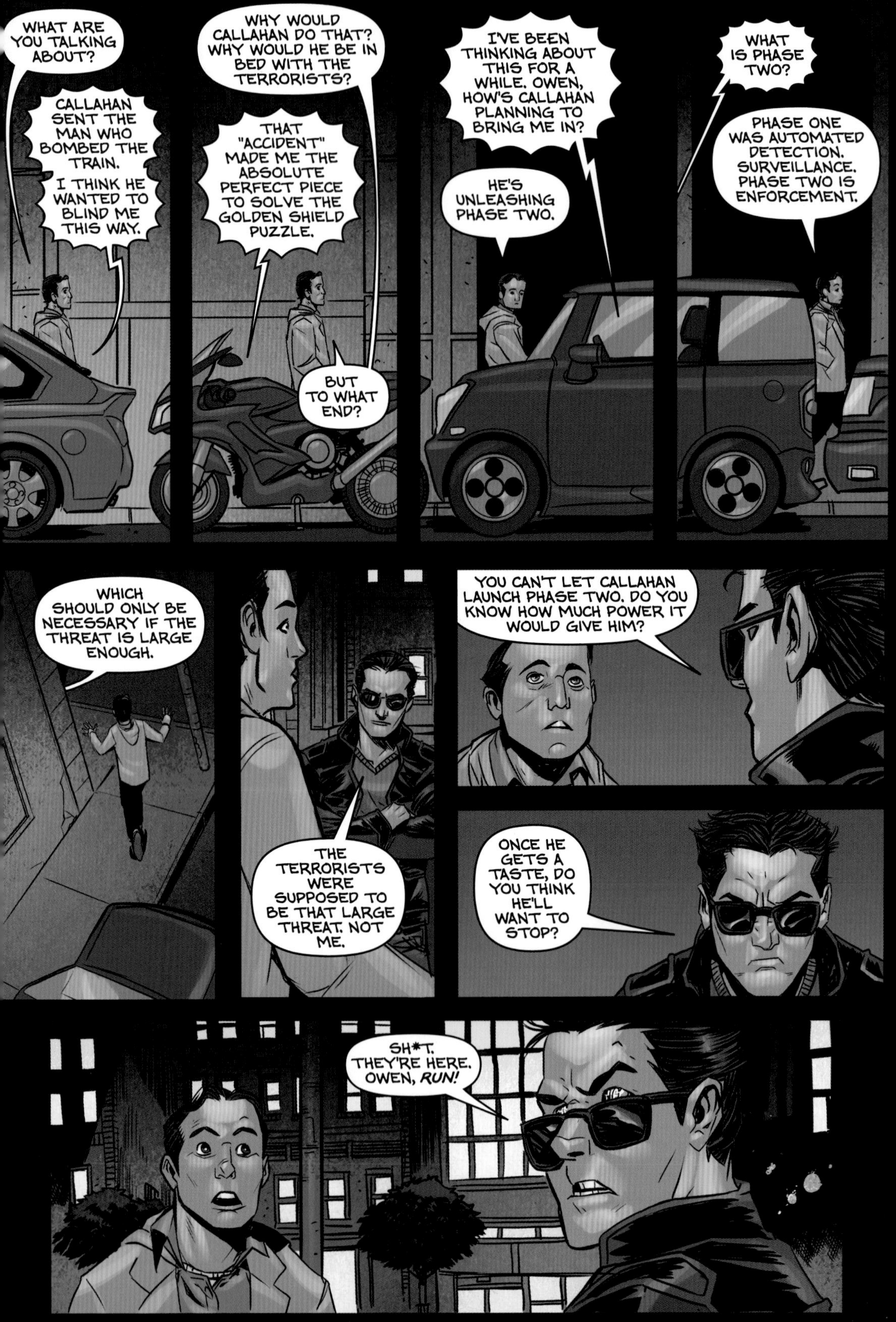
WHAT ARE YOU TALKING ABOUT?
CALLAHAN SENT THE MAN WHO BOMBED THE TRAIN.
I THINK HE WANTED TO BLIND ME THIS WAY.
WHY WOULD CALLAHAN DO THAT? WHY WOULD HE BE IN BED WITH THE TERRORISTS?
THAT "ACCIDENT" MADE ME THE ABSOLUTE PERFECT PIECE TO SOLVE THE GOLDEN SHIELD PUZZLE.
BUT TO WHAT END?
I'VE BEEN THINKING ABOUT THIS FOR A WHILE. OWEN, HOW'S CALLAHAN PLANNING TO BRING ME IN?
HE'S UNLEASHING PHASE TWO.
WHAT IS PHASE TWO?
PHASE ONE WAS AUTOMATED DETECTION. SURVEILLANCE. PHASE TWO IS ENFORCEMENT.
WHICH SHOULD ONLY BE NECESSARY IF THE THREAT IS LARGE ENOUGH.
THE TERRORISTS WERE SUPPOSED TO BE THAT LARGE THREAT. NOT ME.
YOU CAN'T LET CALLAHAN LAUNCH PHASE TWO. DO YOU KNOW HOW MUCH POWER IT WOULD GIVE HIM?
ONCE HE GETS A TASTE, DO YOU THINK HE'LL WANT TO STOP?
SH*T. THEY'RE HERE. OWEN, *RUN!*

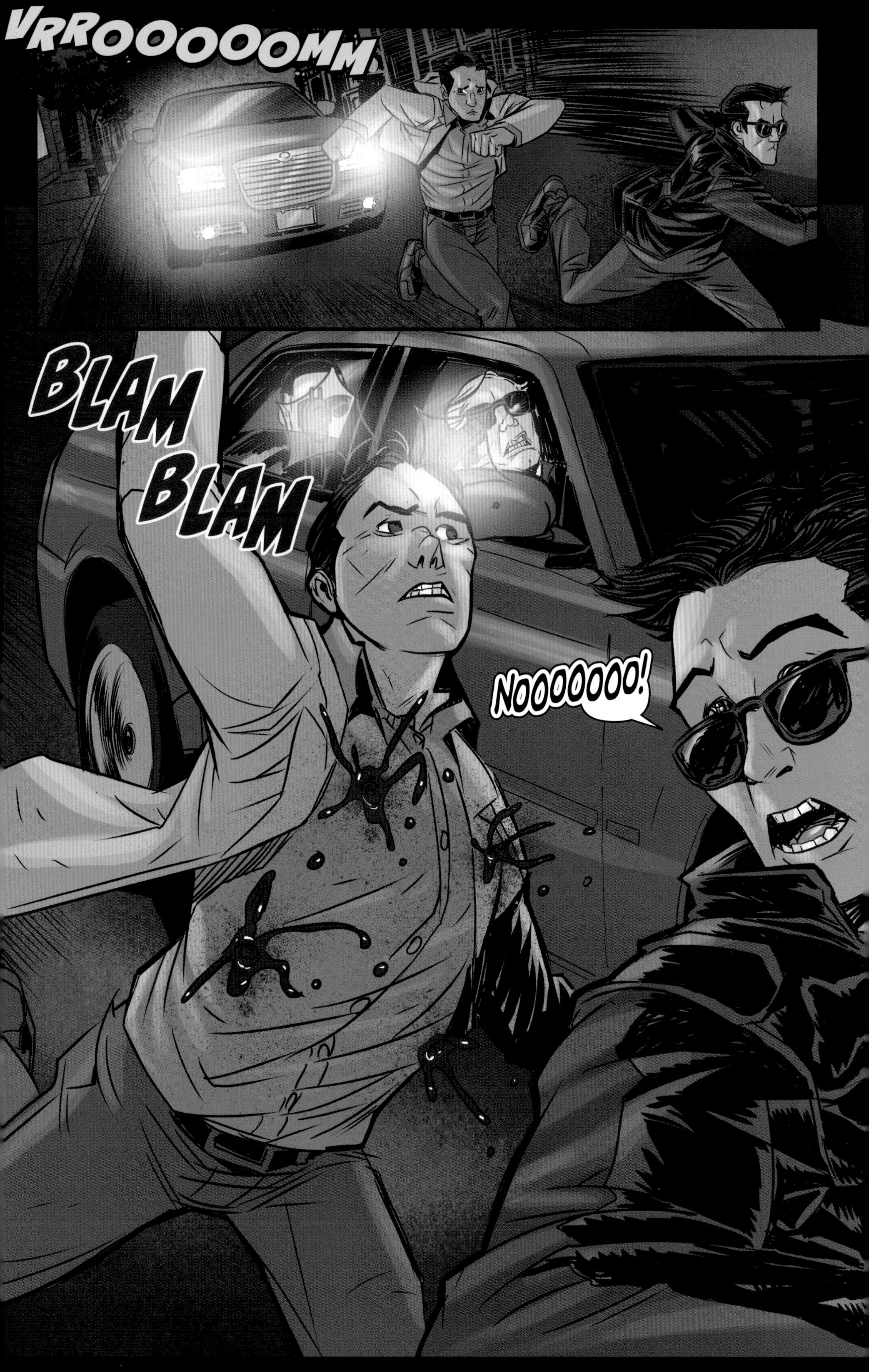
VRROOOOOMM
BLAM
BLAM
NOOOOOOO!

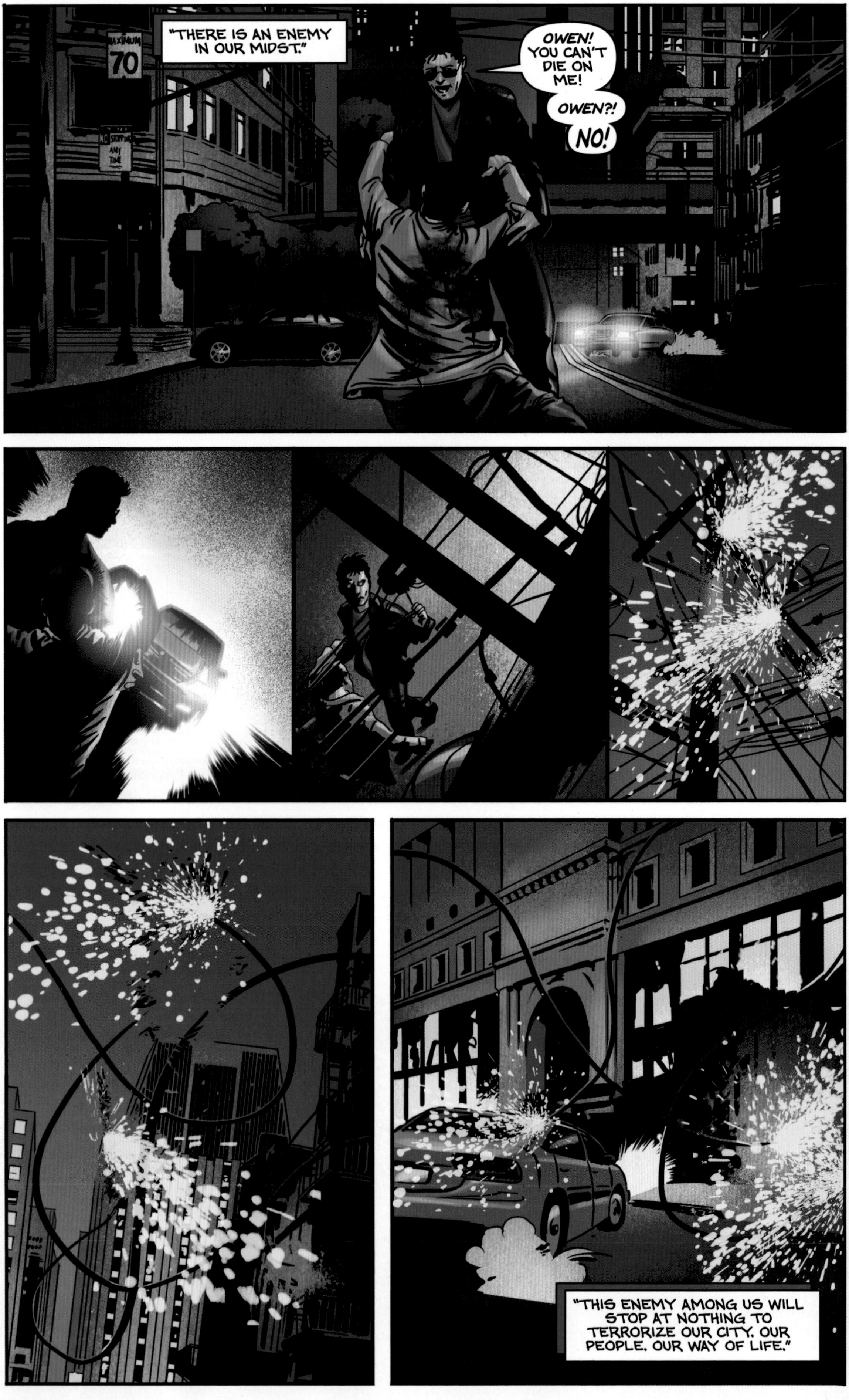
"THERE IS AN ENEMY IN OUR MIDST."
OWEN! YOU CAN'T DIE ON ME!
OWEN?!
NO!
"THIS ENEMY AMONG US WILL STOP AT NOTHING TO TERRORIZE OUR CITY. OUR PEOPLE. OUR WAY OF LIFE."

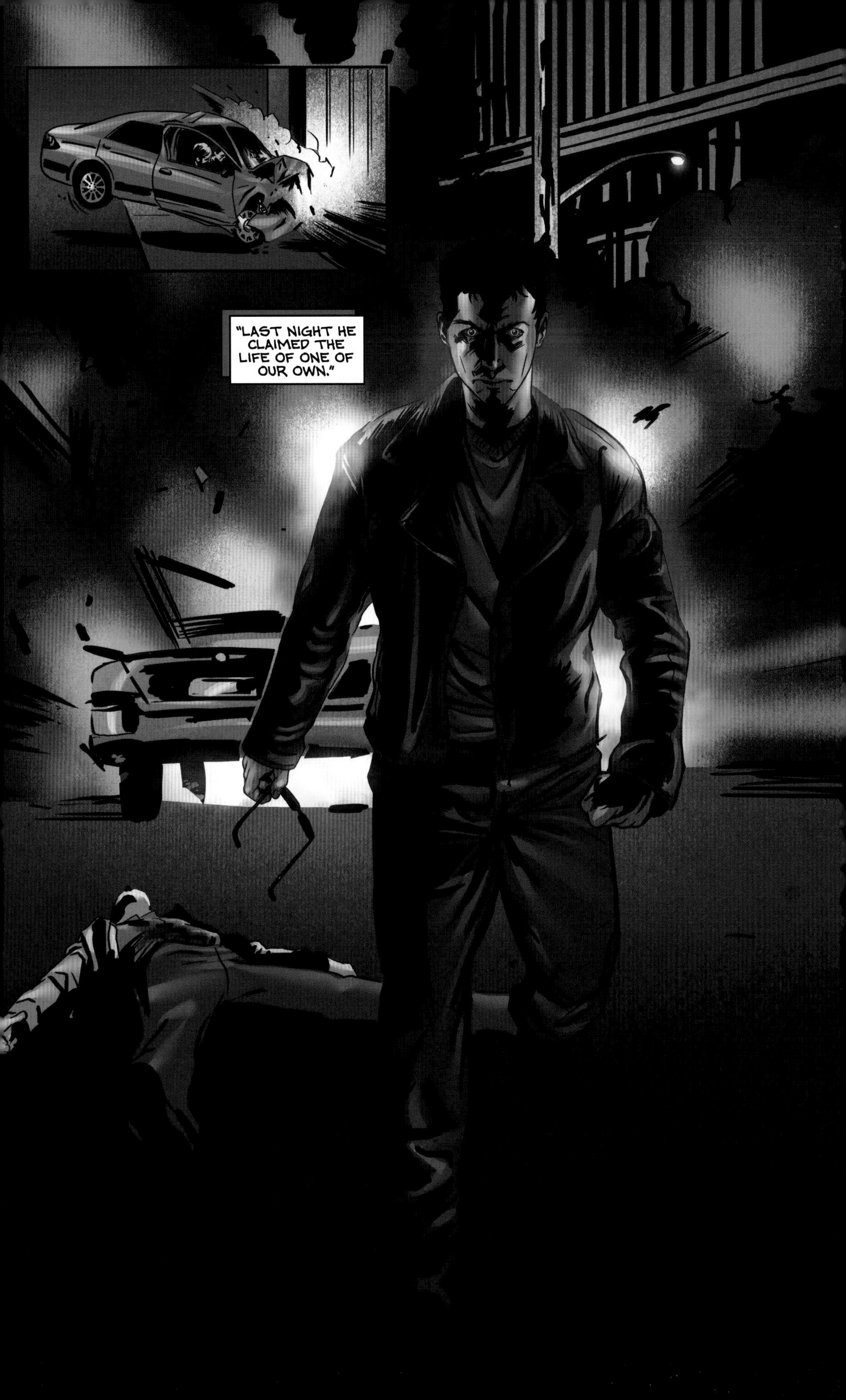
"LAST NIGHT HE CLAIMED THE LIFE OF ONE OF OUR OWN."

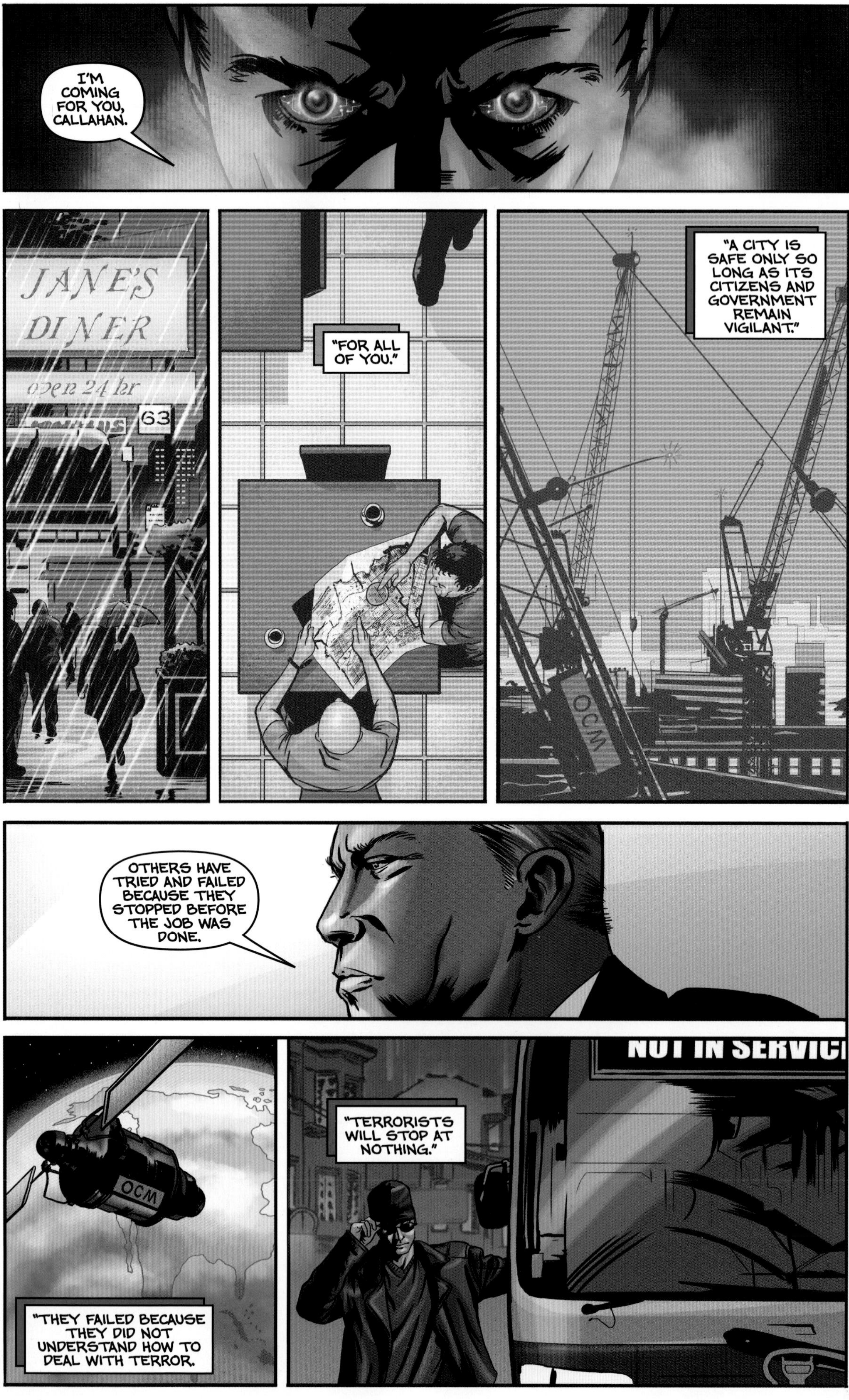
I'M COMING FOR YOU, CALLAHAN.
JANE'S DINER
open 24 hr
63
"FOR ALL OF YOU."
"A CITY IS SAFE ONLY SO LONG AS ITS CITIZENS AND GOVERNMENT REMAIN VIGILANT."
OCM
OTHERS HAVE TRIED AND FAILED BECAUSE THEY STOPPED BEFORE THE JOB WAS DONE.
OCM
"THEY FAILED BECAUSE THEY DID NOT UNDERSTAND HOW TO DEAL WITH TERROR.
NOT IN SERVICE
"TERRORISTS WILL STOP AT NOTHING."

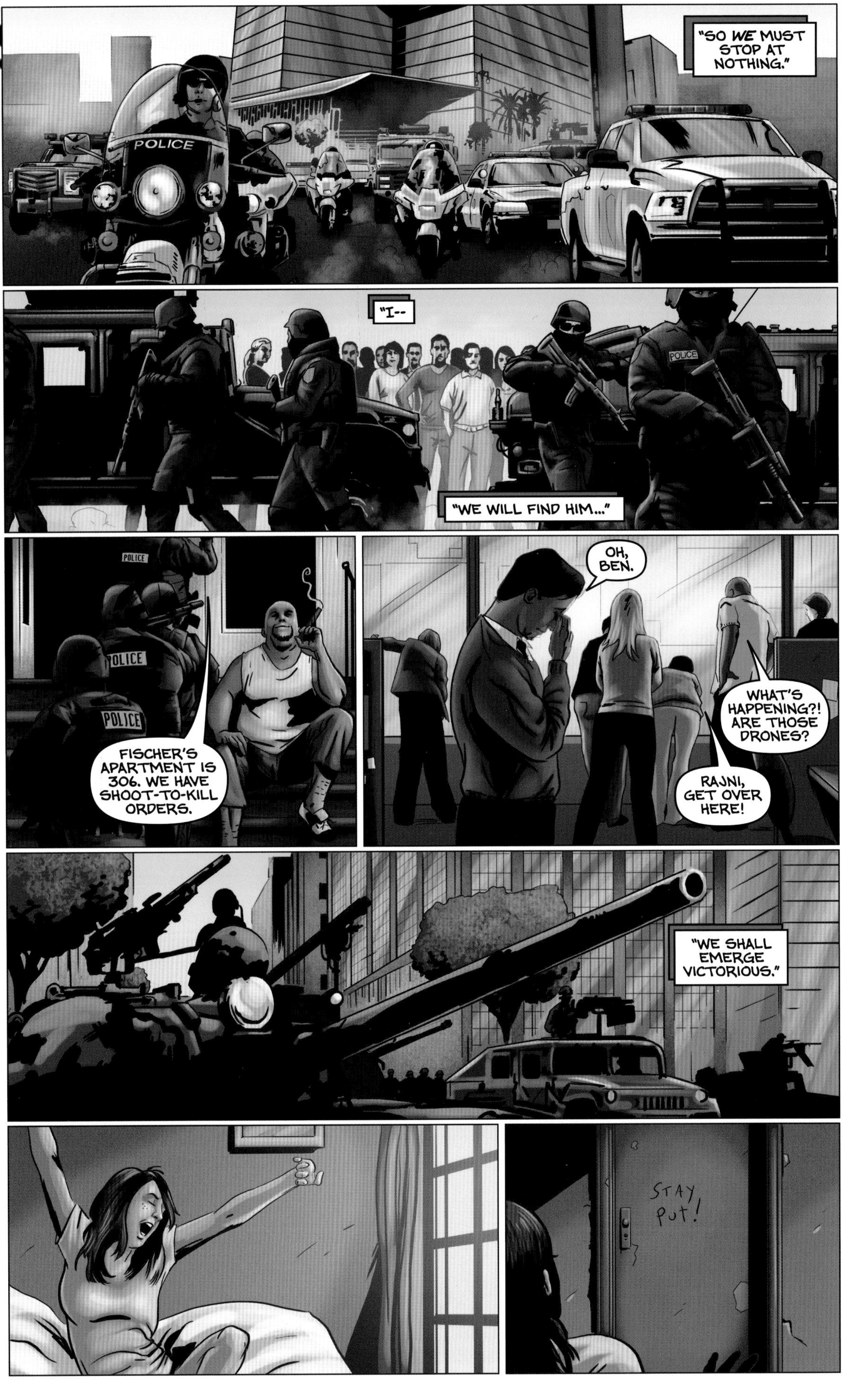
"SO WE MUST STOP AT NOTHING."
POLICE
"I--
"WE WILL FIND HIM..."
POLICE
POLICE
POLICE
POLICE
FISCHER'S APARTMENT IS 306. WE HAVE SHOOT-TO-KILL ORDERS.
OH, BEN.
WHAT'S HAPPENING?! ARE THOSE DRONES?
RAJNI, GET OVER HERE!
"WE SHALL EMERGE VICTORIOUS."
STAY PUT!

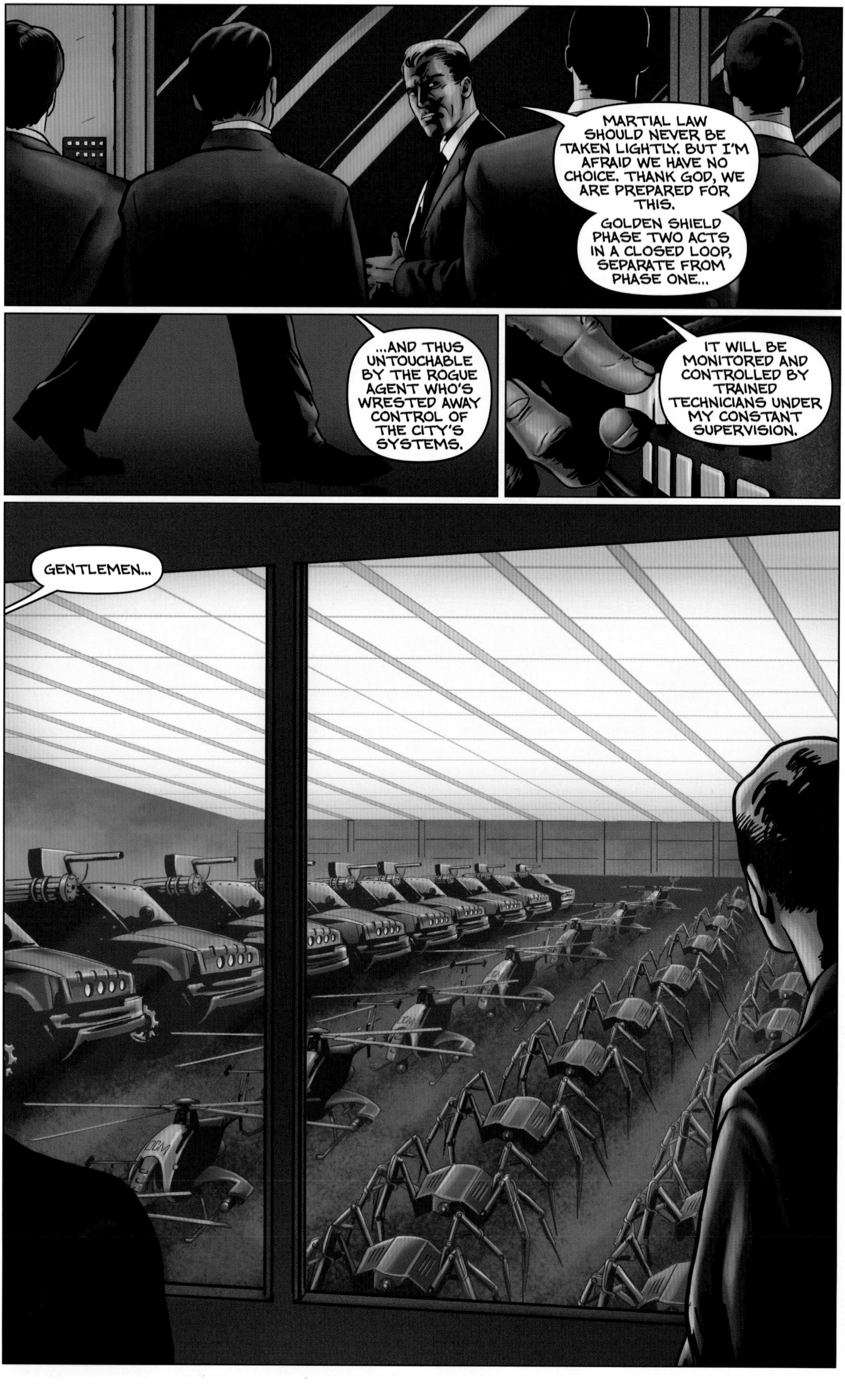
MARTIAL LAW SHOULD NEVER BE TAKEN LIGHTLY. BUT I'M AFRAID WE HAVE NO CHOICE. THANK GOD, WE ARE PREPARED FOR THIS.
GOLDEN SHIELD PHASE TWO ACTS IN A CLOSED LOOP, SEPARATE FROM PHASE ONE...
...AND THUS UNTOUCHABLE BY THE ROGUE AGENT WHO'S WRESTED AWAY CONTROL OF THE CITY'S SYSTEMS.
IT WILL BE MONITORED AND CONTROLLED BY TRAINED TECHNICIANS UNDER MY CONSTANT SUPERVISION.
GENTLEMEN...

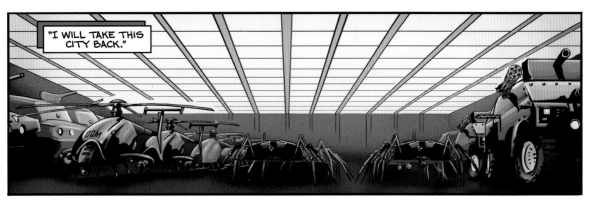

"I WILL TAKE THIS CITY BACK."

FIRE IT UP!

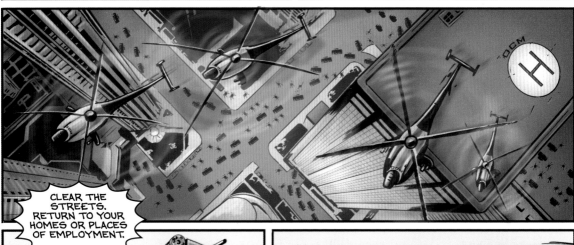

CLEAR THE STREETS. RETURN TO YOUR HOMES OR PLACES OF EMPLOYMENT.

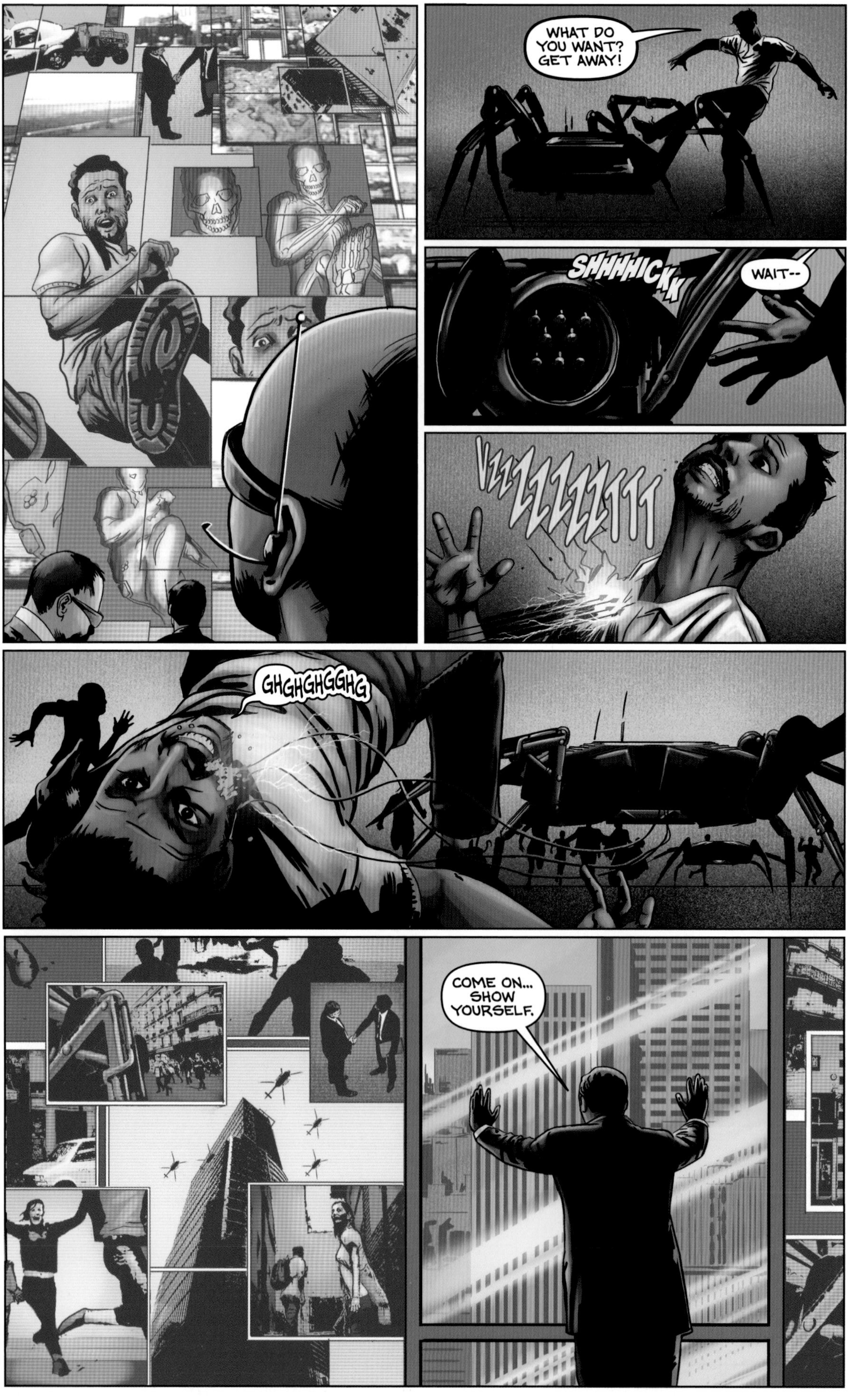
WHAT DO YOU WANT? GET AWAY!
SHHHHICKK
WAIT--
VZZZZZZZTTT
GHGHGHGGHG
COME ON... SHOW YOURSELF.

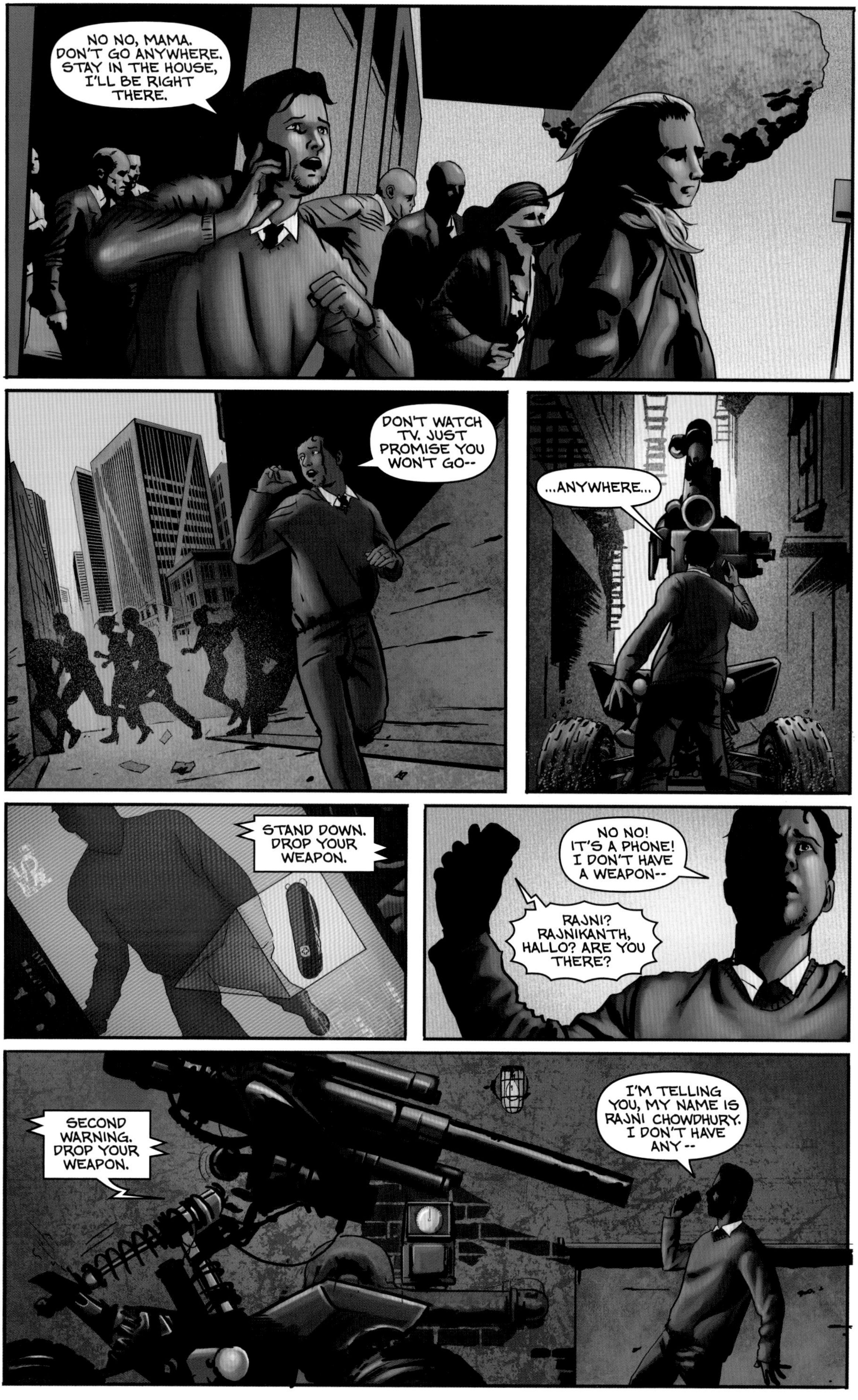
NO NO, MAMA. DON'T GO ANYWHERE. STAY IN THE HOUSE, I'LL BE RIGHT THERE.
DON'T WATCH TV. JUST PROMISE YOU WON'T GO--
...ANYWHERE...
STAND DOWN. DROP YOUR WEAPON.
NO NO! IT'S A PHONE! I DON'T HAVE A WEAPON--
RAJNI? RAJNIKANTH, HALLO? ARE YOU THERE?
SECOND WARNING. DROP YOUR WEAPON.
I'M TELLING YOU, MY NAME IS RAJNI CHOWDHURY. I DON'T HAVE ANY --

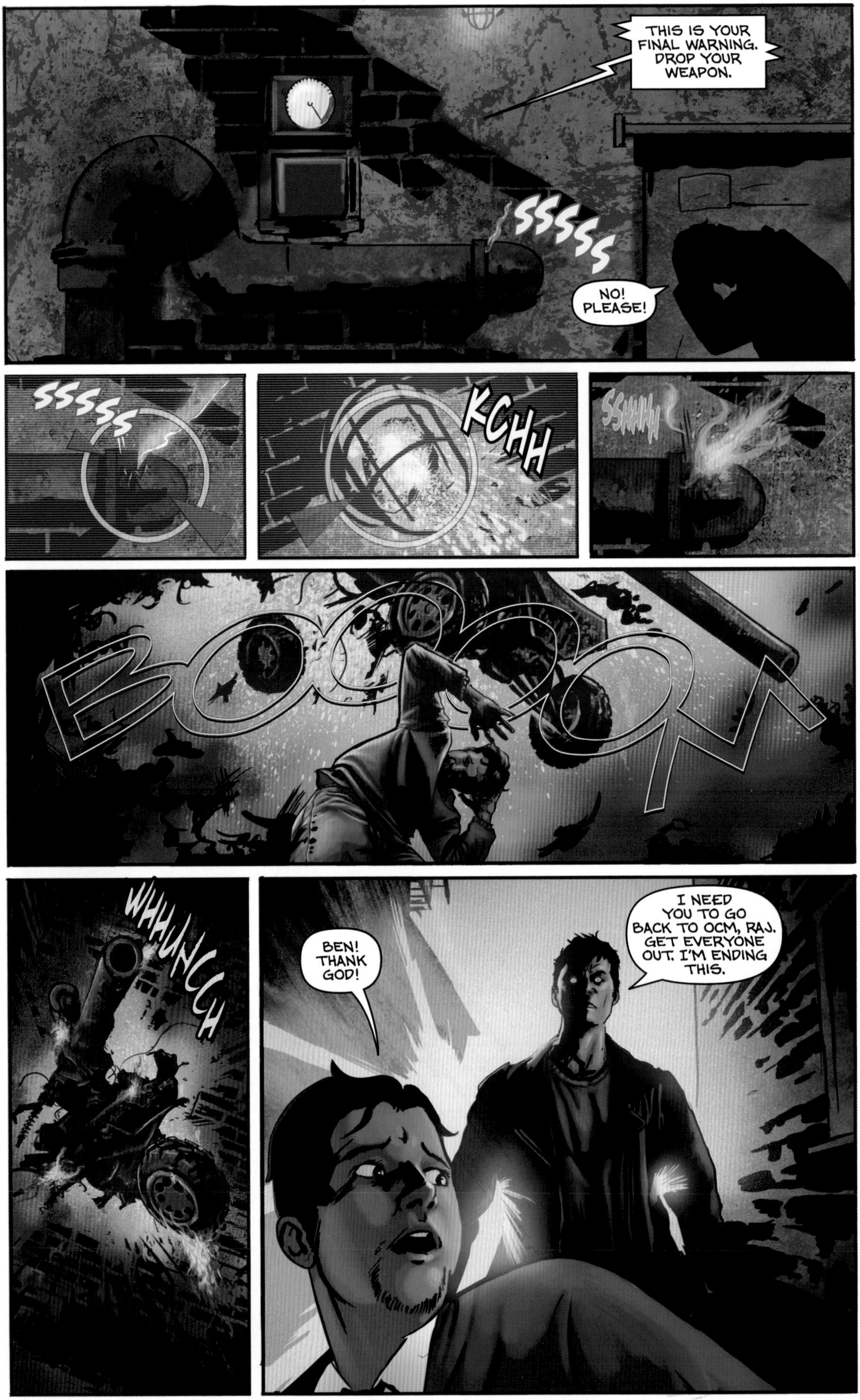
THIS IS YOUR FINAL WARNING. DROP YOUR WEAPON.
SSSSS
NO! PLEASE!
SSSSS
KCHH
SSHHHH
BOOOOM
WHHUNCCH
BEN! THANK GOD!
I NEED YOU TO GO BACK TO OCM, RAJ. GET EVERYONE OUT. I'M ENDING THIS.

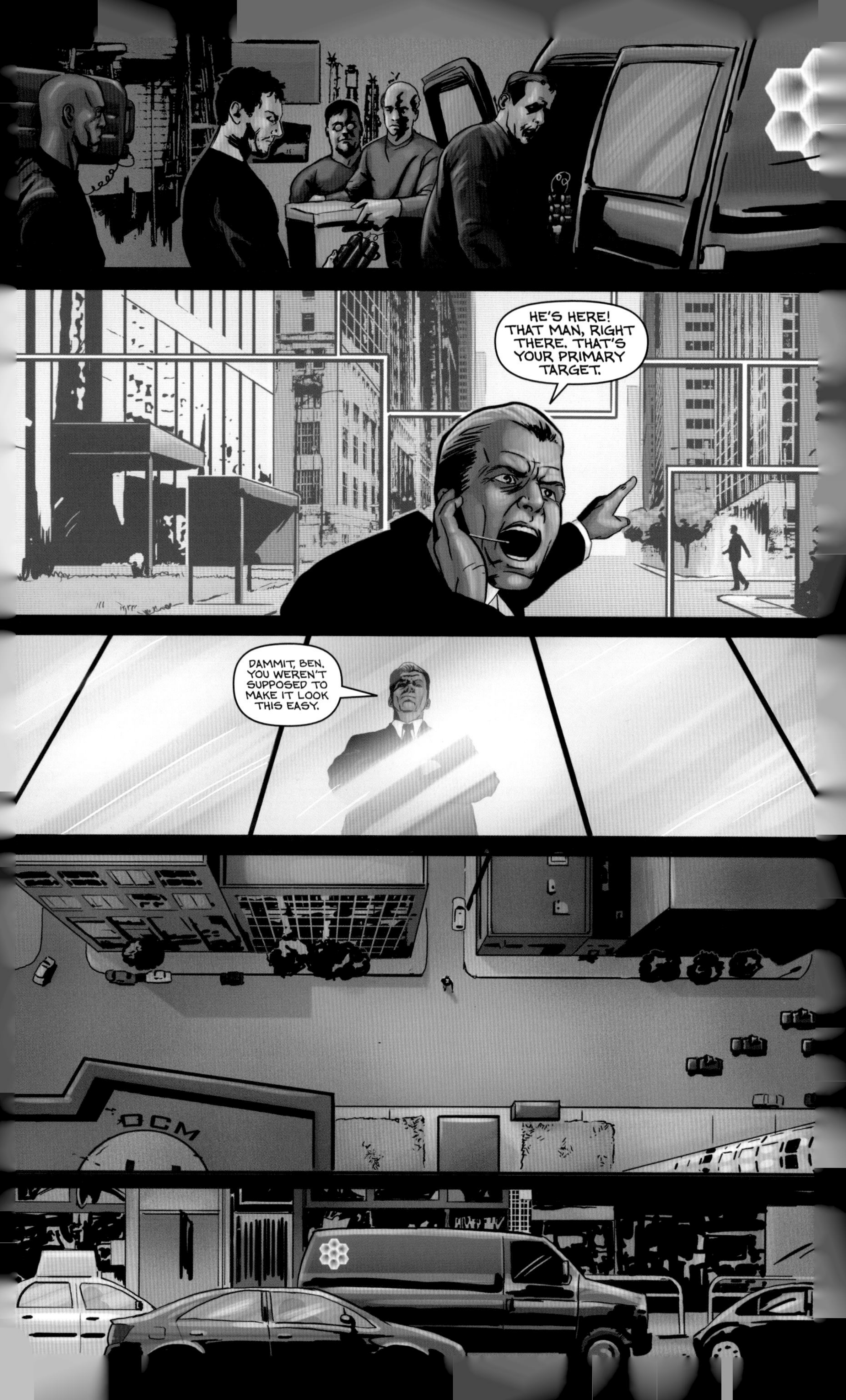
HE'S HERE! THAT MAN, RIGHT THERE. THAT'S YOUR PRIMARY TARGET.
DAMMIT, BEN. YOU WEREN'T SUPPOSED TO MAKE IT LOOK THIS EASY.
OCM

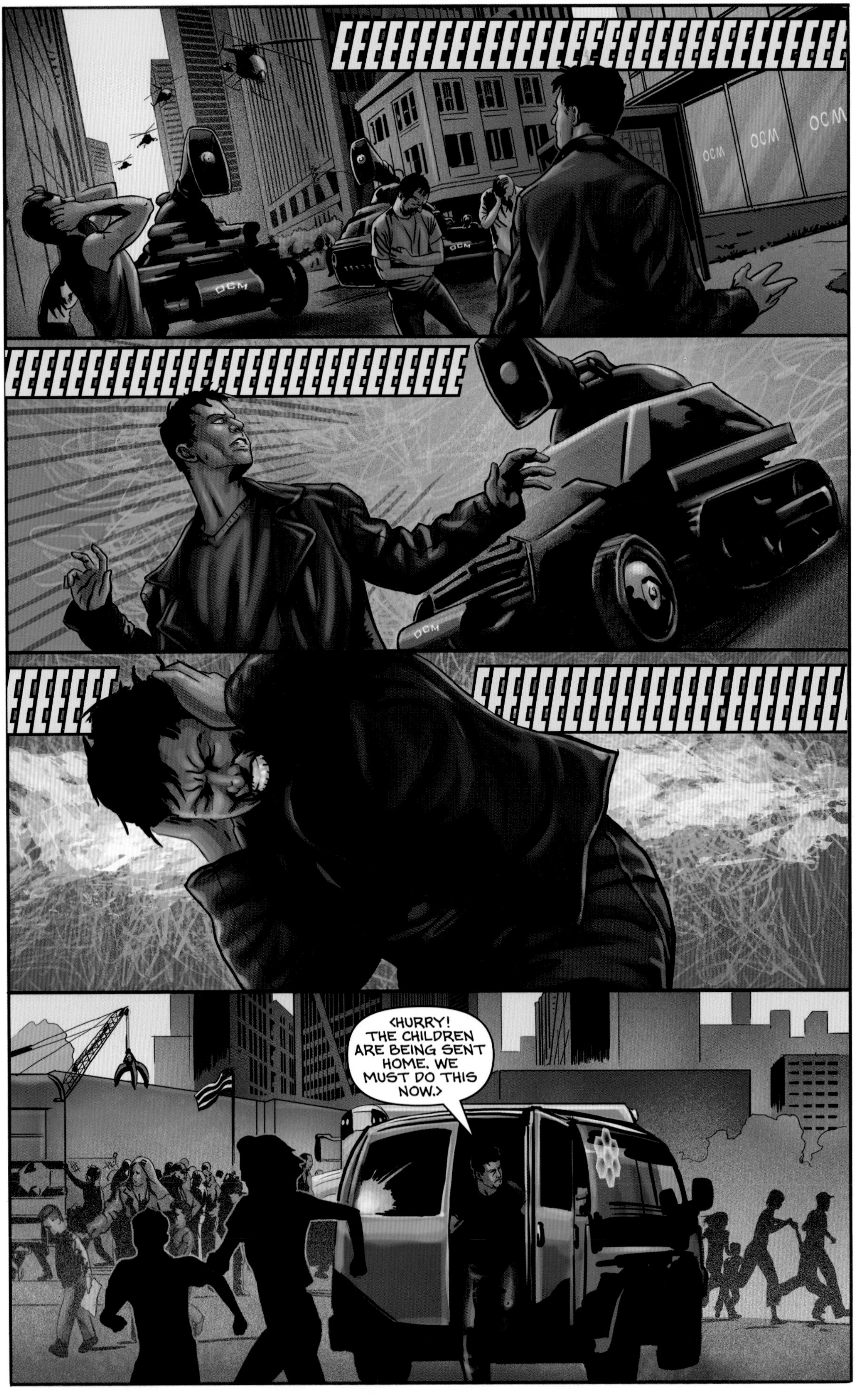
EEEEEEEEEEEEEEEEEEEEEEEEEEEEEEE
OCM
OCM
OCM
OCM
OCM
EEEEEEEEEEEEEEEEEEEEEEEEEEEEEE
OCM
EEEEEEE
EEEEEEEEEEEEEEEEEEEEEEEEEE
<HURRY! THE CHILDREN ARE BEING SENT HOME. WE MUST DO THIS NOW.>

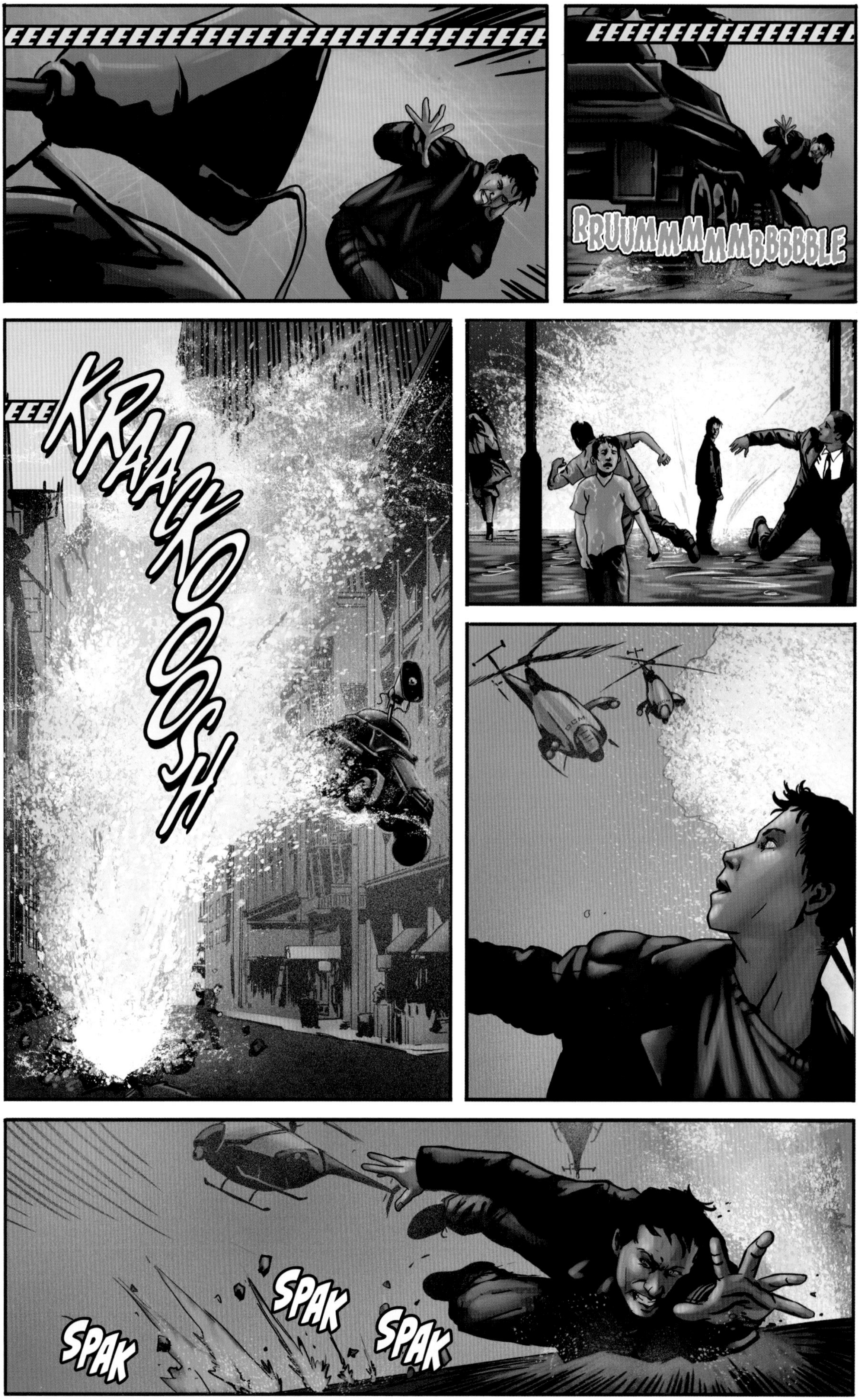

EEEEEEEEEEEEEEEEEEEEEEEEEEEEEEEEEEEEE
EEEEEEEEEEEEEEEEEEL
RRUUMMMMMMBBBBBLE
EEE
KRAACKOOOOSH
SPAK
SPAK
SPAK

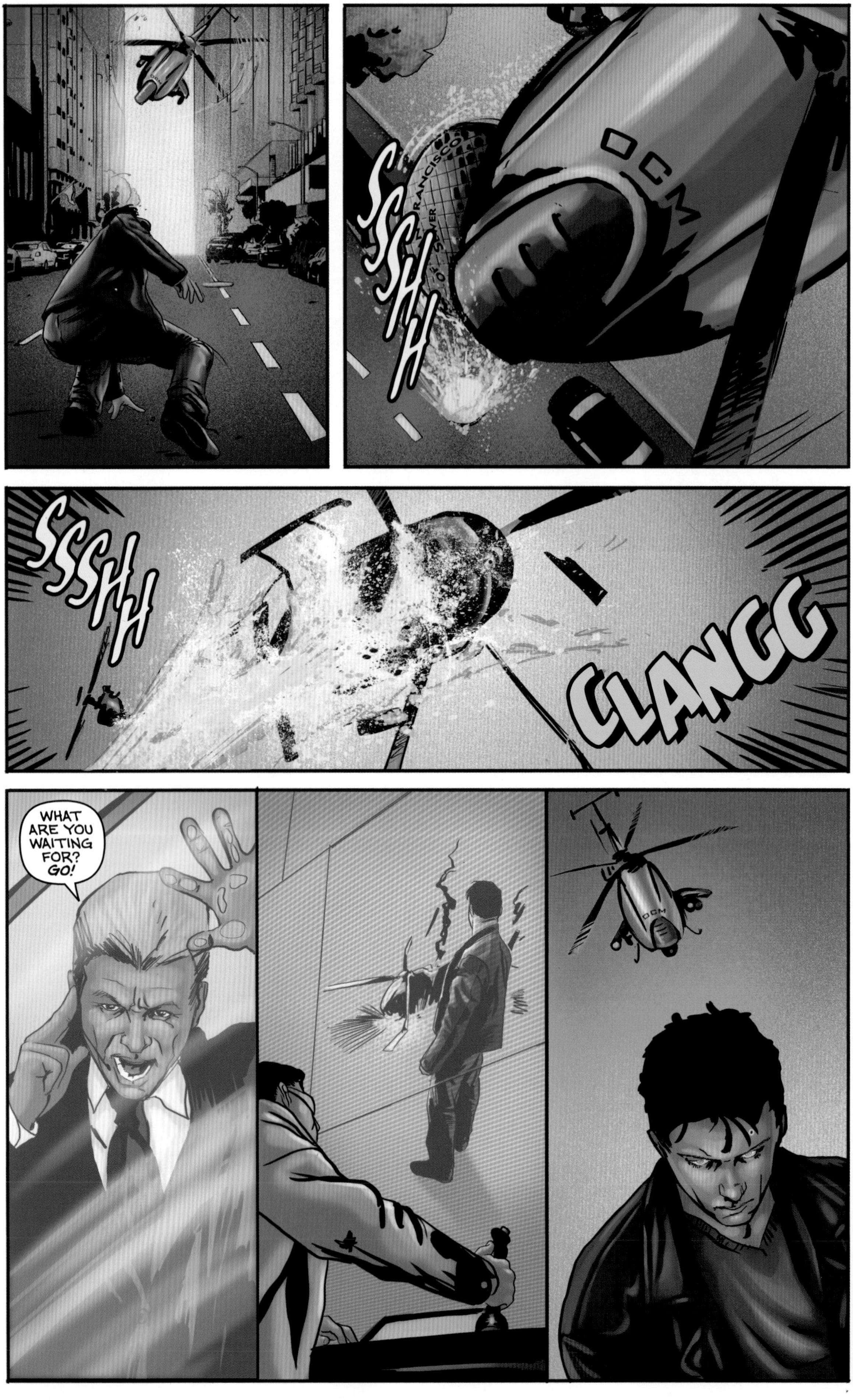
SSSHH
DCM
SSSHH
CLANGG
WHAT ARE YOU WAITING FOR? GO!
DCM

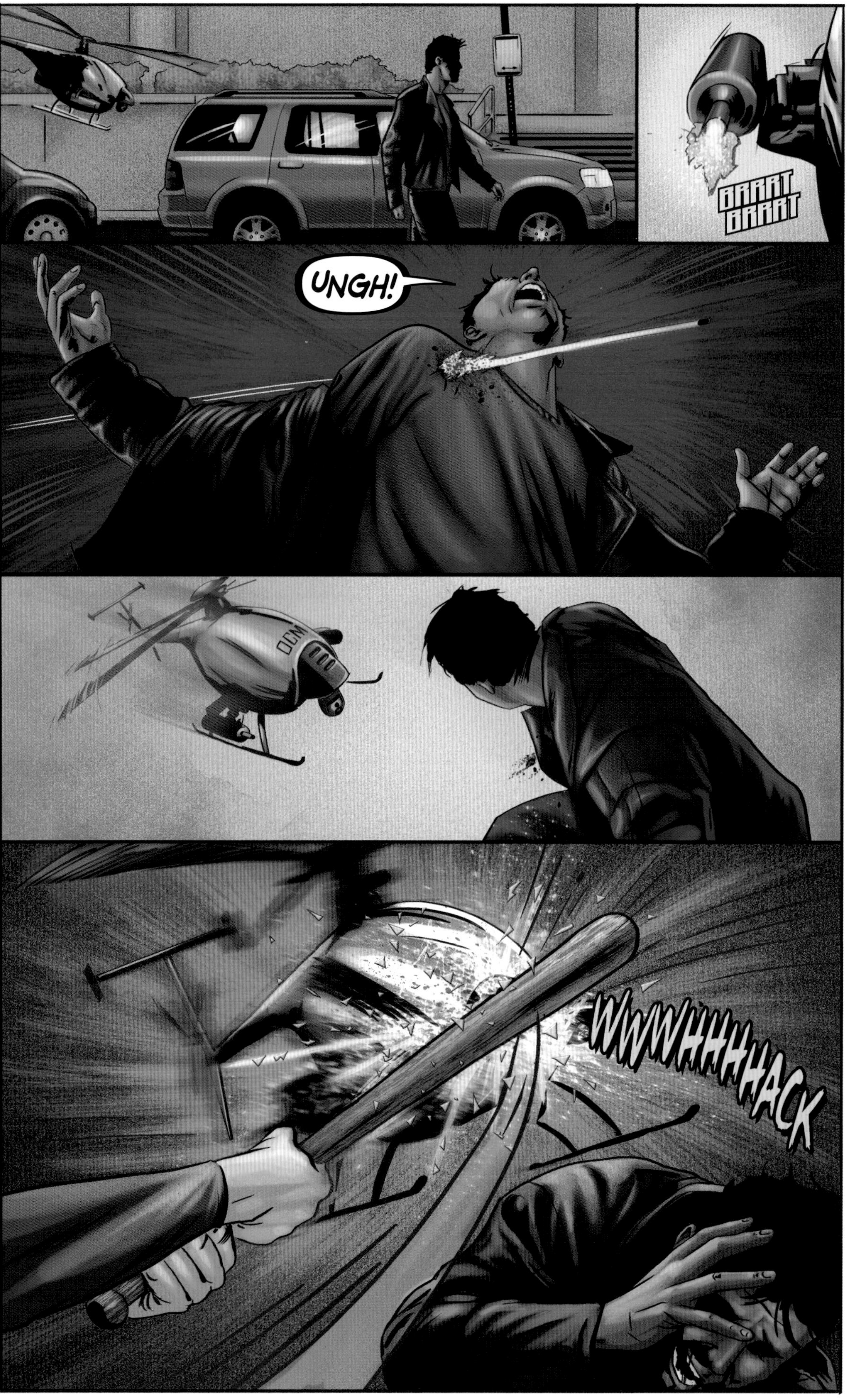
BRRRT
BRRRT
UNGH!
OCM
WWWHHHHACK

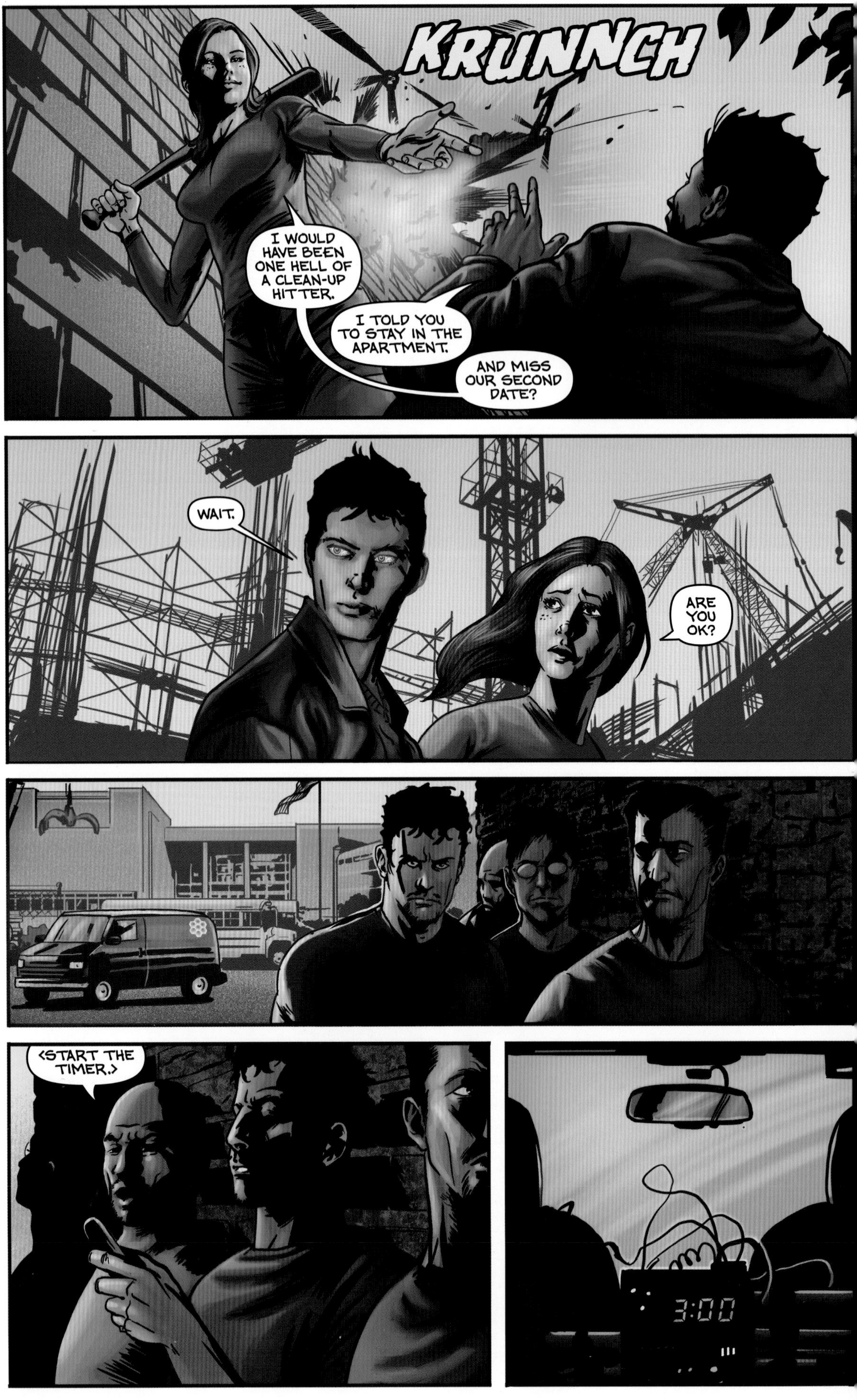
KRUNNCH
I WOULD HAVE BEEN ONE HELL OF A CLEAN-UP HITTER.
I TOLD YOU TO STAY IN THE APARTMENT.
AND MISS OUR SECOND DATE?
WAIT.
ARE YOU OK?
<START THE TIMER.>
3:00

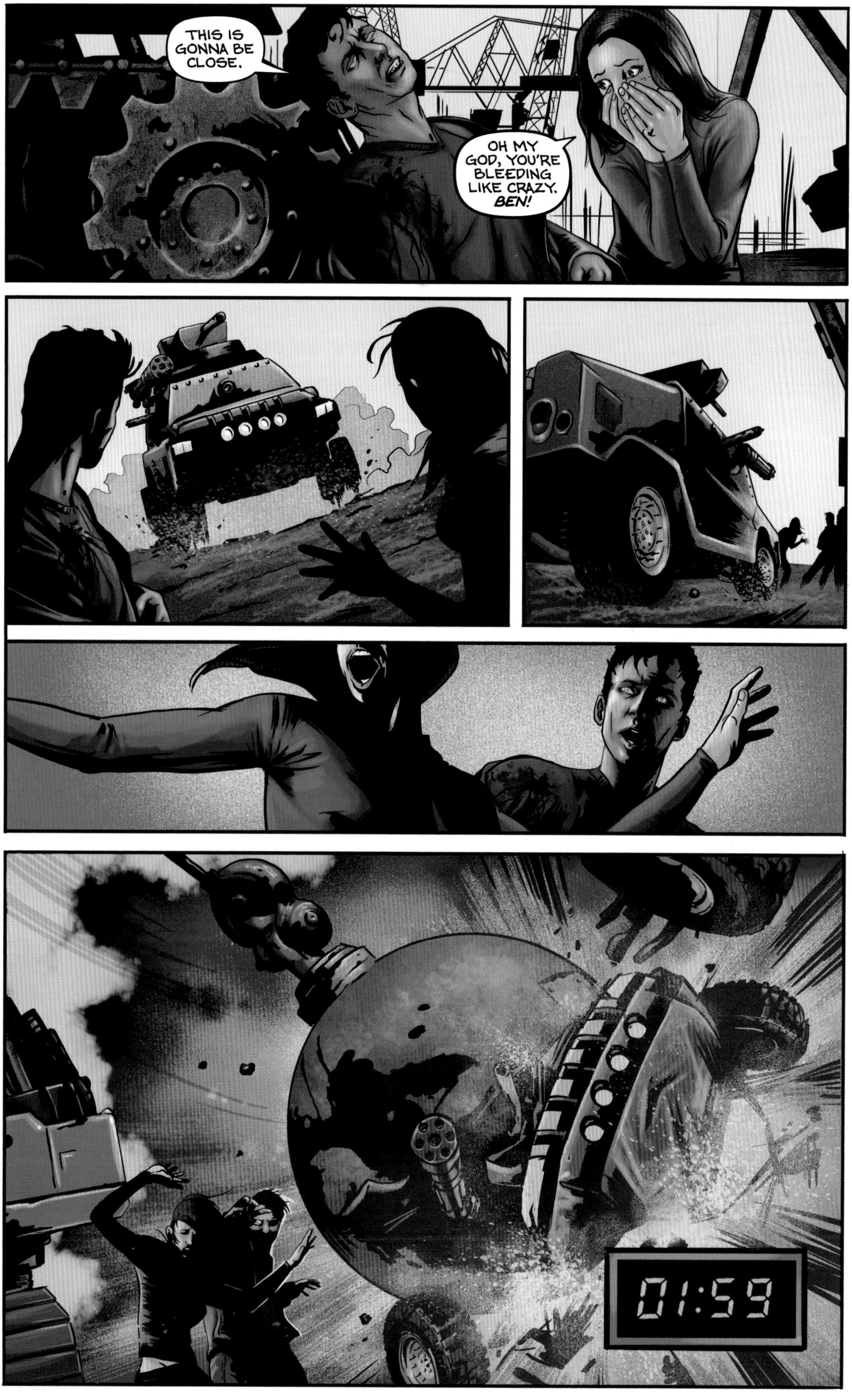
THIS IS GONNA BE CLOSE.
OH MY GOD, YOU'RE BLEEDING LIKE CRAZY. *BEN!*
01:59

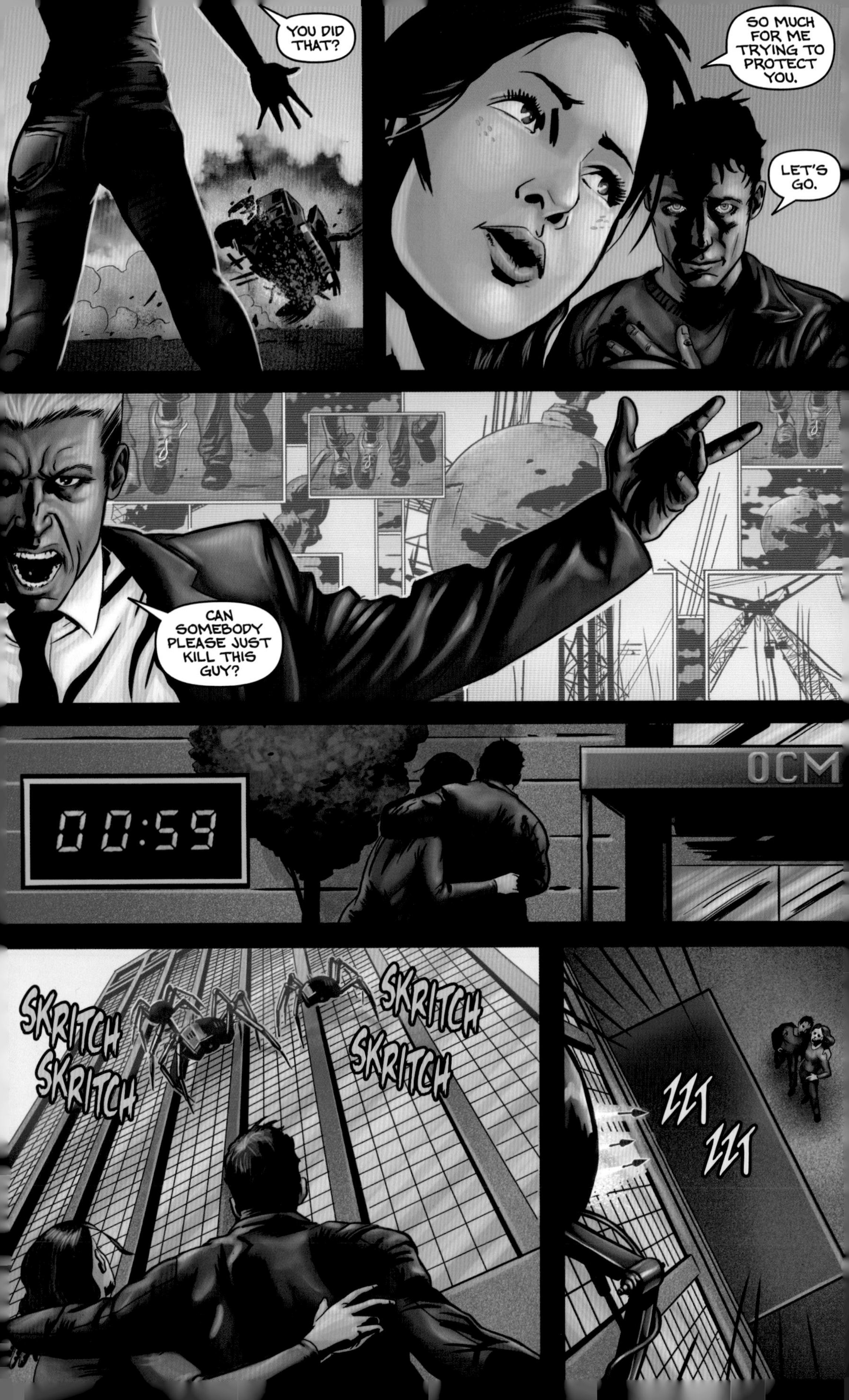
YOU DID THAT?
SO MUCH FOR ME TRYING TO PROTECT YOU.
LET'S GO.
CAN SOMEBODY PLEASE JUST KILL THIS GUY?
00:59
OCM
SKRITCH SKRITCH
SKRITCH SKRITCH
ZZT ZZT

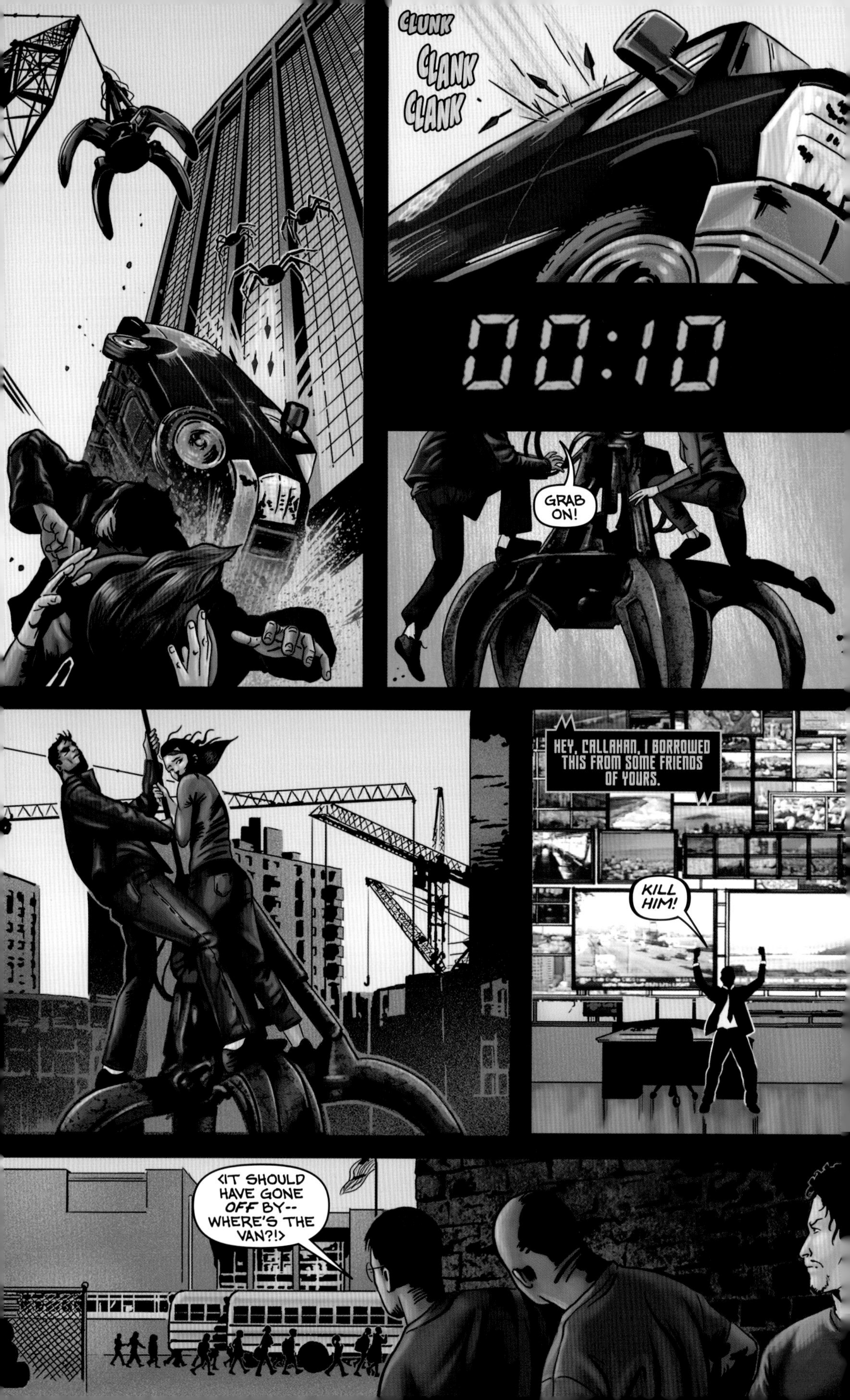
CLUNK
CLANK
CLANK
00:10
GRAB ON!
HEY, CALLAHAN, I BORROWED THIS FROM SOME FRIENDS OF YOURS.
KILL HIM!
<IT SHOULD HAVE GONE *OFF* BY-- WHERE'S THE VAN?!>

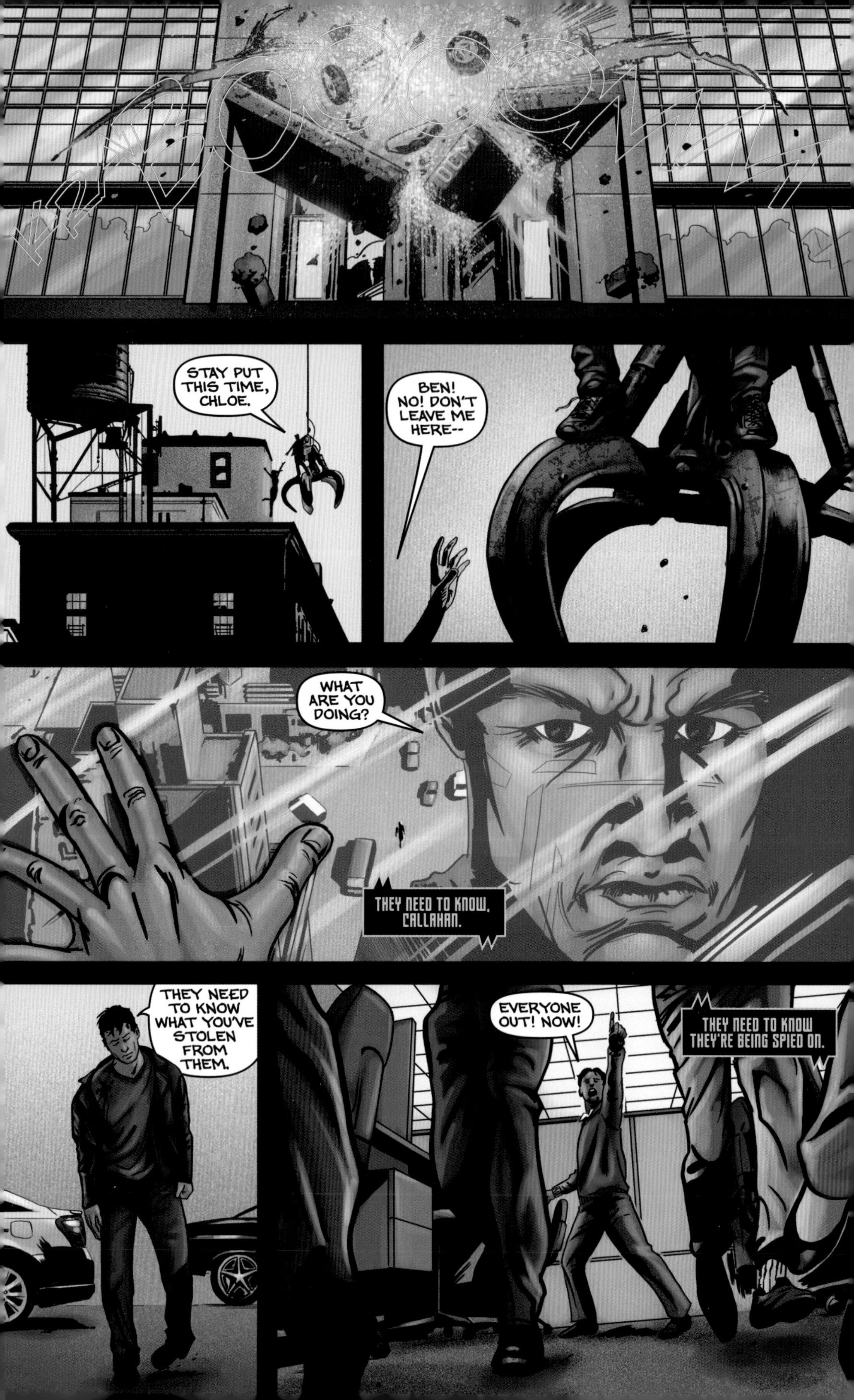
STAY PUT THIS TIME, CHLOE.
BEN! NO! DON'T LEAVE ME HERE--
WHAT ARE YOU DOING?
THEY NEED TO KNOW, CALLAHAN.
THEY NEED TO KNOW WHAT YOU'VE STOLEN FROM THEM.
EVERYONE OUT! NOW!
THEY NEED TO KNOW THEY'RE BEING SPIED ON.

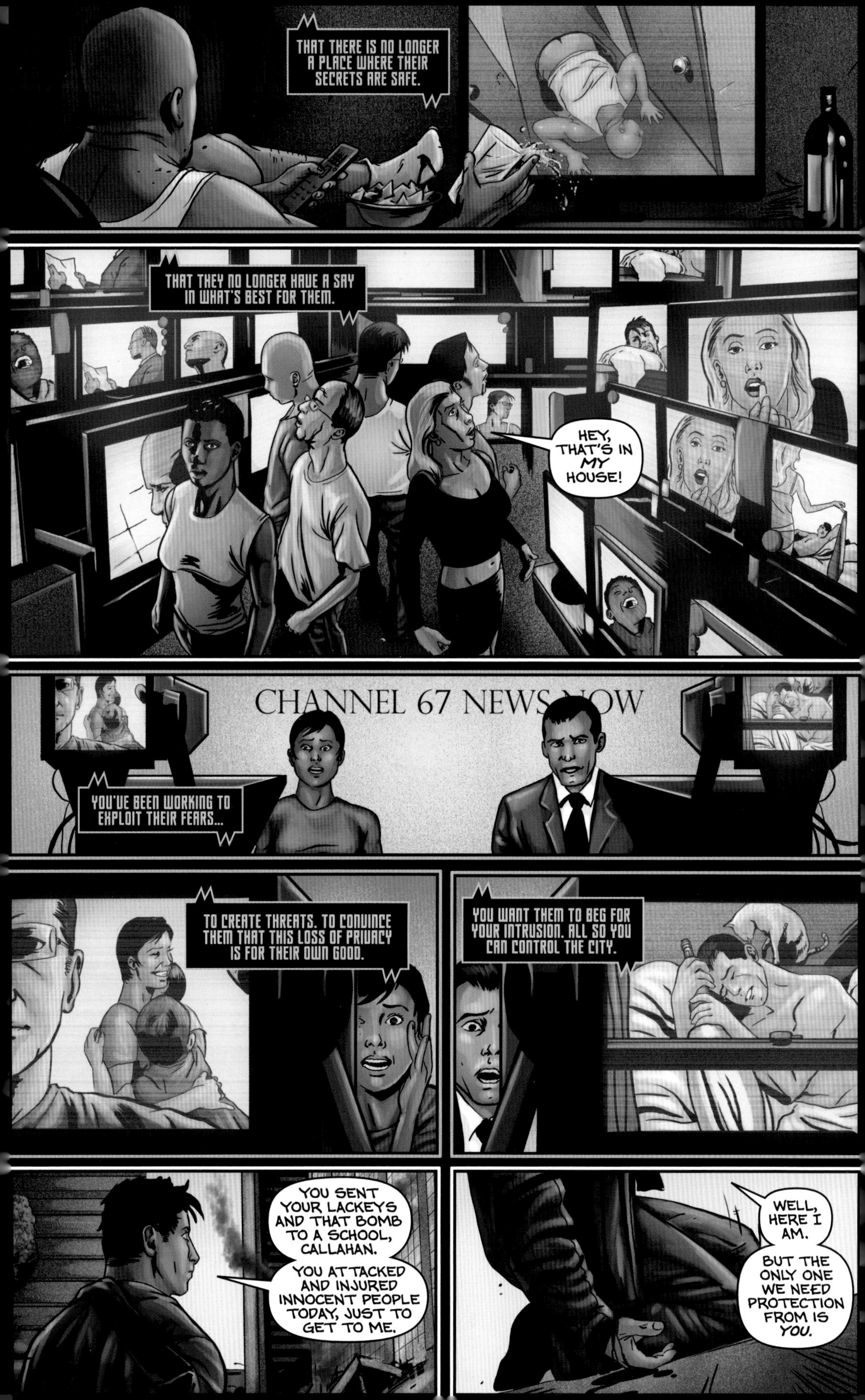
THAT THERE IS NO LONGER A PLACE WHERE THEIR SECRETS ARE SAFE.
THAT THEY NO LONGER HAVE A SAY IN WHAT'S BEST FOR THEM.
HEY, THAT'S IN MY HOUSE!
CHANNEL 67 NEWS NOW
YOU'VE BEEN WORKING TO EXPLOIT THEIR FEARS...
TO CREATE THREATS. TO CONVINCE THEM THAT THIS LOSS OF PRIVACY IS FOR THEIR OWN GOOD.
YOU WANT THEM TO BEG FOR YOUR INTRUSION. ALL SO YOU CAN CONTROL THE CITY.
YOU SENT YOUR LACKEYS AND THAT BOMB TO A SCHOOL, CALLAHAN.
YOU ATTACKED AND INJURED INNOCENT PEOPLE TODAY, JUST TO GET TO ME.
WELL, HERE I AM.
BUT THE ONLY ONE WE NEED PROTECTION FROM IS YOU.

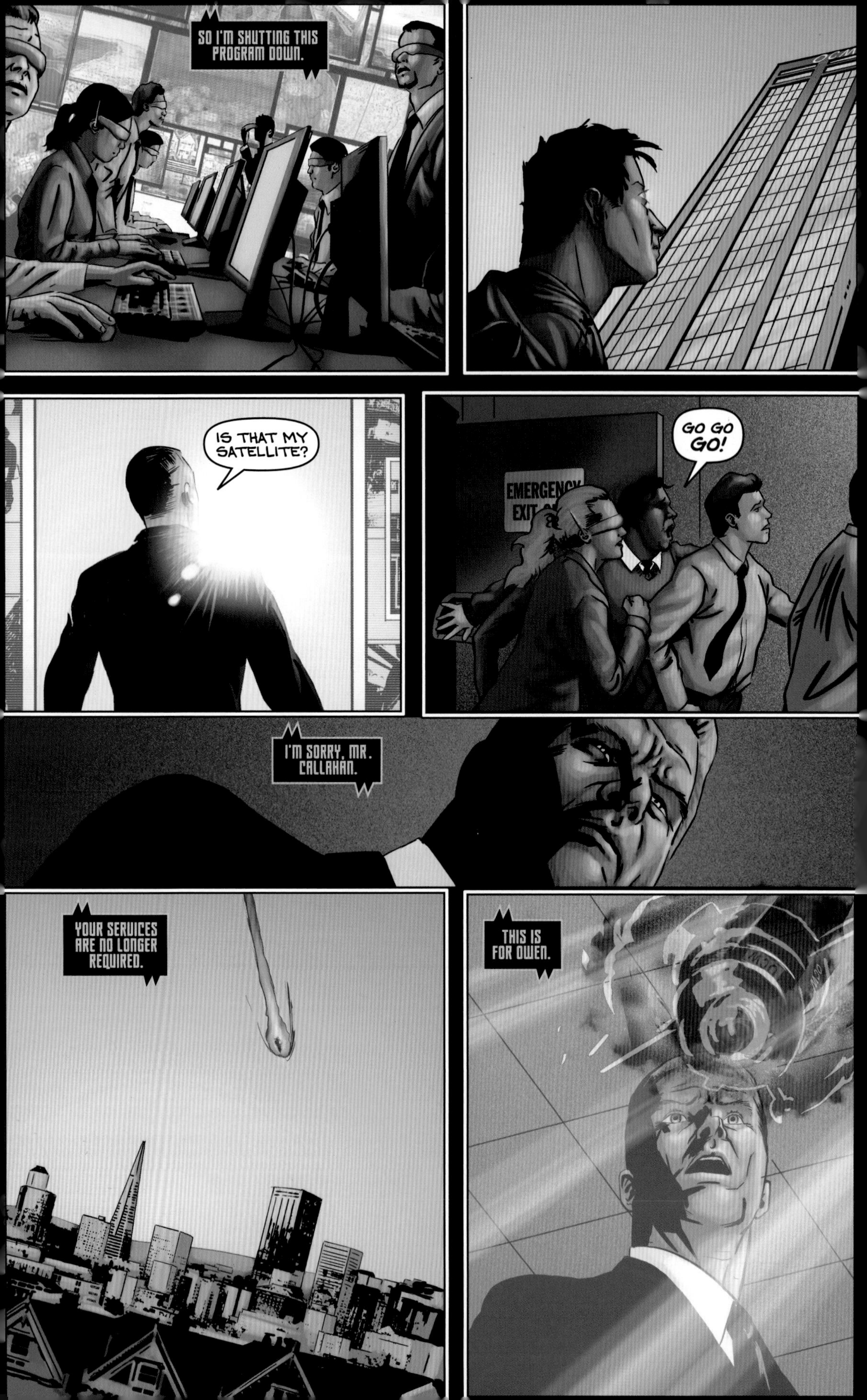
SO I'M SHUTTING THIS PROGRAM DOWN.
IS THAT MY SATELLITE?
GO GO GO!
EMERGENCY EXIT
I'M SORRY, MR. CALLAHAN.
YOUR SERVICES ARE NO LONGER REQUIRED.
THIS IS FOR OWEN.

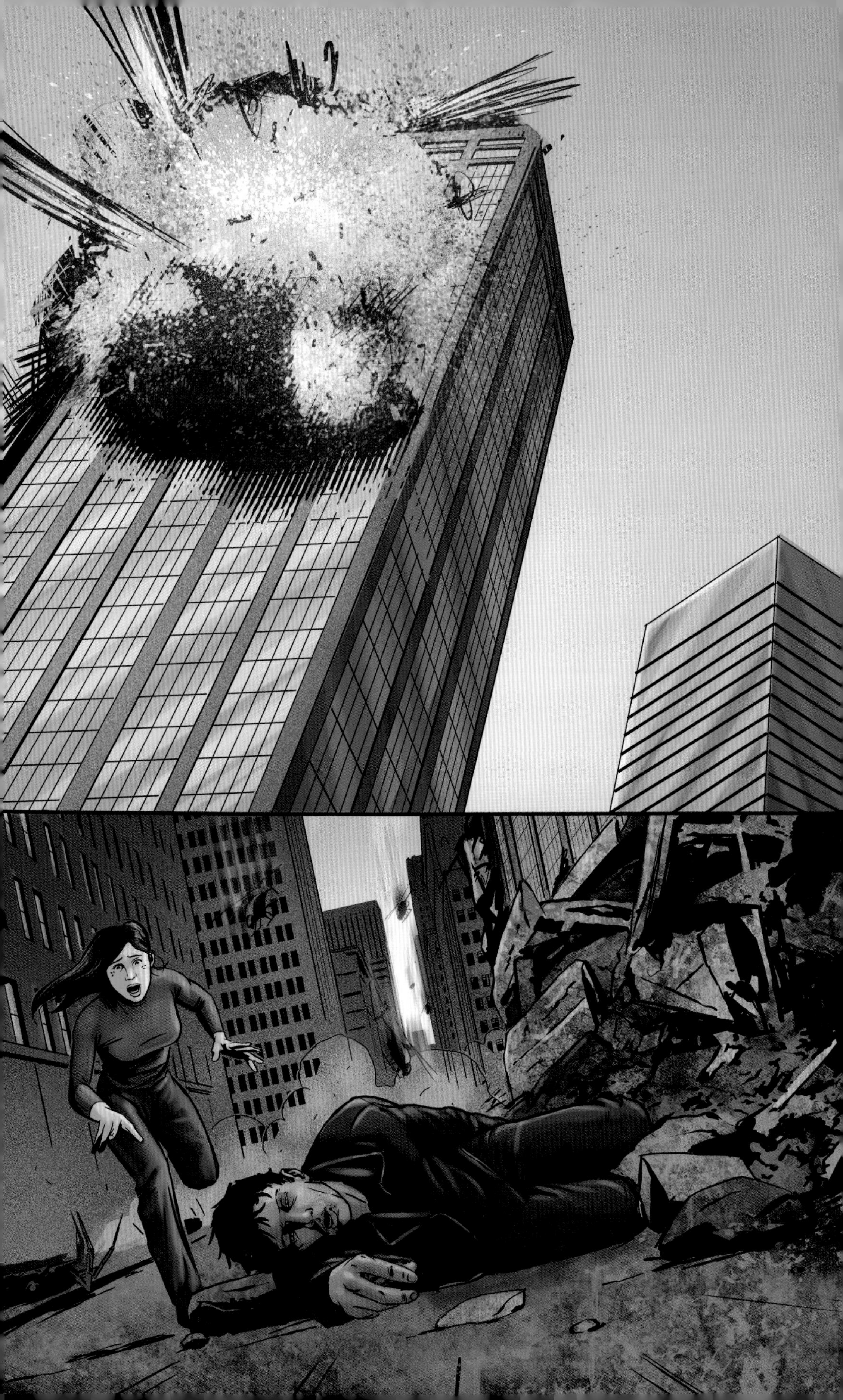

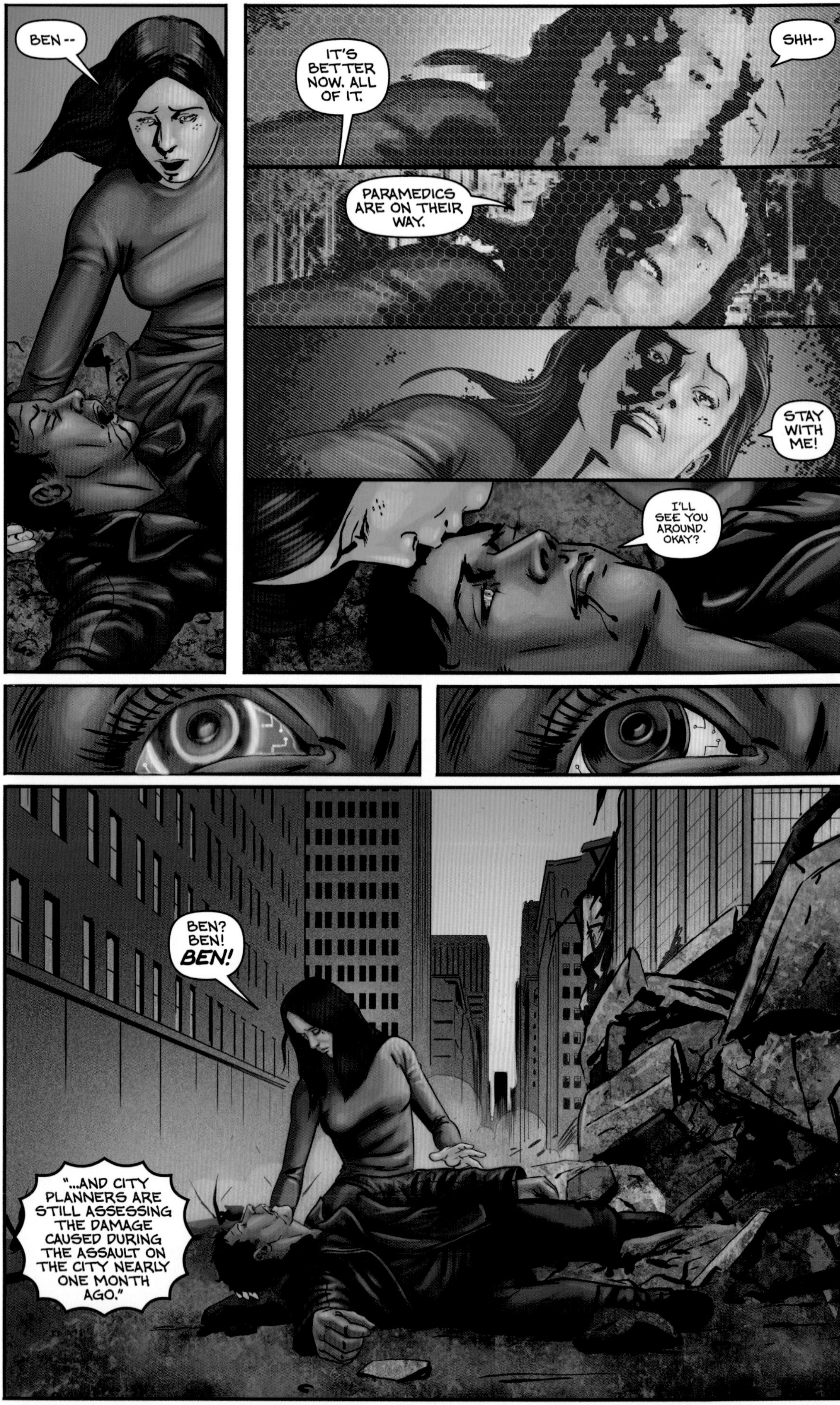
BEN --
IT'S BETTER NOW. ALL OF IT.
SHH--
PARAMEDICS ARE ON THEIR WAY.
STAY WITH ME!
I'LL SEE YOU AROUND. OKAY?
BEN? BEN! BEN!
"...AND CITY PLANNERS ARE STILL ASSESSING THE DAMAGE CAUSED DURING THE ASSAULT ON THE CITY NEARLY ONE MONTH AGO."

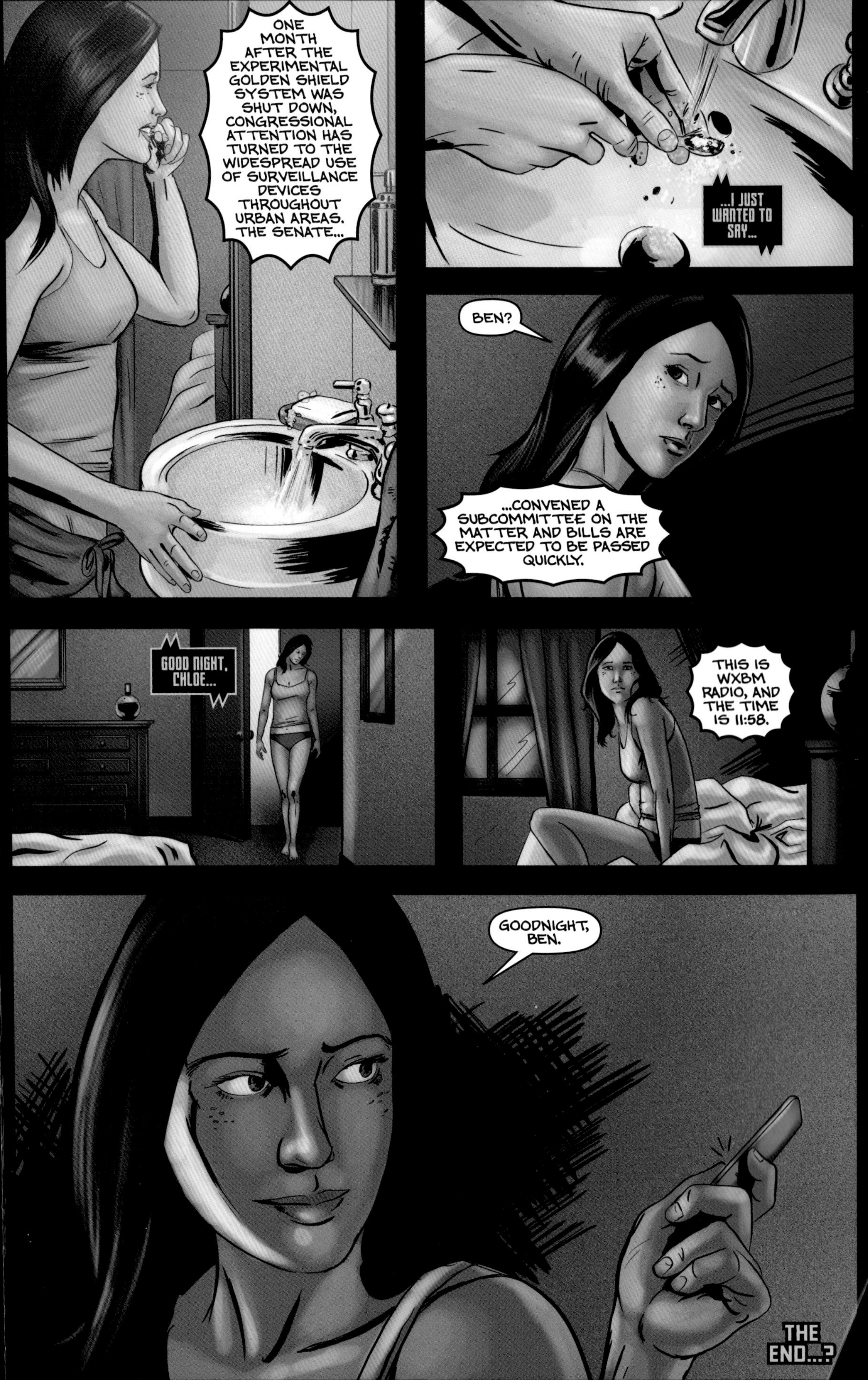
ONE MONTH AFTER THE EXPERIMENTAL GOLDEN SHIELD SYSTEM WAS SHUT DOWN, CONGRESSIONAL ATTENTION HAS TURNED TO THE WIDESPREAD USE OF SURVEILLANCE DEVICES THROUGHOUT URBAN AREAS. THE SENATE...
...I JUST WANTED TO SAY...
BEN?
...CONVENED A SUBCOMMITTEE ON THE MATTER AND BILLS ARE EXPECTED TO BE PASSED QUICKLY.
GOOD NIGHT, CHLOE...
THIS IS WXBM RADIO, AND THE TIME IS 11:58.
GOODNIGHT, BEN.
THE END...?

THE VANISHING VANISHING-POINT OF...
CITY: THE MIND IN THE MACHINE

by Eric Garcia

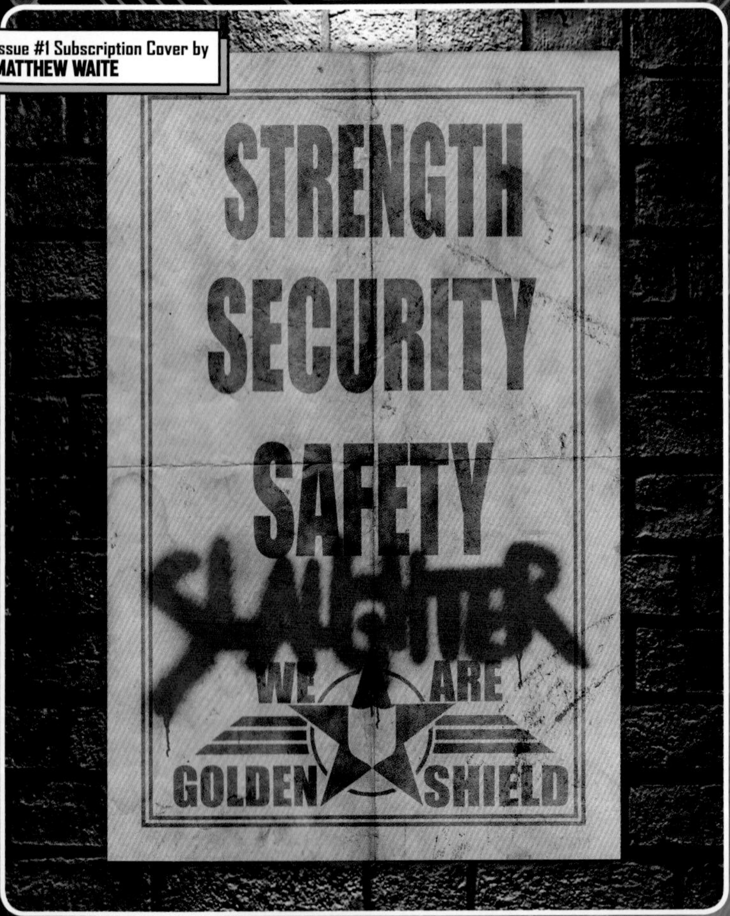
STRENGTH
SECURITY
SAFETY
WE ARE
GOLDEN SHIELD
Issue #1 Subscription Cover by **MATTHEW WAITE**

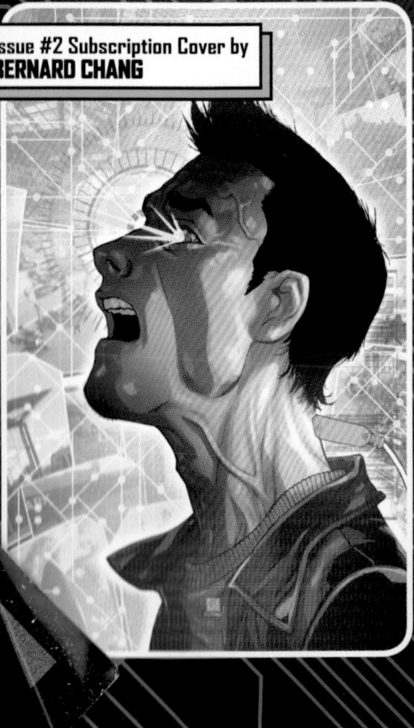
Issue #2 Subscription Cover by **BERNARD CHANG**

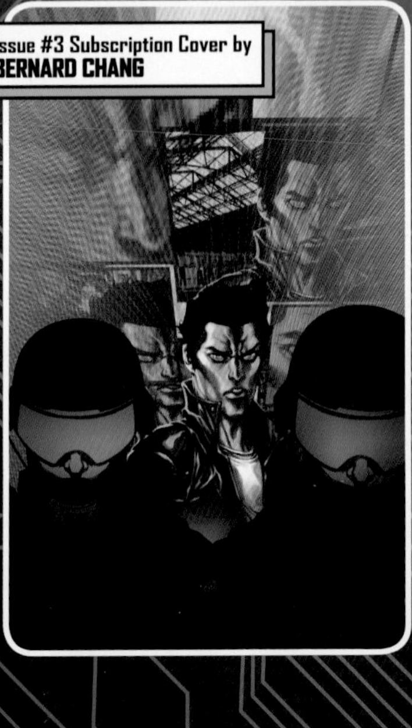
Issue #3 Subscription Cover by **BERNARD CHANG**

I am an only child, and I cannot see the future.

Fine, first things first:

The fact that I'm the only son of an only son of an only son most likely explains quite a lot about me. I'm terrible at sharing, I harbor vague notions of world conquest, and I'm relatively sure that Copernicus was wrong and the world actually revolves around me – but I'm not going to hold it against the guy. He's got enough to deal with, being dead and all. What it also means is that without any siblings to boss about during my formative years, I had a lot of time on my hands to entertain myself. One of my preferred methods was reading, as it was (and remains to this day) low-impact and easy on the knees.

I read a lot of science-fiction, especially over long car rides during summer vacations. Heinlein and Philip K. Dick were my missing brothers, and while they didn't tussle for control over the back seat, they did yeoman's work keeping me enthralled while my father refused to ask for directions in multiple languages. Despite the fact that I had a functional family and childhood, I was still drawn to stories that took me into impossible realms. Ringworlds and strangers in strange lands and hitchhikers with towels and policemen who ingested drugs that bisected their personalities – if it was weird and future-forward, I devoured it.

The stories that gripped me the most, though, were those which posited a world gone slightly off track – those which were recognizable as our own, but for the want of a single, reality-altering twist. I loved *DUNE*, for example, because damn it, I have a soul, but I was blown ass-over-cranium by *NEUROMANCER*. I knew that it was never written in my stars to mine for spice or ride a sandworm, but the idea that I might, one day, explore the Matrix... It put the experience into something I could really grok.

NEUROMANCER began a fascination not just with "cyberpunk" (a term I've loathed since I was old enough to be holier-than-thou, which is officially 14), but with all forms of "realistic" sci-fi. Didn't matter if it was hard or soft or in the comfortable goo between; if it presented a world that was wholly different from ours and yet still retained a semblance of our world, a bridge into reality, I was good to go. I wanted to read it, inhale it, be it, write it.

Then I went and wrote a trilogy about dinosaurs dressing up as humans.

I know. Shut up.

But here's the second part I mentioned earlier: I cannot see the future.

You'd think this would put me at a disadvantage as an occasional sci-fi writer, but the secret they don't want you to know is that nobody can see the future. It's not just me, thank God. Still, that leaves me with some fairly rudimentary tools: research, imagination, and literary slight of hand. This puts me, as a writer, at a crossroads:

Road #1: Conceive of a future so far out as to be unimaginable, or at least far removed from our concept of the world as it currently is. There's some amazing work in this realm, but I don't know that it keeps me excited as much as the nearly possible does.

Road #2: Try and aim at the vanishing point, that spot juuust at the horizon. We're continually rushing toward it at breakneck speed, and yet it's always there, always something new, even as the future becomes the present becomes the past.

It's this second road that sets my brain humming, both as a reader and as a writer – and yet I believe it's a much harder road to travel, precisely because our speed, as a society – as a society further involved in technology than ever before – is increasing at exponential rates. The vanishing point is becoming little more than a blur rushing toward us, and what seems so distant one moment is right on top of us and in our rear-view the next.

When I first wrote the story that would become *THE REPOSSESSION MAMBO*, for example, artificial organs were little more than anomalies, and primarily noble failures. So when I set my story in that world, I'd assumed we were many decades away from the reality. Today, less than fifteen years later, we're talking about printing the damned things on a 3D maker.

So when I first started thinking about *CITY: THE MIND IN THE MACHINE* a few years ago, I knew that I was playing in technological quicksand. Cameras were all over cities already, that was a given. Google Glass had yet to be sprung on us but we all had an inkling it was coming. I'd read a couple of articles about so-called "smart" appliances and the approaching wave of rudimentary brain-machine interfaces, but the idea of putting them all together into one system hadn't yet been explored.

As I worked on the story and it started coming together, I'd stumble across articles about new crime-fighting techniques that I thought were just pie-in-the-sky concepts (automatic facial recognition combined with instant background checks to be used in riot/mob situations), or Big Brother-type government programs that rivaled the fictional Golden Shield in their sheer intrusiveness and Orwellian doublespeak (check out Oakland's Domain Awareness Center). Some of them helped in my research. Some I ignored. They all spurred me on to work even faster.

Now here we are in 2014 (for those reading this in the future, you can remember it as the year that Net Neutrality ended and the Internet as we know it began its slow degradation into an Applebee's-covered wasteland), and the world of *CITY* seems less like science fiction and more like science might-actually-be-happening-somewhere-in-the-world-right-now (which would be a hard section to label at a bookstore, so thank God there aren't any more of those). As a writer, I'm both gratified that I was right, in a way, and yet mortified that I couldn't see beyond what was apparently coming down the pike, larger than life.

Yet I'm trying to imagine how I'd feel if I were that kid in the backseat again, if I was that young, impressionable reader, and I picked up a book like *CITY* – how would I feel about the world presented within? I'd recognize it, certainly. But I wonder if, by the time my father finally stopped to ask for directions and located our next destination, I'd be looking further down the road – past the vanishing point, past the moment that had already shot by, and onto the next technological leap.

I like to think I'd be energized by Ben and his journey, by the Golden Shield technology – that I'd see it not just as a way to present a possible future, but as something that represents both the potential we've got to do good and the incredible danger that comes from moving too quickly without pausing to wonder if we should. That's an idea that I hope, in its own way, is timeless.

Oh, and I also write about con men. ∎

Issue #1 Cover by TOMMY LEE EDWARDS

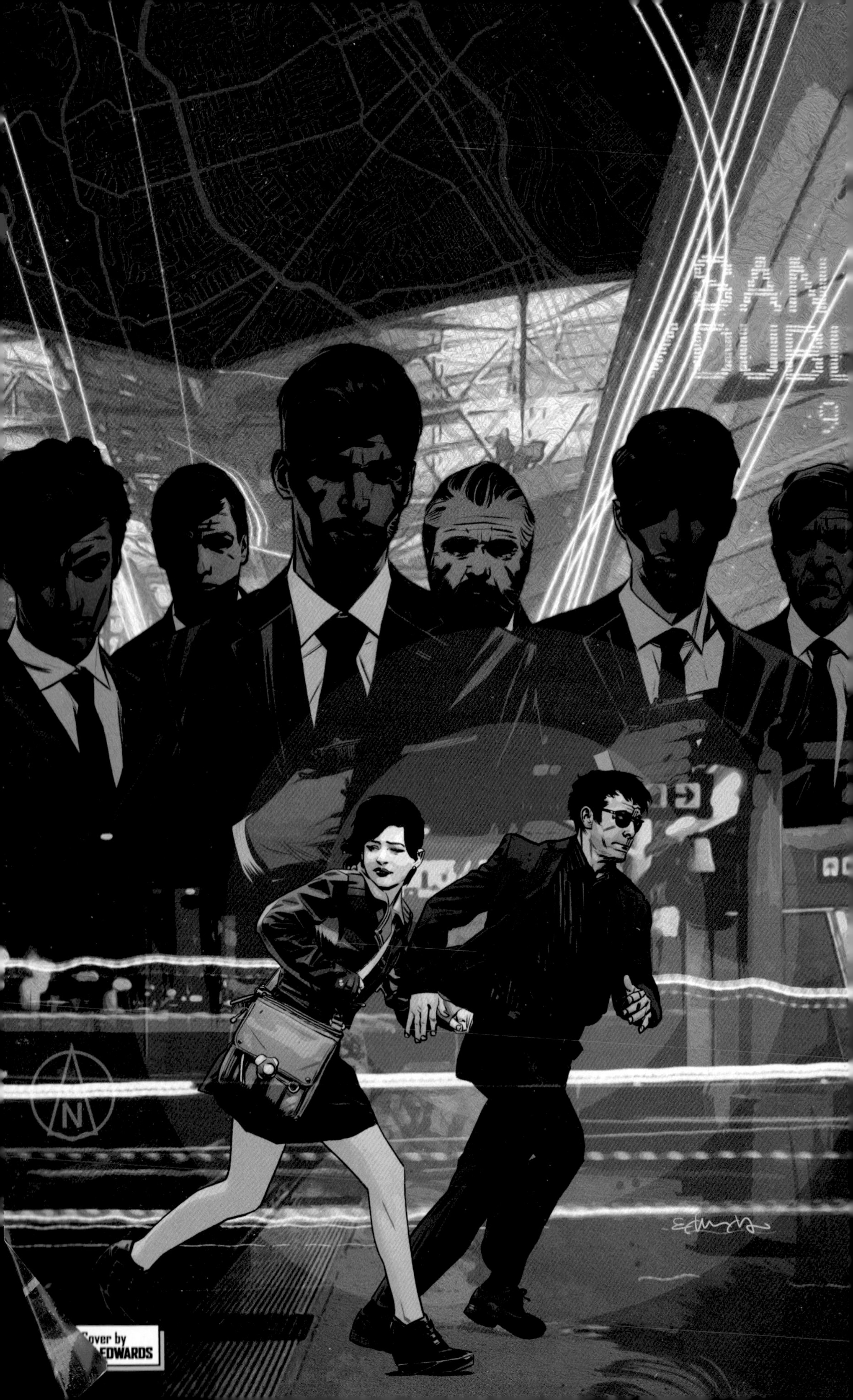
Cover by
EDWARDS